# Greenock, Johnstone.
# Paisley & R
# Street A

## CONTENTS

| | | | |
|---|---|---|---|
| Area of Coverage | 2 | Lochwinnoch & index | 40 - 41 |
| Key to Map Symbols | 3 | Neilston & index | 42 - 43 |
| Barrhead & index | 4 - 7 | Paisley | 44 - 52 |
| Bishopton | 8 - 9 | Quarriers Village & index | 53 |
| Bridge of Weir & index | 10 - 11 | Port Glasgow | 54 - 55 |
| Erskine & Inchinnan | 12 - 15 | Renfrew | 56 - 61 |
| Gourock & Levan | 16 - 17 | Uplawmoor & indices | 62 |
| Greenock | 18 - 25 | Wemyss Bay | 63 |
| Houston & index | 26 - 27 | Index section | 64 - 77 |
| Howwood & index | 28 | Erskine, (including Bishopton & | |
| Inverkip & index | 29 | Inchinnan), Greenock (including | |
| Johnstone & Linwood | 30 - 34 | Gourock, Levan & Port Glasgow), | |
| Kilbarchan & Brookfield | 35 | Johnstone, (including Linwood, | |
| Kilmacolm & index | 36 - 37 | Kilbarchan & Brookfield), Paisley & | |
| Langbank & index | 38 - 39 | Renfrew | |

ISBN 978 1 86097 368 0

Shandon
B833
Clynder
Rhu
Cove
Kilcreggan
A82
B832
Helensburgh
Loch Lomond
A811
Balloch
Alexandria
Bonhill
Croftamie
Killearn
A809
A81
Strathblane
Gourock
Greenock
A770
Cardross
A814
Dumbarton
A78
Port Glasgow
A8
Langbank
M8
Milngavie
Bearsden
Inverkip
Kilmacolm
Bishopton
Erskine
Clydebank
Wemyss Bay
B788
B789
Renfrew
Skelmorlie
Clyde
Quarriers Village
A761
Houston
M8
GLASGOW
Bridge of Weir
Linwood
Muirshiel
Brookfield
Paisley
M8
Kilbarchan
Johnstone
Elderslie
Regional
B786
Howwood
Barrhead
M77
Giffnock
Largs
Lochwinnoch
Busby
Park
B775
A78
A760
A737
B776
A736
Neilston
Newton Mearns
Fairlie
Kilbirnie
Beith
B777
Uplawmoor
A77
A726
Glengarnock
B706
Lugton
Eaglesham
B780
Burnhouse
B769
B781
Dunlop
West Kilbride
Dalry
B707
A735
Seamill
M77
B778
B780
B778
Stewarton
A736
Annick
A77
Ardrossan
Kilwinning
Fenwick
Kilmaurs
Stevenston
B769
A719
Saltcoats
A77
Irvine
Crosshouse
Kilmarnock
Newmilns
A71
A71

| | | | |
|---|---|---|---|
| M8 | Motorway | F | Filling station |
| A737 | Primary route dual / single | H | Hospital |
| A736 | A road dual / single | S | Superstore |
| B790 | B road dual / single | B | Bus station |
| | Unclassified road | m | Museum |
| | Pedestrian / one way street | a | Antiquity |
| | Track / path | | Historic house |
| | Railway / tunnel and station | | Garden |
| | Vehicle ferry route | i | Tourist information centre |
| | Foot ferry route | | Viewpoint |
| | Primary school | | Caravan site |
| | Secondary school | | Camping |
| | Special / independent school | | Other tourist attraction |
| P | Police station | | Place of worship |
| F | Fire station | | Woodland |
| A | Ambulance station | | Recreation, park or cemetery |
| C | Coastguard station | | Built up area |
| L | Lifeboat station | | Rocks |
| PO | Post office | | Shingle |
| L | Library | | Sand |
| P | Parking | | Marsh |

**Scale 1:14 000**

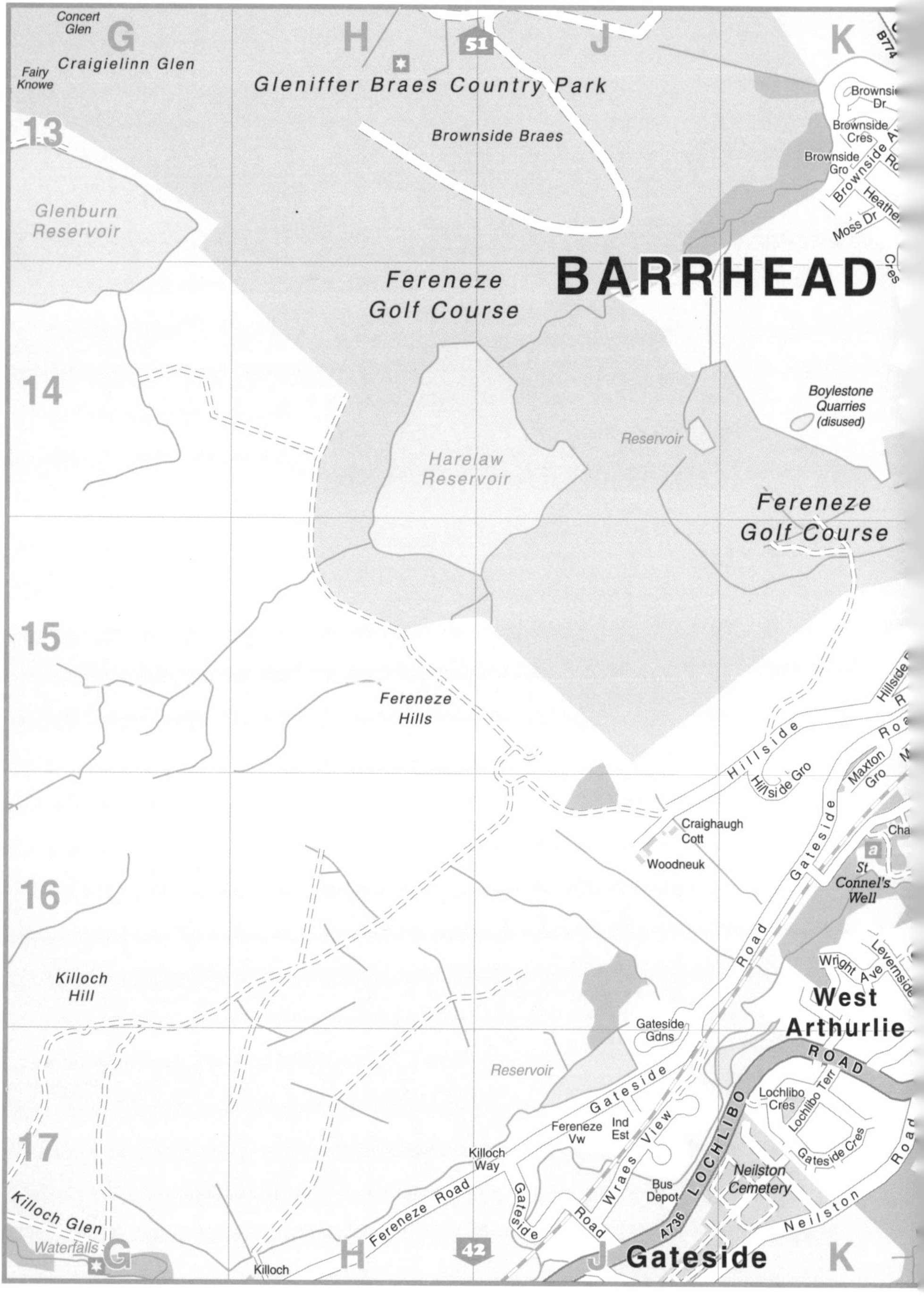

G
H
J
K
Concert Glen
Craigielinn Glen
Fairy Knowe
51
Gleniffer Braes Country Park
Brownside Braes
B774
Brownside Dr
Brownside Cres
Brownside Gro
Brownside Rd
Heather
Moss Dr
Cres
13
Glenburn Reservoir
Fereneze Golf Course
BARRHEAD
14
Harelaw Reservoir
Reservoir
Boylestone Quarries (disused)
Fereneze Golf Course
15
Fereneze Hills
Hillside Road
Hillside Gro
Maxton Gro
Craighaugh Cott
Woodneuk
Gateside Road
Cha
St Connel's Well
16
Killoch Hill
Wright Ave
Levernside
West Arthurlie
Gateside Gdns
Reservoir
ROAD
Lochlibo Cres
Lochlibo Terr
Gateside Cres
Road
17
Gateside
Fereneze Vw
Ind Est
Wraes View
Killoch Way
LOCHLIBO
Neilston Cemetery
Bus Depot
A736
Neilston
Killoch Glen
Fereneze Road
Gateside
Road
Waterfalls
Killoch
42
Gateside
G
H
J
K

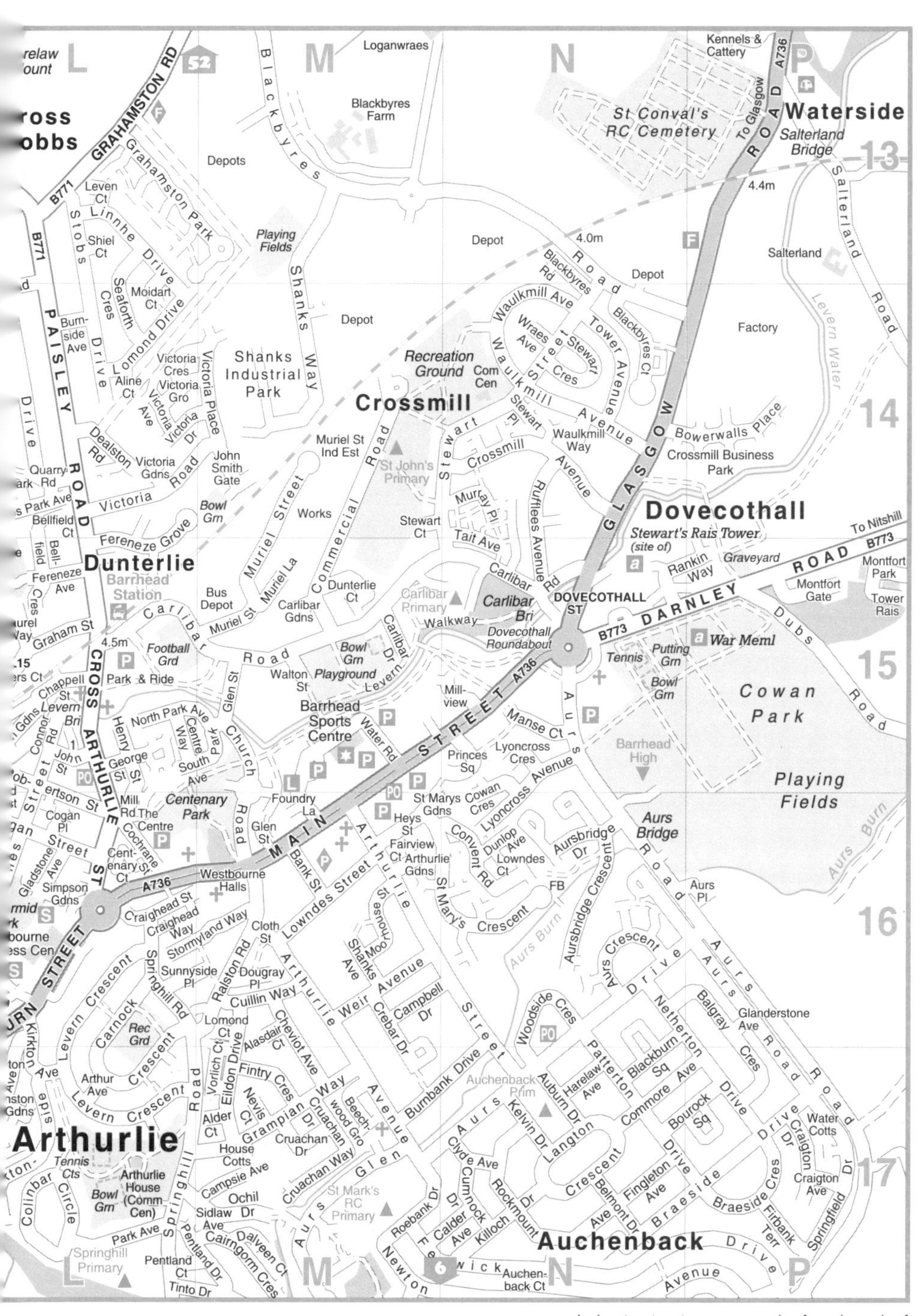


Index to street names can be found overleaf

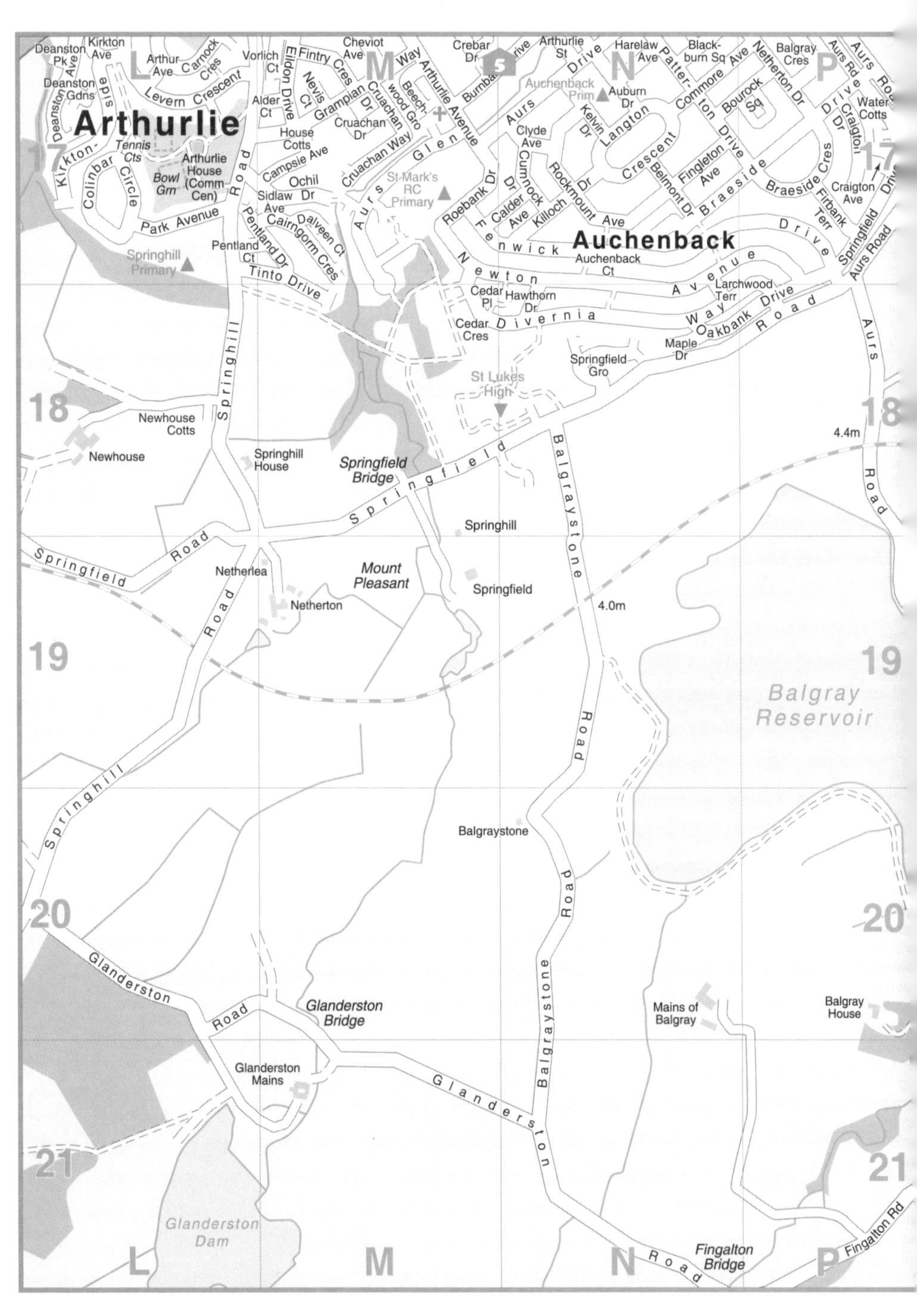
Arthurlie
Auchenback
Arthurlie House (Comm Cen)
Bowl Grn
Tennis Cts
Springhill Primary
St Mark's RC Primary
Auchenback Prim
St Lukes High
Springhill House
Springfield Bridge
Springhill
Springfield
Mount Pleasant
Netherlea
Netherton
Newhouse Cotts
Newhouse
Balgraystone
Balgray Reservoir
Mains of Balgray
Balgray House
Glanderston Bridge
Glanderston Mains
Glanderston Dam
Fingalton Bridge
Fingalton Rd
Springfield Road
Springhill Road
Balgraystone Road
Glanderston Road
Aurs Road
Oakbank Road
Park Avenue
Tinto Drive
Levern Crescent
Arthurlie Avenue
Newton Avenue
Fenwick Drive
Braeside Drive
Langton Crescent
Diverna Way
4.4m
4.0m
L
M
N
P
17
18
19
20
21

## ex to Barrhead


a Drive L13
lair Court M16
Court M17
Court L14
r Avenue L17
rlie M16, M17
nue
rlie M16
dens
rlie Street M16, N17
rn Drive N17
enback N17
urt
Crescent N16
Drive N17
Glen M17
Place P16
Road N15, P16
rrhead)
Road P17, P18
uchenback)
bridge N16
escent
sbridge Drive N16
ray P16, P17
escent
graystone N18, N21
ad
k Street M16
nes Street L16
chwood M17
ove
field Court L14
field Crescent L15
mont Drive N17
ckburn Square N17
ckbyres Court N14
ckbyres Road M13, N13
ckwood Street L16
rock Square N17
verwalls Place N14
lestone Road K14
eside Crescent P17
eside Drive N17
om Crescent K13
wnside Avenue K13
ownside Crescent K13
ownside Drive K13
ownside Grove K13
nbank Drive M17
rnside Avenue L14
irngorm Crescent M17
lder Avenue N17
mpbell Drive M16
mpsie Avenue M17
plethill Road K13
rlibar Drive M15
rlibar Gardens M15
rlibar Road L15, N15
rnock Crescent L16
edar Crescent M18
edar Place M18
entenary Court L16

Centre, The L16
Centre Way L15
Chappell Street L15
Cheviot Avenue M16, M17
Church Road M15
Cloth Street M16
Clyde Avenue N17
Cochrane Street L16
Cogan Place L16
Cogan Street L16
Colinbar Circle L17
Commercial Road M15
Commore Avenue N17
Connor Road L15
Convent Road N16
Cowan Crescent N16
Craighead Street L16
Craighead Way L16
Craigton Avenue P17
Craigton Drive P17
Crebar Drive M16, M17
Cross Arthurlie Street L15
Crossmill Avenue N14
Cruachan Drive M17
Cruachan Way M17
Cuillin Way M16
Cumnock Drive N17
Dalmeny Drive K16
Dalveen Court M17
Darnley Road N15
Dealston Road L14
Deanston Avenue L17
Deanston Gardens L17
Deanston Park L17
Divernia Way N18
Dougray Place M16
Dovecothall Street N15
Dubs Road P15
Dunlop Avenue N16
Dunterlie Court M15
Eildon Drive M17
Fairview Court M16
Fenwick Drive M17
Fereneze Avenue L15
Fereneze Grove L15
Fereneze Road H17
Fereneze View J17
Fern Drive L14
Fingalton Road P21
Fingleton Avenue N17
Fintry Crescent M17
Firbank Terrace P17
Foundry Lane M16
Gateside Crescent K17
Gateside Gardens J16
Gateside Road J17, K16
George Street L15
Gertrude Place K16
Gladstone Avenue L16
Glanderston Road L20, M21
Glanderstone Avenue P16
Glasgow Road N14

Glen Street M15, M16
Gleniffer Drive K13
Gorse Drive L14
Graham Street L15
Grahamston Park L13
Grahamston Road L13
Grampian Way M17
Harelaw Avenue N17
Hawthorn Drive N18
Heather Avenue K13
Henry Street L15
Heys Street M16
Hillside Drive K15
Hillside Grove K16
Hillside Road K15
House Cottages M17
John Smith Gate M14
John Street L15
Kelburn Street L16
Kelvin Drive N17
Kerr Street K16
Killoch Drive N17
Killoch Way J17
Kirkton Avenue L16
Kirktonside L17
Langton Crescent N17
Larchwood Terrace N18
Laurel Way L15
Leven Court L13
Levernside Avenue K16
Levern Crescent L17
Levern Gardens L15
Levern Walkway M15
Linnhe Drive L13
Lochlibo Crescent K17
Lochlibo Road J17
Lochlibo Terrace K17
Lomond Court M16
Lomond Drive L14
Lowndes Court N16
Lowndes Street M16
Lyoncross Avenue N16
Lyoncross Crescent N15
Main Street M16
Manse Court N15
Maple Drive N18
Maxton Avenue K15
Maxton Grove K15
Mill Road L16
Millview N15
Moidart Court L14
Montfort Gate P15
Montfort Park P15
Moorhouse Street M16
Moss Drive K13
Muriel Lane M15
Muriel Street M15
Murray Place N14
Neilston Road K17
Netherton Drive N16, P17
Nevis Court M17
Newhouse Cottages L18
Newton Avenue M17
North Park Avenue L15
Oakbank Drive N18

Ochil Drive M17
Paisley Road L14
Park Avenue L17
Patterton Drive N17
Pentland Court L17
Pentland Drive L17
Princes Square N15
Quarry Road L14
Ralston Road M16
Rankin Way N15
Robertson Street L15
Rockmount Avenue N17
Roebank Drive M17
Rowanpark Drive K13
Rufflees Avenue N14
St Marys Crescent N16
St Marys Gardens M16
Salterland Road P13
Saunders Court (1) L15
Seaforth Crescent L14
Shanks Avenue M16
Shanks Way M13
Shiel Court L13
Sidlaw Avenue M17
Simpson Gardens L16
South Park Avenue L15
Springfield Drive P17
Springfield Grove N18
Springfield Road L19, M18
Springhill Road L16, L17
Springhill Road L18, L20
Stewart Court M14
Stewart Crescent N14
Stewart Place N14
Stewart Street N14
Stobs Drive L13
Stormyland Way L16
Sunnyside Place L16
Tait Avenue N14
Tinto Drive L17
Tower Avenue N14
Tower Rais P15
Trees Park Avenue L14
Trees Park Gardens L14
Victoria Avenue L14
Victoria Crescent L14
Victoria Drive L14
Victoria Gardens L14
Victoria Grove L14
Victoria Place M14
Victoria Road L14
Vorlich Court M17
Walton Street M15
Water Cottages P17
Water Road M15
Waulkmill Avenue N14
Waulkmill Way N14
Weir Avenue M16
Westbourne Halls M16
Whin Avenue L14
Woodside Crescent N16
Wraes Avenue N14
Wraes View J17
Wright Avenue K16

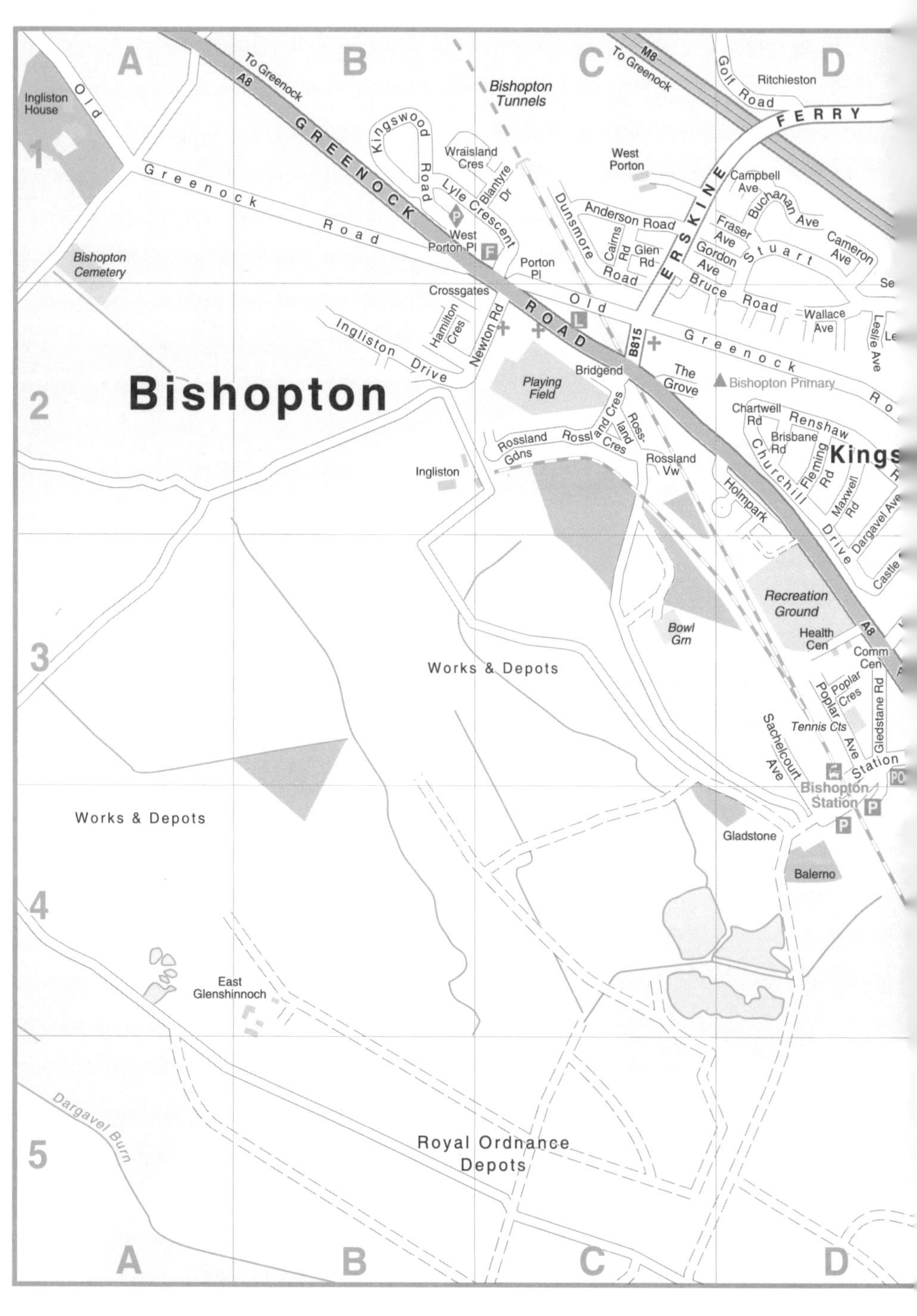
A
B
C
D
1
2
3
4
5
Ingliston House
Old
To Greenock
A8
GREENOCK ROAD
Bishopton Tunnels
To Greenock
M8
Golf Road
Ritchieston
FERRY
ERSKINE
Kingswood Road
Wraisland Cres
Blantyre Dr
Lyle Crescent
West Porton
Campbell Ave
Buchanan Ave
Cameron Ave
Fraser Ave
Gordon Ave
Stuart Ave
Bruce Road
Greenock Road
West Porton Pl
Porton Pl
Anderson Road
Dunsmore Road
Cairns Rd
Glen Rd
Bishopton Cemetery
Crossgates
Hamilton Cres
Newton Rd
Old
B815
Wallace Ave
Leslie Ave
Ingliston Drive
Bishopton
Playing Field
Bridgend
The Grove
Bishopton Primary
Greenock Ro
Chartwell Rd
Renshaw
Brisbane Rd
Churchill Drive
Fleming Rd
Maxwell Rd
Dargavel Ave
Kings
Rossland Gdns
Rossland Cres
Ross-land Cres
Rossland Vw
Ingliston
Holmpark
Castle
Recreation Ground
Health Cen
Comm Cen
Bowl Grn
Works & Depots
Poplar Cres
Poplar Ave
Gledstane Rd
Tennis Cts
Sachelcourt Ave
Station
Bishopton Station
Gladstone
Balerno
Works & Depots
East Glenshinnoch
Dargavel Burn
Royal Ordnance Depots

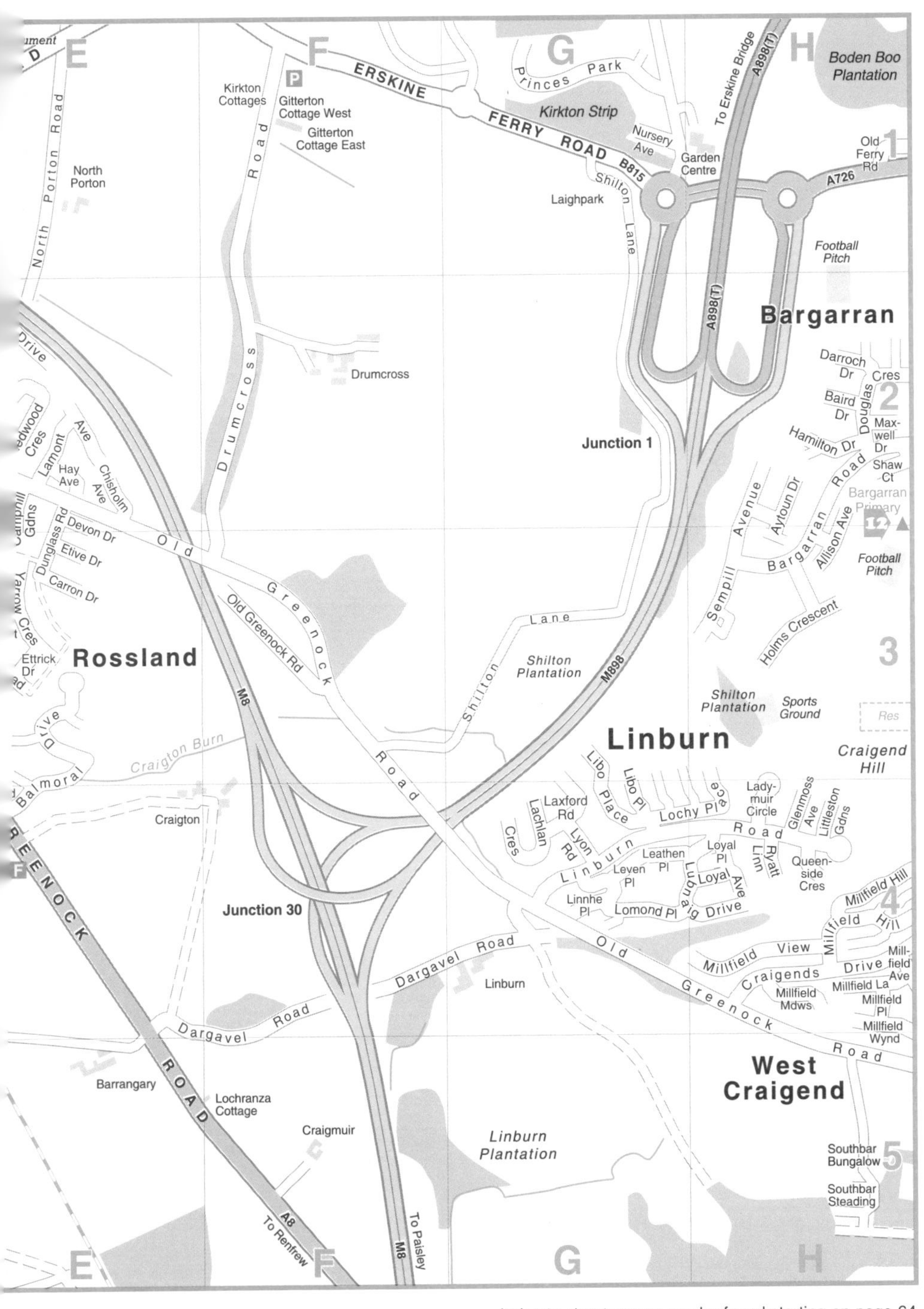


Index to street names can be found starting on page 64

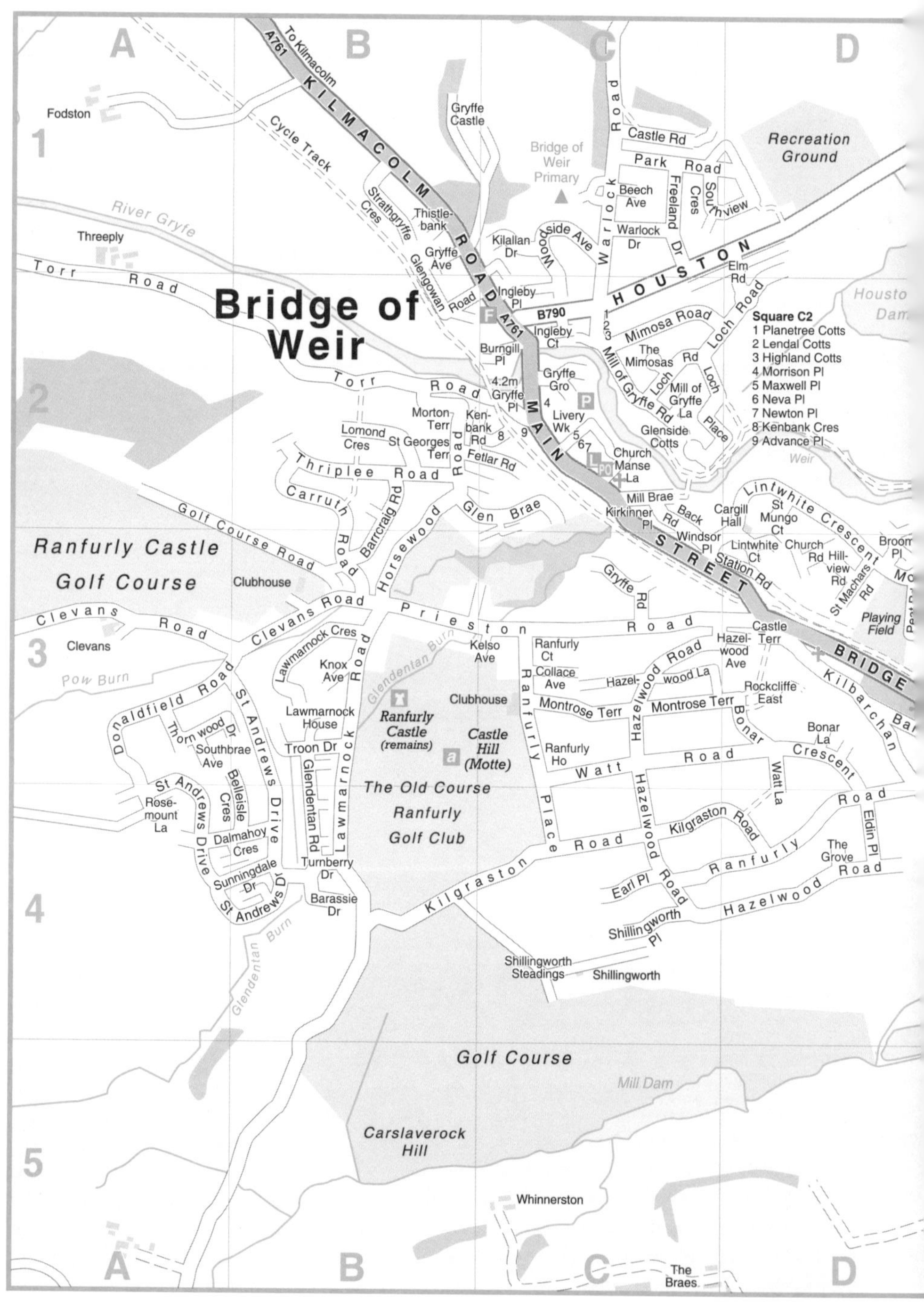

Bridge of Weir
Square C2
1 Planetree Cotts
2 Lendal Cotts
3 Highland Cotts
4 Morrison Pl
5 Maxwell Pl
6 Neva Pl
7 Newton Pl
8 Kenbank Cres
9 Advance Pl
To Kilmacolm
A761
KILMACOLM ROAD
MAIN STREET
BRIDGE
HOUSTON
B790
Fodston
Cycle Track
Gryffe Castle
Bridge of Weir Primary
Recreation Ground
Castle Rd
Park Road
Beech Ave
Freeland Dr
Cres
Southview
Warlock Road
Warlock Dr
Woodside Ave
Kilallan Dr
Strathgryffe Cres
Thistle-bank
Gryffe Ave
Glengowan Road
Ingleby Pl
Ingleby Ct
Burngill Pl
River Gryffe
Threeply
Torr Road
Elm Rd
Loch Road
Mimosa Road
The Mimosas
Rd
Loch Place
Mill of Gryffe Rd
Mill of Gryffe La
Glenside Cotts
Gryffe Gro
Livery Wk
4.2m
Gryffe Pl
Church Manse La
Weir
Housto Dam
Morton Terr
Ken-bank Rd
Lomond Cres
St Georges Terr
Road
Fetlar Rd
Thriplee Road
Carruth Road
Barrcraig Rd
Glen Brae
Horsewood
Mill Brae
Kirkinner Pl
Back Rd
Cargill Hall
St Mungo Ct
Lintwhite Crescent
Windsor Pl
Lintwhite Ct
Church Rd
Hill-view Rd
Station Rd
St Machars Rd
Broom Pl
Playing Field
Golf Course Road
Ranfurly Castle Golf Course
Clubhouse
Clevans Road
Clevans
Pow Burn
Prieston Road
Gryffe Rd
Castle Terr
Hazel-wood Ave
Kilbarchan
Lawmarnock Cres
Knox Ave
Lawmarnock Road
Glendentan Burn
Kelso Ave
Ranfurly Ct
Collace Ave
Hazel-wood La
Hazelwood Road
Rockcliffe East
Clubhouse
Ranfurly Castle (remains)
Castle Hill (Motte)
Lawmarnock House
Troon Dr
Glendentan Rd
Montrose Terr
Ranfurly Ho
Bonar Crescent
Bonar La
Watt Road
Watt La
Ranfurly Place
The Old Course
Ranfurly Golf Club
Donaldfield Road
Thorn wood Dr
Southbrae Ave
St Andrews Drive
Belleisle Cres
Rose-mount La
Dalmahoy Cres
Sunningdale Dr
Turnberry Dr
Barassie Dr
Kilgraston Road
Ranfurly Road
Eldin Pl
The Grove
Earl Pl
Hazelwood Road
Shillingworth Pl
Shillingworth Steadings
Shillingworth
Golf Course
Mill Dam
Carslaverock Hill
Whinnerston
The Braes

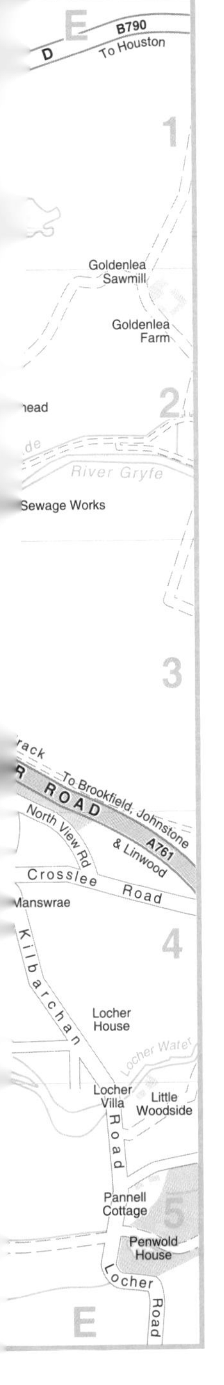

## Index to Bridge of Weir

Advance Place (9) C2
Back Road C2
Bankend Road D3
Barassie Drive B4
Barrcraig Road B3
Beech Avenue C1
Belleisle Crescent B4
Bonar Crescent D3
Bonar Lane D3
Bracken Place D2
Bridge of Weir Road D3
Broom Place D3
Burngill Place C2
Carruth Road B2
Castle Road C1
Castle Terrace D3
Church Manse Lane C2
Church Road D3
Clevans Road B3
Collace Avenue C3
Crosslee Road E4
Dalmahoy Crescent A4
Donaldfield Road A3
Earl Place C4
Eldin Place D4
Elm Road D1
Fetlar Road B2
Freeland Drive C1
Glen Brae B2
Glendentan Road B3
Glengowan Road B2
Glenside Cottages C2
Golf Course Road A2
Gorse Crescent D3
Grove, The D4
Gryfe Road C3
Gryffe Avenue B1
Gryffe Castle B1
Gryffe Grove C2
Gryffe Place C2
Hazelwood Avenue D3
Hazelwood Lane C3
Hazelwood Road C3
Highland Cottages (3) C2
Hillview Road D3
Horsewood Road B3
Houston Road C2
Ingleby Court C2
Ingleby Place C2
Kelso Avenue C3
Kenbank Crescent (8) C2
Kenbank Road B2
Kilallan Avenue C1
Kilbarchan Road D3
Kilgraston Road C4
Kilmacolm Road B1
Kirkinner Place C3
Knox Avenue B3
Lawmarnock Crescent B3
Lawmarnock House B3
Lawmarnock Road B4
Lendal Cottages (2) C2
Lintwhite Court D3
Lintwhite Crescent D2
Livery Walk C2
Loch Place C2
Loch Road C2
Locher Road E5
Lomond Crescent B2
Main Street C2
Maxwell Place (5) C2
Mill Brae C2
Mill of Gryffe Lane C2
Mill of Gryffe Road C2
Mimosa Road C2
Mimosas, The C2
Montrose Terrace C3
Morrison Place (4) C2
Morton Terrace B2
Moss Road D3
Neva Place (6) C2
Newton Place (7) C2
North View Road E4
Park Road C1
Peat Road D3
Planetree Cottages (1) C2
Preiston Road B3
Ranfurly Court C3
Ranfurly House C3
Ranfurly Place C3
Ranfurly Road D4
Rockcliffe East D3
Rosemount Lane A4
St Andrews Drive B3
St Georges Terrace B2
St Machars Road D3
St Mungo Court D2
Shillingworth Place C4
Shillingworth Steadings C4
Southbrae Avenue A3
Southview Crescent C1
Station Road D3
Strathgryffe Crescent B1
Sunningdale Drive B4
Thistlebank B1
Thornwood Drive A3
Thriplee Road B2
Torr Road B2
Troon Drive B3
Turnberry Drive B4
Warlock Drive C1
Warlock Road C1
Watt Lane D3
Watt Road C3
Windsor Place C3
Woodside Avenue C1

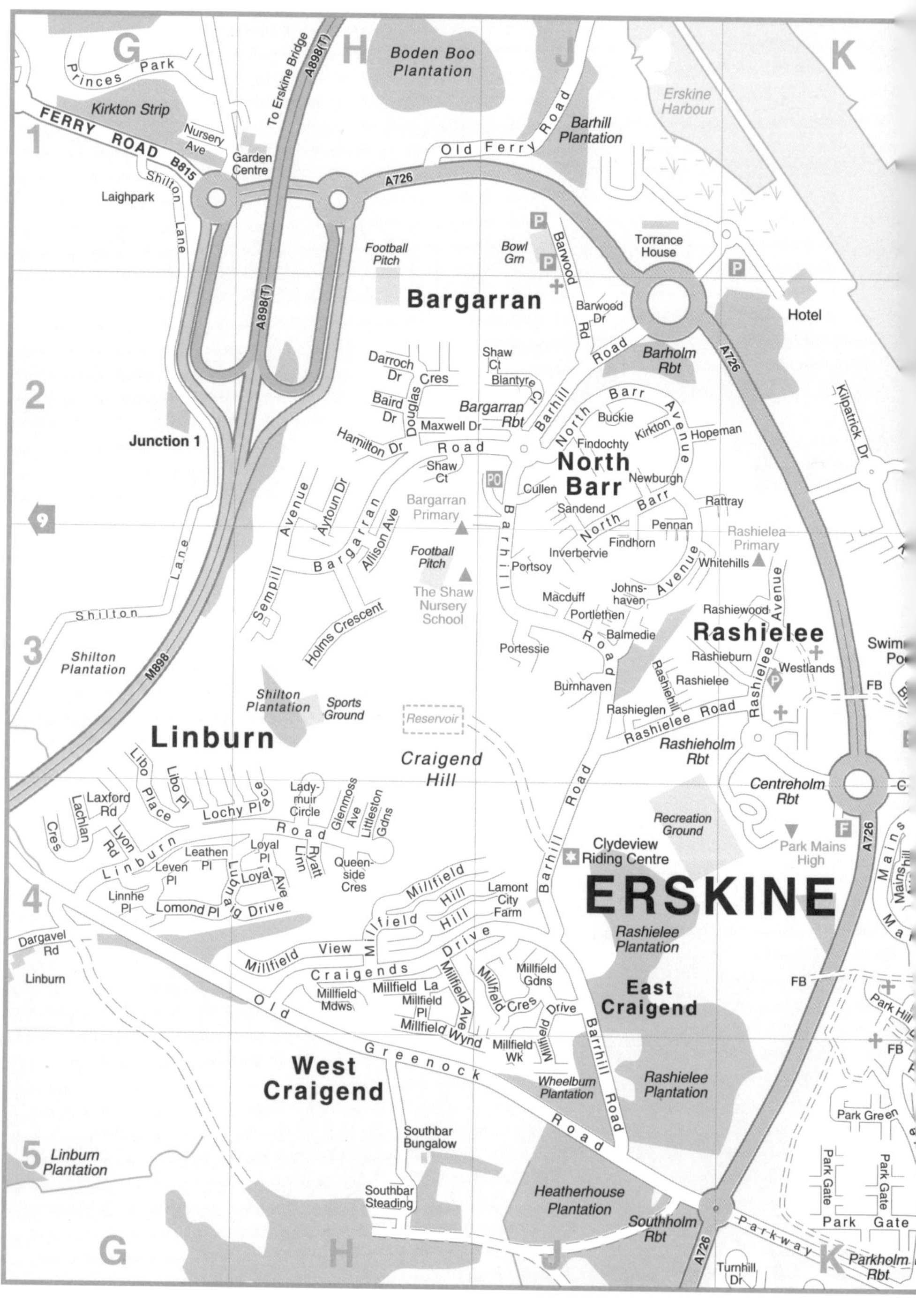

ERSKINE
Bargarran
North Barr
Rashielee
Linburn
East Craigend
West Craigend
Craigend Hill
Boden Boo Plantation
Barhill Plantation
Erskine Harbour
Kirkton Strip
Princes Park
FERRY ROAD B815
Nursery Ave
Garden Centre
To Erskine Bridge
A898(T)
A726
Old Ferry Road
Shilton Lane
Laighpark
Football Pitch
Bowl Grn
Barwood Rd
Barwood Dr
Torrance House
Hotel
Barholm Rbt
Darroch Dr
Cres
Shaw Ct
Blantyre Ct
Baird Dr
Douglas Cres
Bargarran Rbt
Maxwell Dr
Hamilton Dr
Road
Barhill
North Barr Avenue
Buckie
Kirkton
Hopeman
Findochty
Newburgh
Cullen
Sandend
Rattray
Pennan
Findhorn
Inverbervie
Portsoy
Whitehills
Rashielea Primary
Kilpatrick Dr
Junction 1
Bargarran Primary
Sempill Avenue
Aytoun Dr
Allison Ave
Bargarran
Holms Crescent
The Shaw Nursery School
Johns-haven
Macduff
Portlethen
Balmedie
Portessie
Burnhaven
Rashiewood
Rashieburn
Rashielee
Rashiehill
Rashieglen
Rashielee Road
Rashielee Avenue
Westlands
Rashieholm Rbt
Centreholm Rbt
Swim Po
FB
Shilton
Shilton Plantation
M898
Sports Ground
Reservoir
Libo Place
Libo Pl
Laxford Rd
Lachlan Cres
Lyon Rd
Lochy Place
Lady-muir Circle
Glenmoss Ave
Littleston Gdns
Linburn Road
Leathen Pl
Leven Pl
Loyal Pl
Loyal Ave
Ryatt Linn
Queen-side Cres
Lugnaig Drive
Linnhe Pl
Lomond Pl
Dargavel Rd
Linburn
Recreation Ground
Clydeview Riding Centre
Park Mains High
Mains
Mainshill
Millfield Hill
Lamont
City Farm
Millfield View
Millfield Drive
Craigends
Millfield La
Millfield Mdws
Millfield Pl
Millfield Ave
Millfield Cres
Millfield Gdns
Millfield Wynd
Millfield Wk
Millfield Drive
Old Greenock Road
Barhill Road
Wheelburn Plantation
Rashielee Plantation
Park Hill
Park Green
Park Gate
Southbar Bungalow
Southbar Steading
Heatherhouse Plantation
Southholm Rbt
Parkway
Turnhill Dr
Parkholm Rbt
Linburn Plantation
G
H
J
K
1
2
3
4
5
9

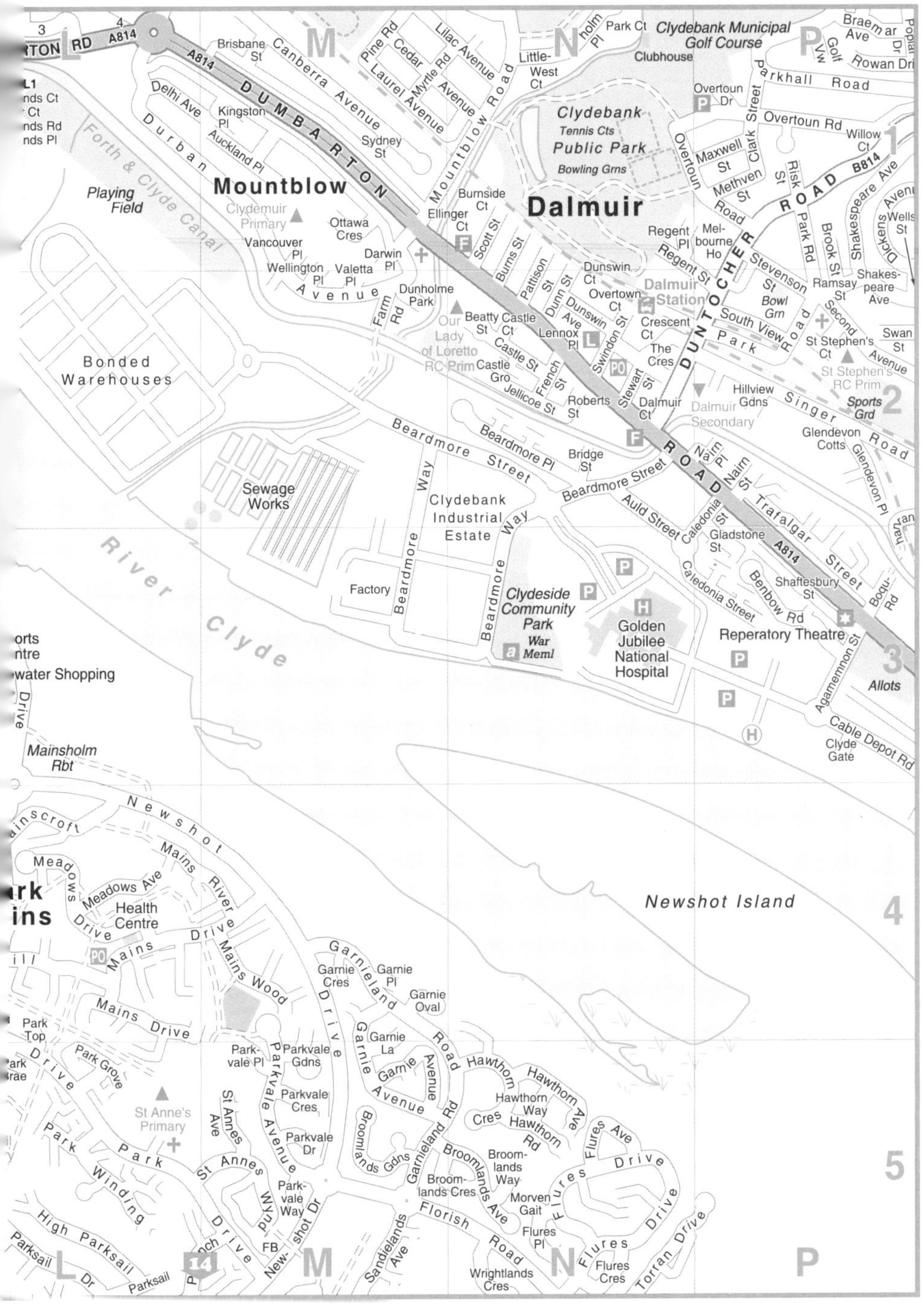


Index to street names can be found starting on page 64

J K L M
6 7 8 9 10

Erskine
Freeland
Inchinna

Turnhill Ave
Turnhill Dr
Turnyland Mdws
Turnyland Way
Turnhill Drive
Freeland Rd
Parkholm Rbt
Broomhill Cres
Low Parksail
Parksail
Park-way
New Dr
13
Inverarish
Dun Cann
Tiana-vaig
Suis-nish
Arnish
Niamh Ct
Cem
Old
Bourne Ct
Park Crescent
Bourne Cres
Park Road
Banchory
Broompark Dr
Craigiehall Ave
Craigiehall Cres
Craigiehall Way
Turnhill Cres
Fern Ave
Turnhill Gdns
Moss Dr
Freeland Road
Broom Ave
Sconser
Umachan
Ollach
Penchorran
Trovaig
Oskaig
Broomlea Cres
Luckingsford Road
Broomlands Ct
Bowl Grn
Greenock
Playing Field
Luckingsford Dr
Luckingsford Ave
Greenhead Road
Freeland Dr
Ladyacres Way
SOUTHBAR ROAD
A726
A8
To Bishopton
Broom Hill
Red Smiddy Rbt
GREENOCK ROAD
GREE
New Mains
Factory
Fountain Crescent
India Drive
Rec Grd
Inchinnan Dr
Inchinnan Drive
BARNSFORD ROAD
Newmains Avenue
Brownsfield Rd
Brownsfield Cres
Allands Avenue
River Dr
Avenue
Fountain Drive
Works
To Houston
HOUSTON ROAD
B790
TA Centre
Barnsford Avenue
Fountain Ave
Cartside Avenue
Inchinnan Industrial Estate
Inchinnan Business Park
South St
Brownsfield
Inchinnan Drive
Barnsford Bridge
Easter Walkinshaw
Wester Yonderton
Easter Yonderton
Walkinshaw Road

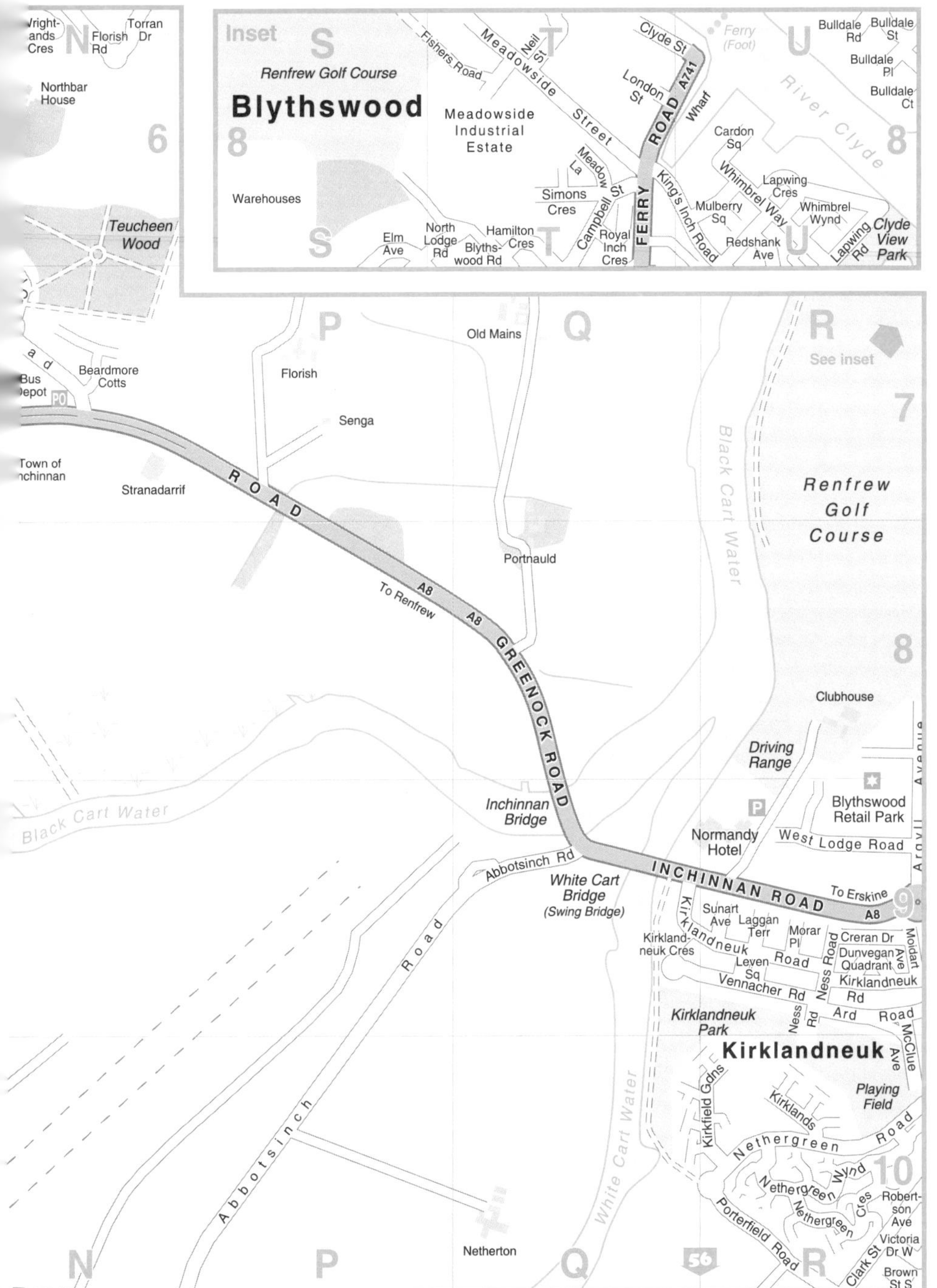


Index to street names can be found starting on page 64

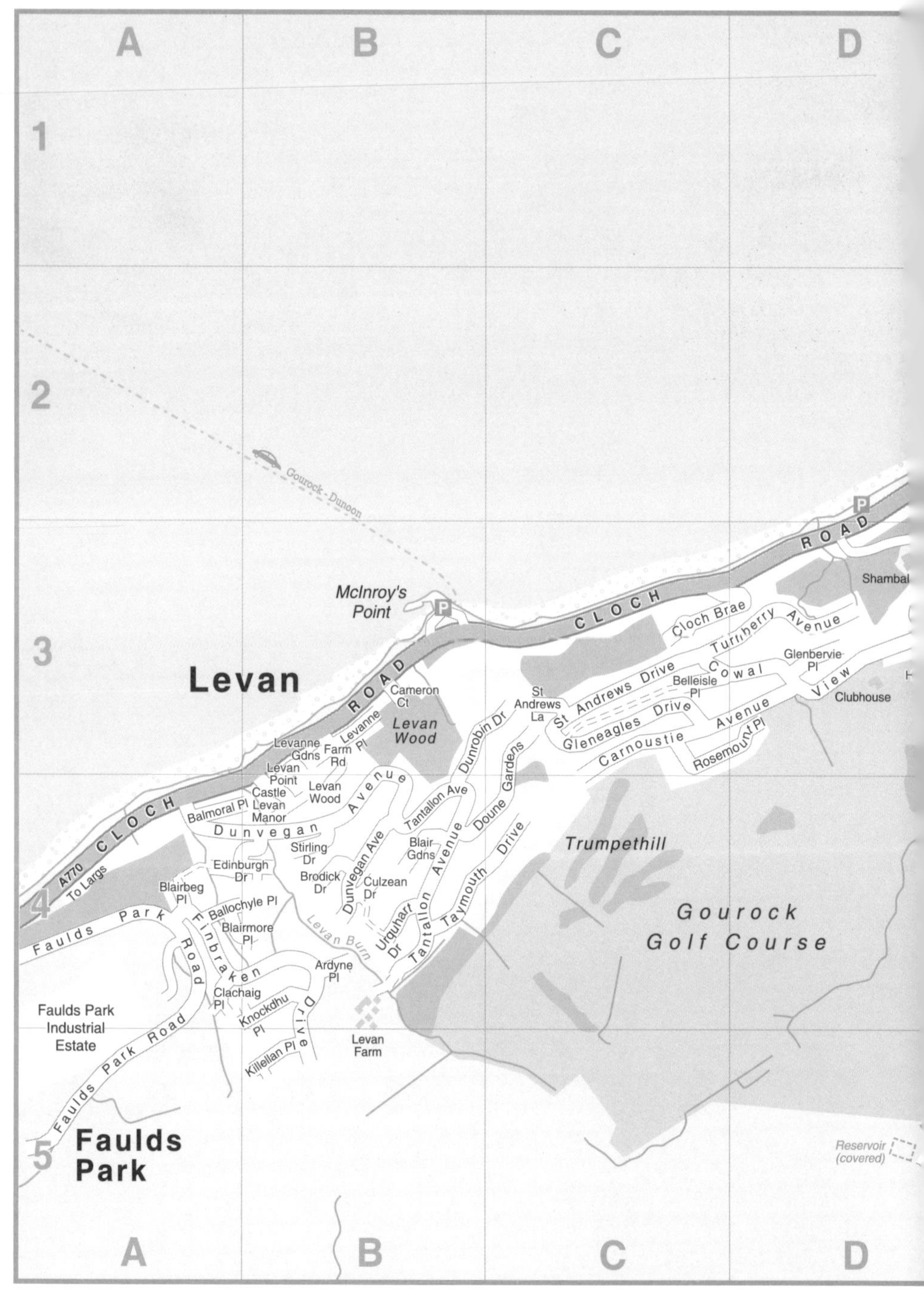
A
B
C
D
1
2
3
4
5
Gourock - Dunoon
McInroy's Point
Levan
CLOCH ROAD
A770 To Largs
Cameron Ct
Levan Wood
Levanne Pl
Levanne Gdns
Farm Rd
Levan Point
Castle Levan Manor
Levan Wood
Balmoral Pl
Dunvegan Avenue
Stirling Dr
Edinburgh Dr
Brodick Dr
Blairbeg Pl
Ballochyle Pl
Blairmore Pl
Finbraken Road
Fauld Park Road
Dunvegan Ave
Culzean Dr
Blair Gdns
Tantallon Ave
Tantallon Avenue
Urquhart Dr
Levan Burn
Ardyne Pl
Clachaig Pl
Knockdhu Pl
Drive
Killellan Pl
Levan Farm
Faulds Park Industrial Estate
Faulds Park Road
Faulds Park
Dunrobin Dr
Doune Gardens
Taymouth Drive
St Andrews La
St Andrews Drive
Gleneagles Drive
Carnoustie Avenue
Rosemount Pl
Belleisle Pl
Cowal View
Cloch Brae
Turnberry Avenue
Glenbervie Pl
Clubhouse
Shambal
Trumpethill
Gourock Golf Course
Reservoir (covered)

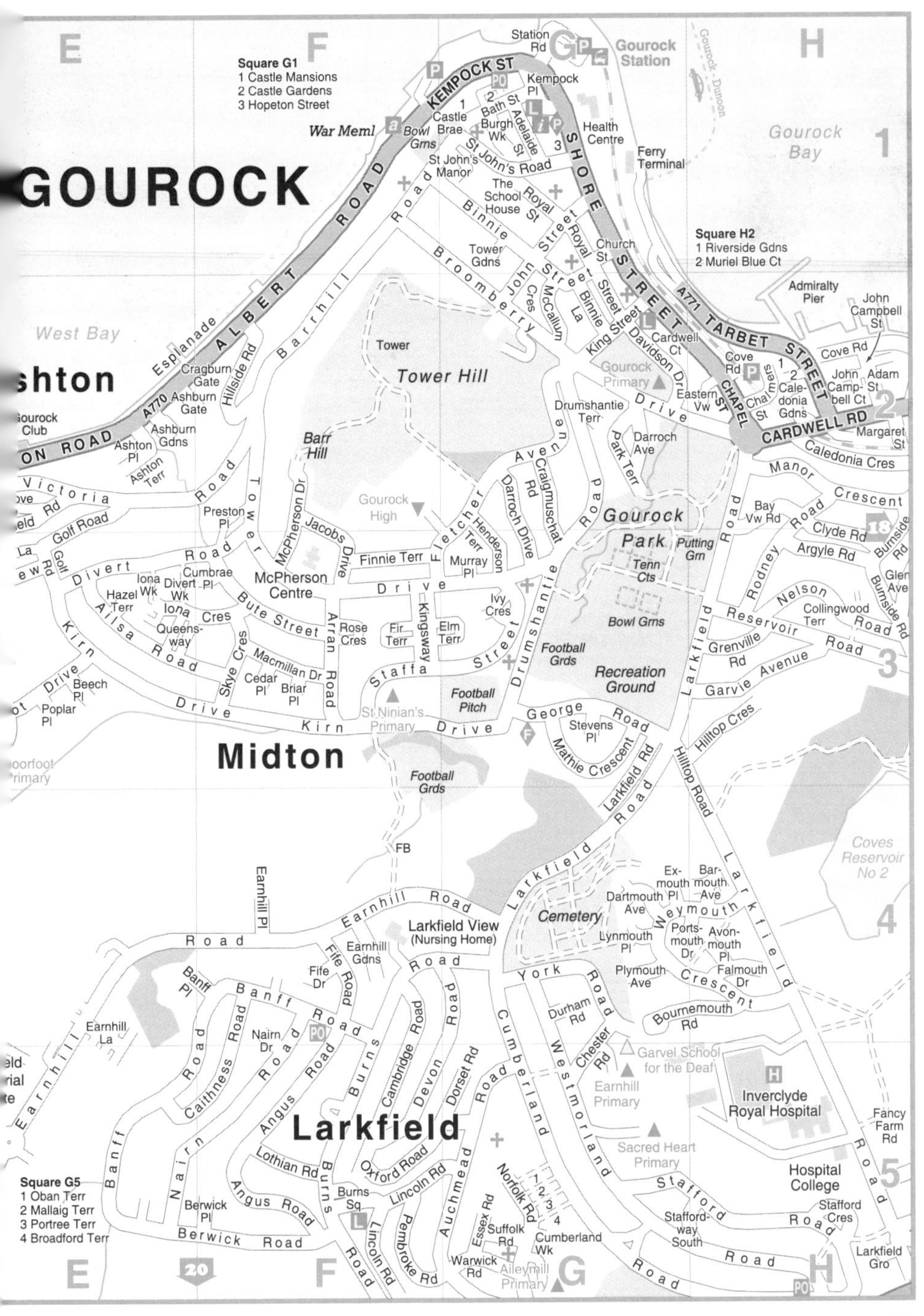


Index to street names can be found starting on page 65

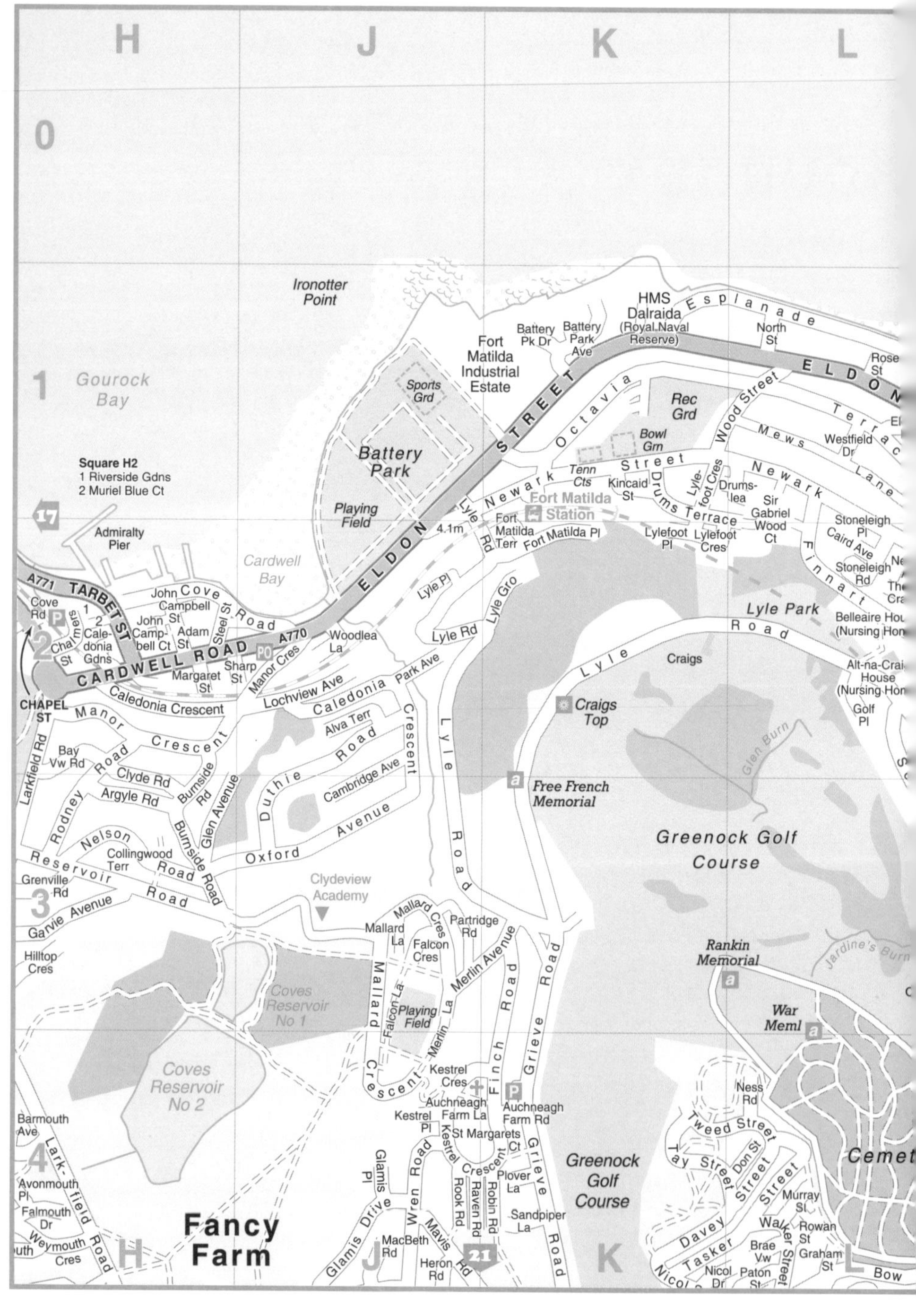
H
J
K
L
0
1
2
3
4
Ironotter Point
Gourock Bay
Square H2
1 Riverside Gdns
2 Muriel Blue Ct
17
Admiralty Pier
Cardwell Bay
HMS Dalraida (Royal Naval Reserve)
Esplanade
North St
Rose St
Eldon
Battery Pk Dr
Battery Park Ave
Fort Matilda Industrial Estate
Sports Grd
Battery Park
Playing Field
Eldon Street
Octavia
Rec Grd
Bowl Grn
Wood Street
Terrace
Mews
Westfield Dr
Lane
Newark Street
Tenn Cts
Kincaid St
Drums Terrace
Lyle-foot Cres
Drums-lea
Sir Gabriel Wood Ct
Fort Matilda Station
Fort Matilda Terr
Fort Matilda Pl
Lyle Rd
4.1m
Lylefoot Pl
Lylefoot Cres
Stoneleigh Pl
Caird Ave
Stoneleigh Rd
Finnart
Lyle Park
Belleaire House (Nursing Home)
Alt-na-Craig House (Nursing Home)
Golf Pl
Craigs
Lyle Road
Craigs Top
Glen Burn
Free French Memorial
Greenock Golf Course
A771 Tarbet St
Cove Rd
Chalmers St
Caledonia Gdns
John Cove Road
Campbell St
John Campbell Ct
Adam St
Steel St
Cardwell Road
A770
PO
Woodlea La
Sharp St
Margaret St
Manor Cres
Lochview Ave
Caledonia Park Ave
Lyle Pl
Lyle Gro
Chapel St
Caledonia Crescent
Manor Crescent
Alva Terr
Duthie Road
Crescent
Cambridge Ave
Oxford Avenue
Lyle Road
Larkfield Rd
Bay Vw Rd
Rodney Road
Clyde Rd
Argyle Rd
Burnside Rd
Glen Avenue
Burnside Road
Nelson
Collingwood Terr
Road
Reservoir Road
Grenville Rd
Garvie Avenue
Clydeview Academy
Hilltop Cres
Mallard Cres
Mallard La
Partridge Rd
Falcon Cres
Merlin Avenue
Mallard Crescent
Falcon La
Playing Field
Merlin La
Finch Road
Grieve Road
Coves Reservoir No 1
Coves Reservoir No 2
Rankin Memorial
Jardine's Burn
War Meml
Kestrel Cres
Auchneagh Farm La
Auchneagh Farm Rd
Kestrel Pl
St Margarets Ct
Kestrel Crescent
Plover La
Sandpiper La
Robin Rd
Raven Rd
Rook Rd
Glamis Pl
Glamis Drive
Wren Road
Mavis Rd
MacBeth Rd
Heron Rd
21
Greenock Golf Course
Ness Rd
Tweed Street
Tay Street
Don St
Street
Murray St
Walker Street
Rowan St
Graham St
Brae Vw
Paton St
Nicol Dr
Tasker
Davey
Bow
Cemet
Barmouth Ave
Lark-field Road
Avonmouth Pl
Falmouth Dr
Weymouth Cres
Fancy Farm

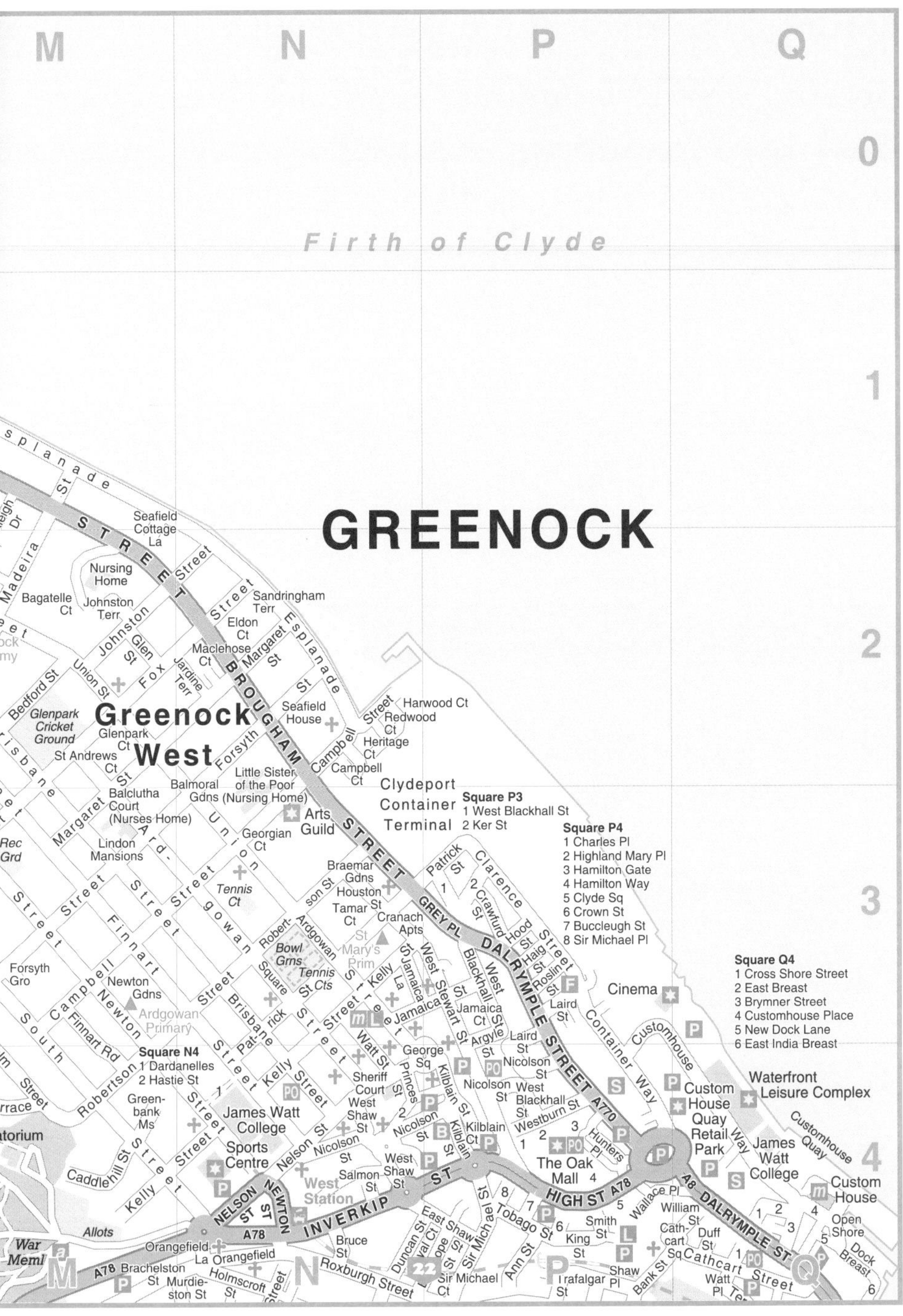
GREENOCK
Firth of Clyde
Greenock West
Clydeport Container Terminal
Square P3
1 West Blackhall St
2 Ker St
Square P4
1 Charles Pl
2 Highland Mary Pl
3 Hamilton Gate
4 Hamilton Way
5 Clyde Sq
6 Crown St
7 Buccleugh St
8 Sir Michael Pl
Square Q4
1 Cross Shore Street
2 East Breast
3 Brymner Street
4 Customhouse Place
5 New Dock Lane
6 East India Breast
Square N4
1 Dardanelles
2 Hastie St
Waterfront Leisure Complex
Custom House Quay
Retail Park
James Watt College
Custom House
Cinema
Arts Guild
The Oak Mall
Sports Centre
West Station
HIGH ST A78
INVERKIP ST
BROUGHAM STREET
DALRYMPLE STREET A770
A8 DALRYMPLE ST
GREY PL
Roxburgh Street
Container Way
Customhouse Quay
Esplanade
Glenpark Cricket Ground
Nursing Home
Seafield Cottage La
Seafield House
Ardgowan Primary
St Mary's Prim
Bowl Grns
Tennis Ct
Allots
War Meml
M
N
P
Q
0
1
2
3
4

Index to street names can be found starting on page 65

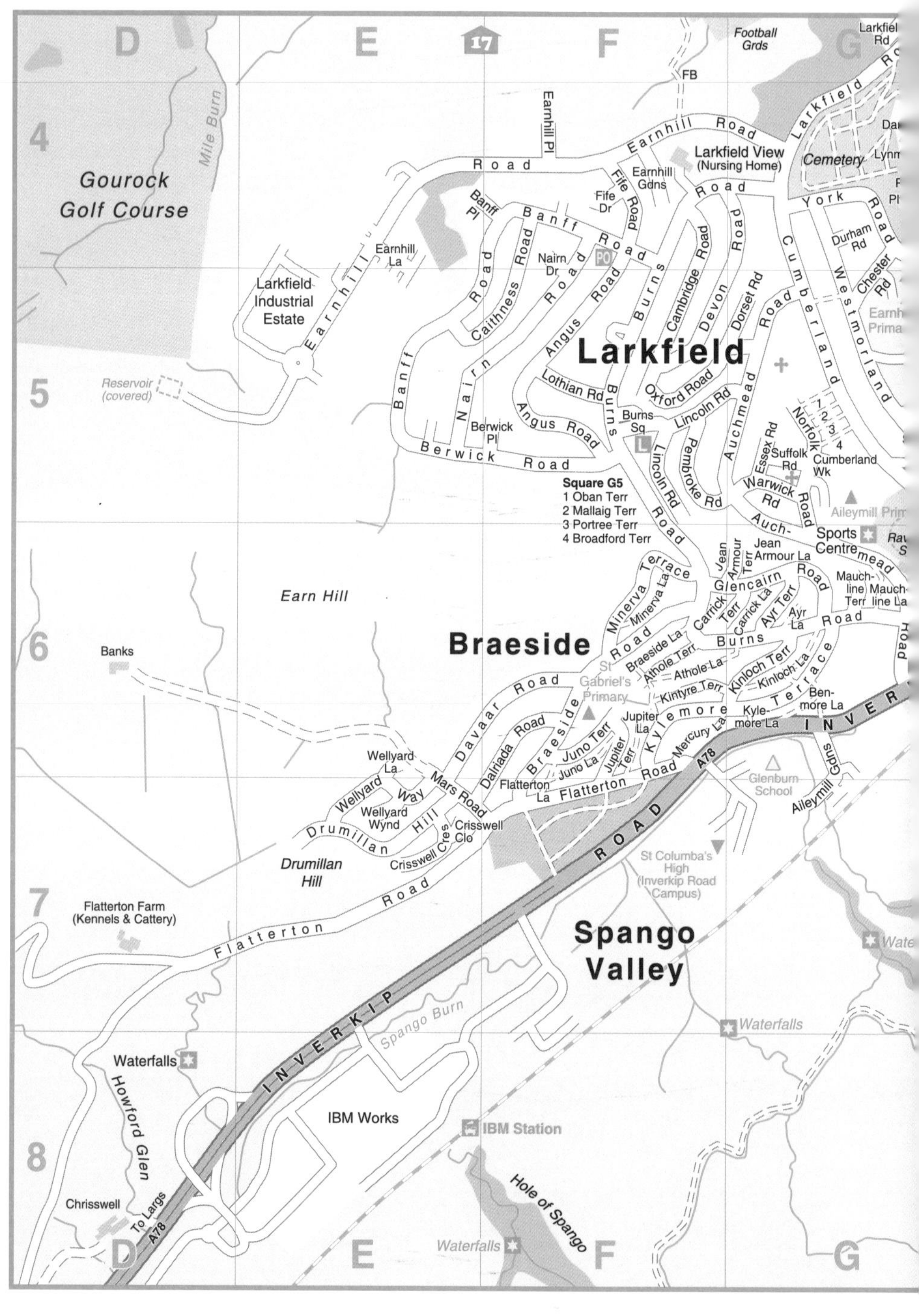

D
E
17
F
G
4
5
6
7
8
Football Grds
FB
Gourock Golf Course
Mile Burn
Earnhill Pl
Earnhill Road
Larkfield View (Nursing Home)
Cemetery
Earnhill Gdns
Fife Dr
Fife Road
Banff Pl
Banff Road
Earnhill La
Larkfield Industrial Estate
Nairn Dr
Caithness Road
Angus Road
Burns Road
Cambridge Road
Devon Road
Dorset Rd
Cumberland Road
Westmorland
York Road
Durham Rd
Chester Rd
Larkfield
Lothian Rd
Oxford Road
Lincoln Rd
Auchmead Road
Burns Sq
Berwick Pl
Berwick Road
Nairn Road
Banff Road
Reservoir (covered)
Pembroke Rd
Essex Rd
Suffolk Rd
Norfolk
Cumberland Wk
Warwick Rd
Aileymill Prim
Sports Centre
Centremead
Square G5
1 Oban Terr
2 Mallaig Terr
3 Portree Terr
4 Broadford Terr
Jean Armour Terr
Jean Armour La
Auch-
Mauch-line Terr
Mauch-line La
Minerva Terrace
Minerva La
Glencairn Road
Carrick Terr
Carrick La
Ayr Terr
Ayr La
Earn Hill
Braeside
Braeside La
Burns Road
Atholl Terr
Atholl La
Kinloch Terr
Kinloch La
Kintyre Terr
Ben-more La
Kyle-more La
Kylemore Terrace
St Gabriel's Primary
Banks
Davaar Road
Jupiter La
Jupiter Terr
Mercury La
Juno Terr
Juno La
Braeside Road
Dalriada Road
Wellyard La
Wellyard Way
Wellyard Wynd
Mars Road
Flatterton La
Flatterton Road
Drumillan Hill
Crisswell Cres
Crisswell Clo
Drumillan Hill
Glenburn School
Aileymill Gdns
A78
INVERKIP ROAD
St Columba's High (Inverkip Road Campus)
Flatterton Farm (Kennels & Cattery)
Flatterton Road
Spango Valley
Spango Burn
Waterfalls
Howford Glen
IBM Works
IBM Station
Hole of Spango
Chrisswell
To Largs

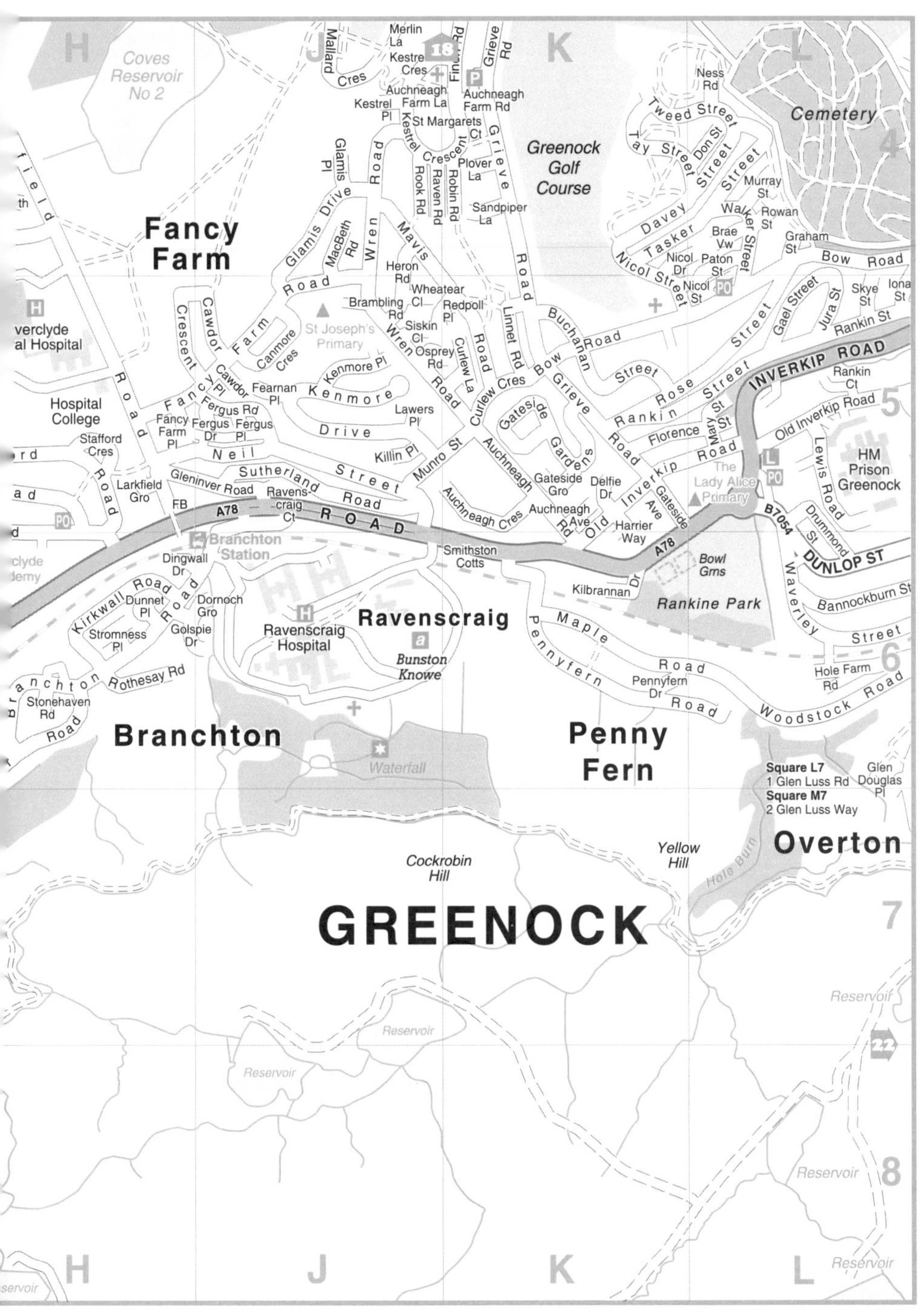


Index to street names can be found starting on page 65

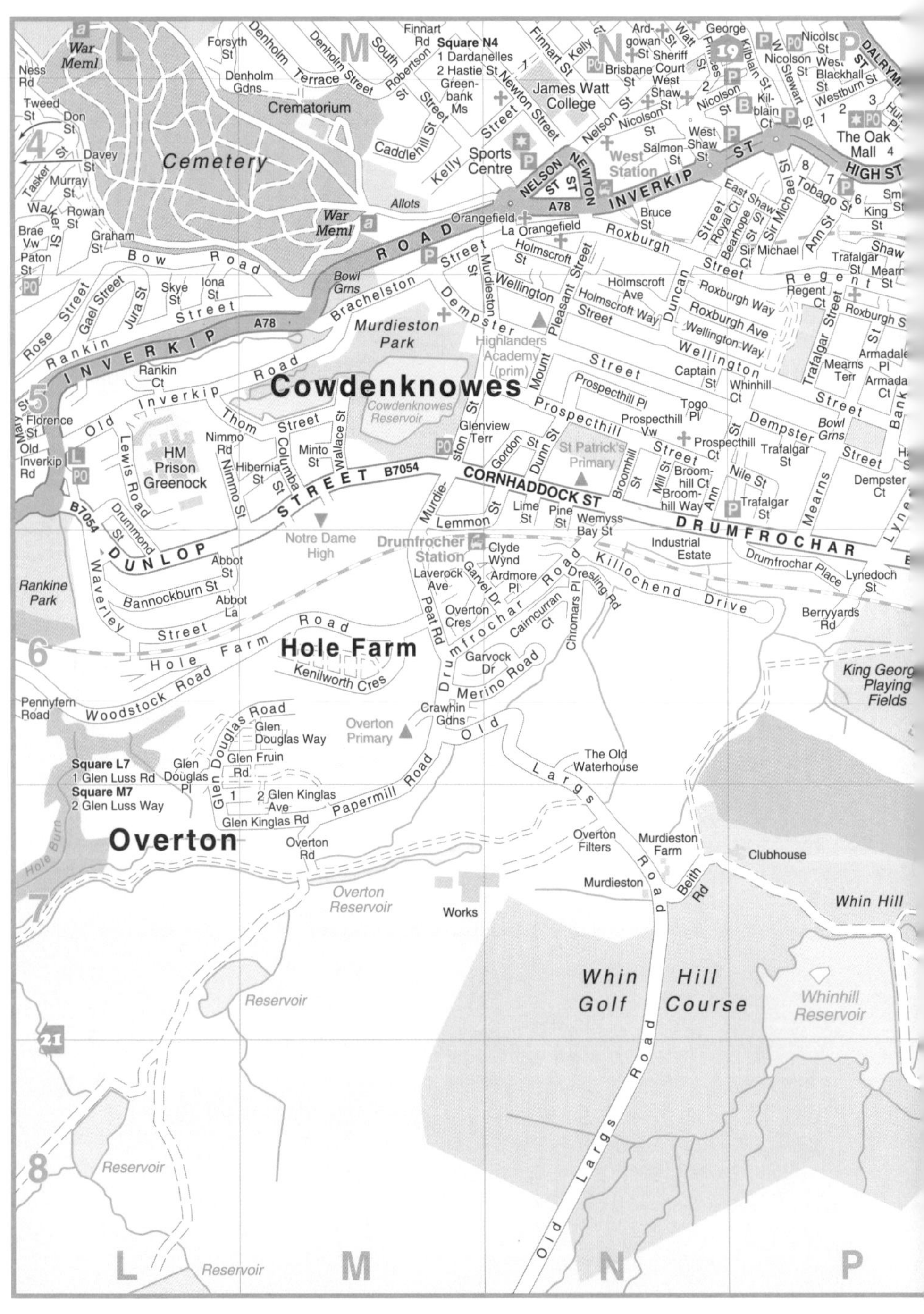
L
M
N
P
4
5
6
7
8
Square N4
1 Dardanelles
2 Hastie St
Square L7
1 Glen Luss Rd
Square M7
2 Glen Luss Way
Cemetery
Crematorium
War Meml
James Watt College
Sports Centre
West Station
The Oak Mall
HIGH ST
INVERKIP ST
INVERKIP ROAD
A78
NELSON ST
NEWTON ST
Orangefield
La Orangefield
Allots
Bow Road
Rankin Street
Rose Street
Gael Street
Jura St
Skye St
Iona St
Brachelston
Bowl Grns
Murdieston Park
Highlanders Academy (prim)
Cowdenknowes
Cowdenknowes Reservoir
HM Prison Greenock
Lewis Road
Old Inverkip Road
Rankin Ct
Thom Street
Nimmo St
Nimmo Rd
Hibernia St
Columba St
Minto St
Wallace St
DUNLOP STREET
B7054
Notre Dame High
Drumfrocher Station
CORNHADDOCK ST
DRUMFROCHAR
Industrial Estate
Drumfrochar Place
Killochend Drive
Lynedoch St
Berryyards Rd
St Patrick's Primary
Prospecthill Street
Dempster Street
Wellington Street
Roxburgh Street
Regent St
Trafalgar Street
Mearns Street
Rankine Park
Waverley Street
Bannockburn St
Abbot St
Abbot La
Drummond St
Hole Farm
Hole Farm Road
Kenilworth Cres
Woodstock Road
Pennyfern Road
Drumfrochar Road
Peat Rd
Overton Cres
Laverock Ave
Garvel Dr
Ardmore Pl
Clyde Wynd
Cairncurran Ct
Chromars Pl
Dresling Rd
Garvock Dr
Merino Road
Crawhin Gdns
Overton Primary
Glen Douglas Road
Glen Douglas Way
Glen Fruin Rd
Glen Kinglas Ave
Glen Kinglas Rd
Papermill Road
Overton
Overton Rd
Hole Burn
Overton Reservoir
Works
Old Largs Road
The Old Waterhouse
Overton Filters
Murdieston Farm
Murdieston
Clubhouse
Beith Rd
Whin Hill
Whin Hill Golf Course
Whinhill Reservoir
King George Playing Fields
Reservoir
21
19

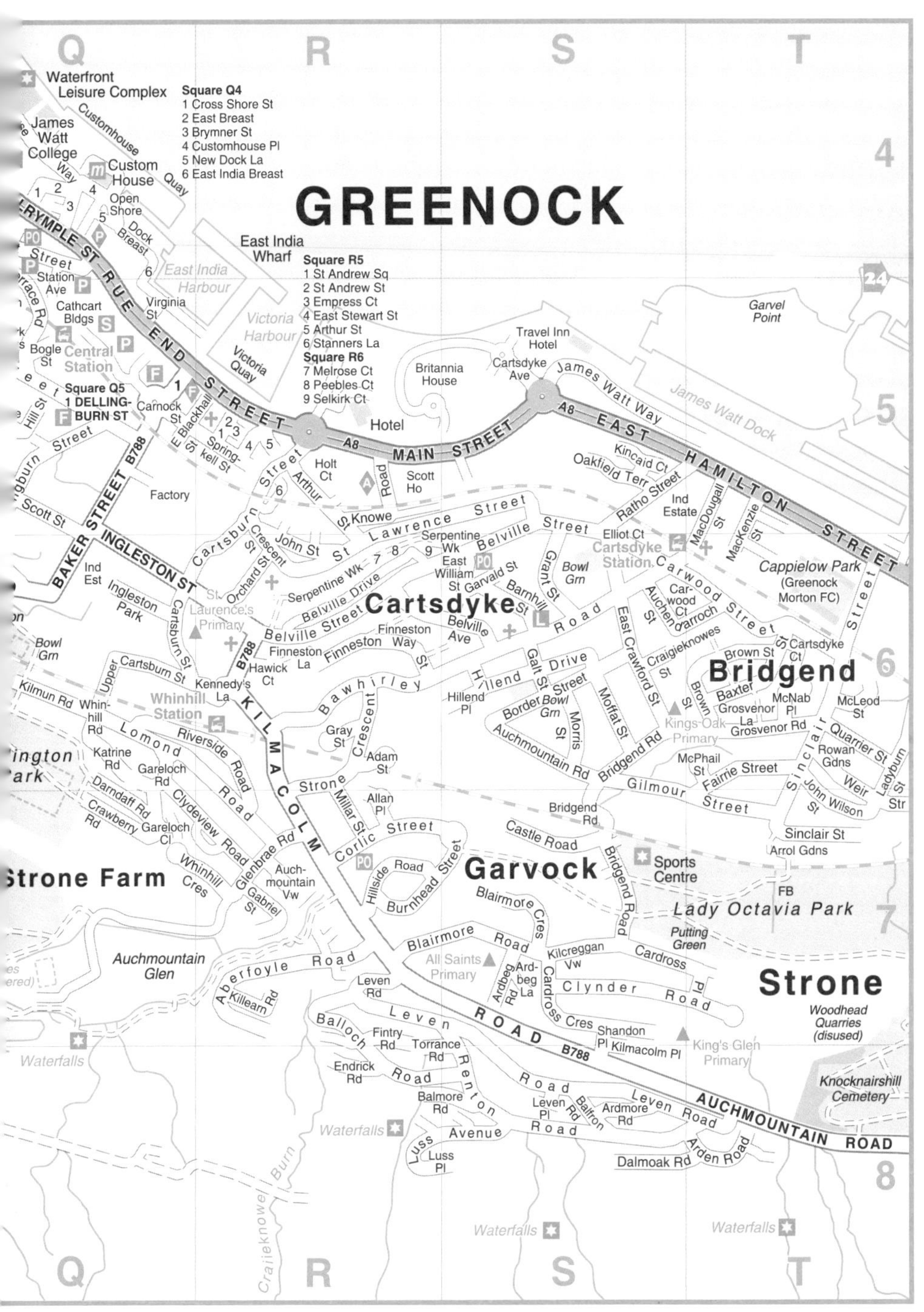


Index to street names can be found starting on page 65

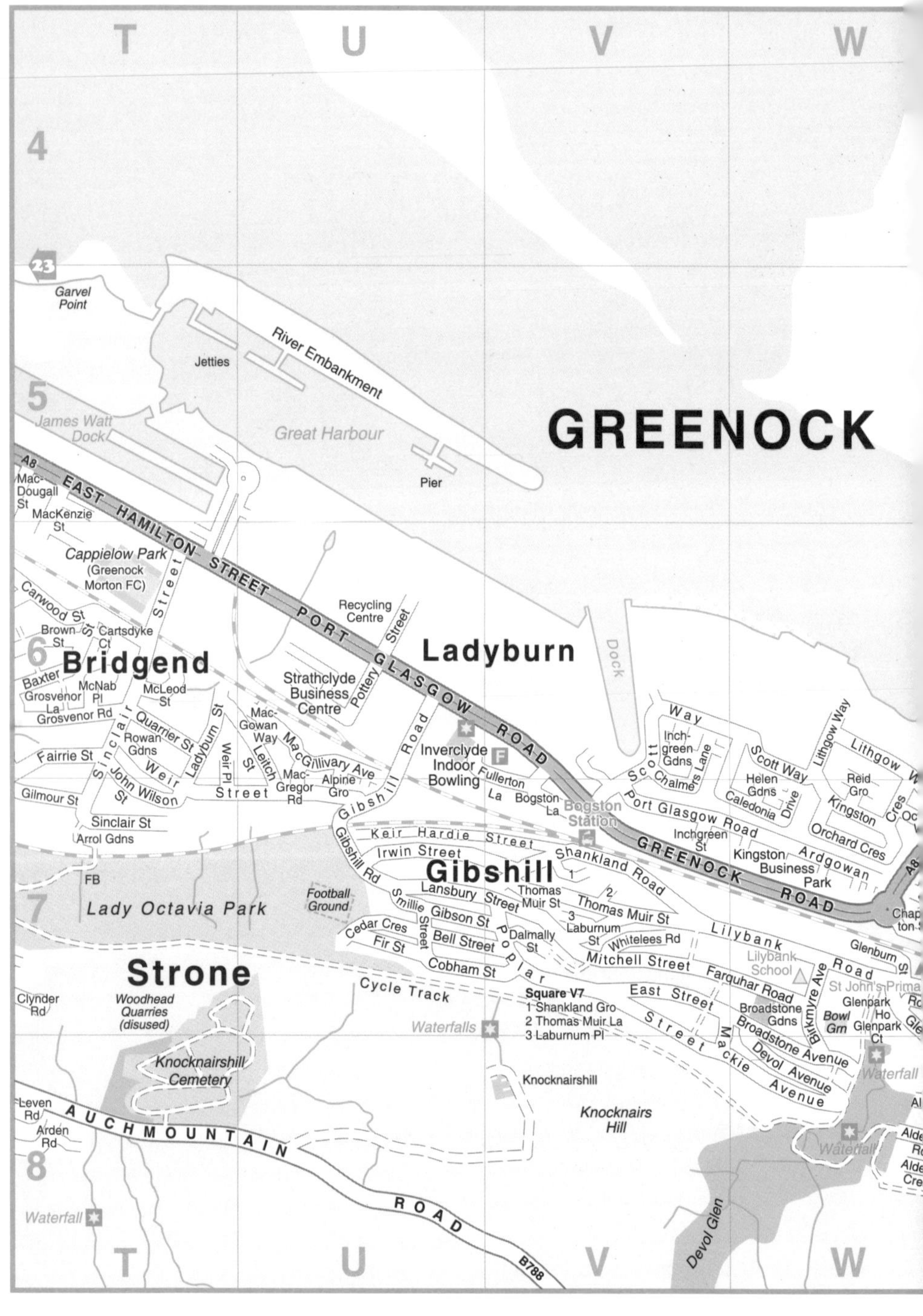
GREENOCK
Ladyburn
Bridgend
Gibshill
Strone
River Embankment
Jetties
Great Harbour
James Watt Dock
Pier
Garvel Point
EAST HAMILTON STREET
PORT GLASGOW ROAD
GREENOCK ROAD
AUCHMOUNTAIN ROAD
Cappielow Park (Greenock Morton FC)
Recycling Centre
Strathclyde Business Centre
Inverclyde Indoor Bowling
Bogston Station
Lady Octavia Park
Football Ground
Woodhead Quarries (disused)
Knocknairshill Cemetery
Knocknairshill
Knocknairs Hill
Waterfalls
Waterfall
Devol Glen
Cycle Track
Square V7
1 Shankland Gro
2 Thomas Muir La
3 Laburnum Pl
Kingston Business Park
Lilybank School
Dock

X Y Z AA

4

5

6

River Clyde

7

8

lybank

**Square X7**

**Square Y7**
1 Water St
2 Falconer St
3 Crawford St
4 Customhouse La

**Square Y8**
5 Thistle Ct
6 Heather Ct

**Square Z8**
1 Kilmory Terrace
2 Caledonia Street
3 Montgomerie Street

Greenock Road
Anderson St
Mirren's Shore
Queen St
West Quay
A8
The Comet (Historic Ship)
Coronation Park
Brown Street
Shore Street
Scarlow St
King Street
Church St
Fore St
Health Cen
Swim Pool
Balfour St
Huntly Terr
Huntly Pl
Princes Street
Jean St
William St
Street
School Ct
Avenue
Newark House
Willison's La
Chapel La
Highholm Ave
John Wood St
Bay St
Rowan Ct
Bay St
Court Road
Station Rd
Craigard
Port Glasgow Station
Ardenclutha Dr
Lochview Rd
Duncan Rd
Hillside Drive
Bowl Grns
Birkmyre Park
Springhill Road
Barrs Brae
Barrs Brae La
Glenhuntly Road
Glenhuntly Terr
Angus Rd
Berwick Rd
Bouverie Street
Ardmore Road
Kinross Ave
Moray Road
Barr's Brae
Roseyard Pl
Whitecroft
Cycle Track
Newark Castle
Castle Rd
Newark Castle Park
A8 Greenock
Newark St
Lwr Bouverie St
Newark Pl
Waterfalls
A761 Clune Brae
Clune Park Primary
Ashgrove La
Wilson St
Glasgow Road
Bruce St
Robert Street
Wallace St
Clune Pk St
Maxwell St
Fyfe Shore Rd
Fyfe Park Rd
Glenclune
Kelburn
Auchinleck Terr
Clune Brae
Benclutha

54

Index to street names can be found starting on page 65

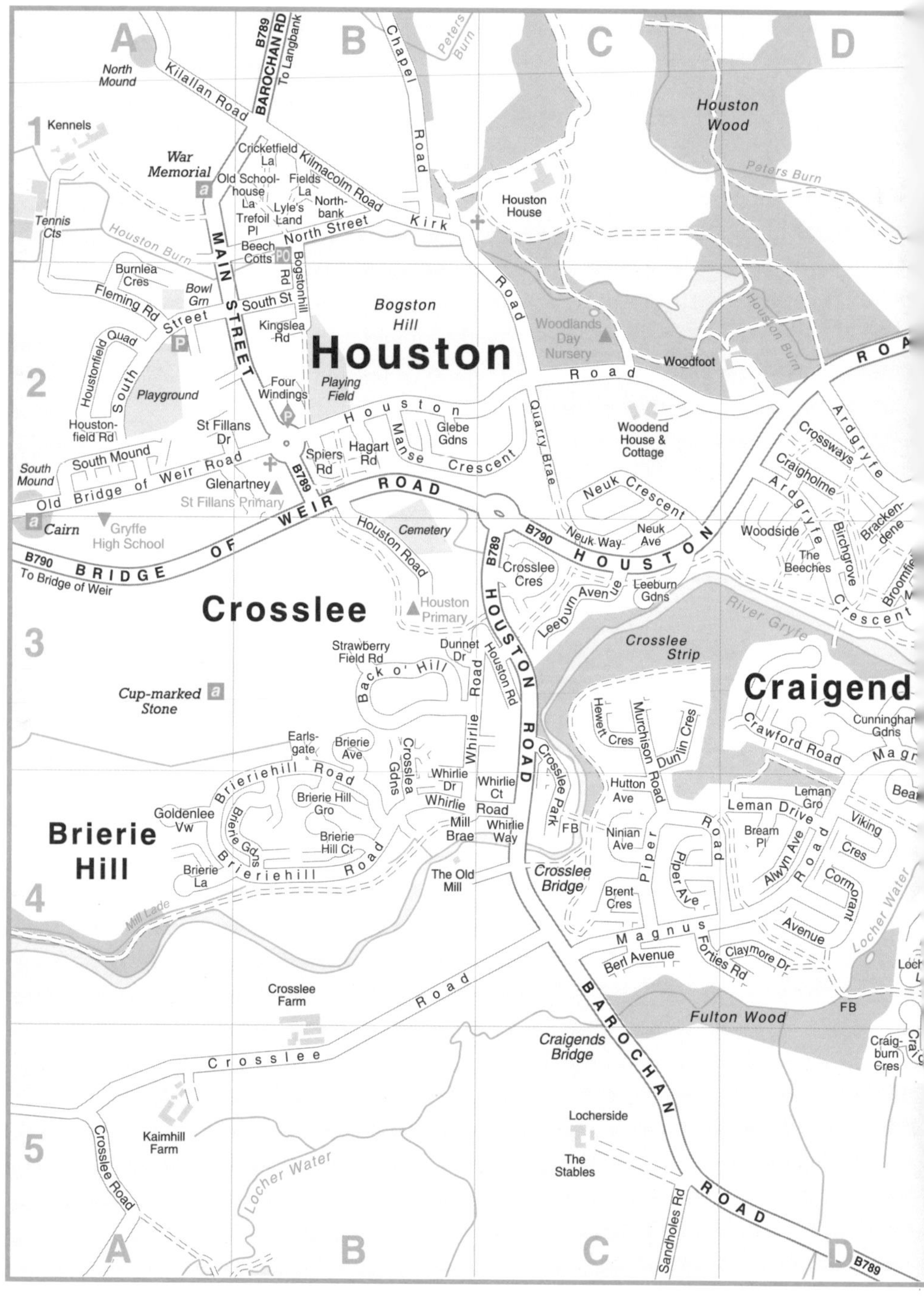

Houston
Crosslee
Craigend
Brierie Hill
Bogston Hill
Houston Wood
Main Street
Barochan Road
Houston Road
Bridge of Weir Road
Kilallan Road
Kilmacolm Road
North Street
Kirk Road
Chapel Road
Crosslee Road
Brieriehill Road
Whirlie Road
Magnus Road
Fulton Wood
Crosslee Strip
River Gryfe
Locher Water
Houston Burn
Peters Burn
Mill Lade
War Memorial
Cup-marked Stone
Cairn
Gryffe High School
St Fillans Primary
Houston Primary
Woodlands Day Nursery
Cemetery
Playground
Playing Field
Tennis Cts
Kennels
North Mound
South Mound
Houston House
Woodend House & Cottage
Crosslee Farm
Kaimhill Farm
Locherside
The Stables
The Old Mill
Crosslee Bridge
Craigends Bridge
To Bridge of Weir
To Langbank
B789
B790

## Index to Houston

Alwyn Avenue D4
Ardgryfe Crescent D2
Back o' Hill C3
Barochan Road B1, C4
Beatrice Gardens D4
Beech Cottages A1
Beeches, The D3
Berl Avenue C4
Birchgrove D3
Bogstonhill Road B2
Brackendene D3
Bream Place D4
Brent Crescent C4
Bridge of Weir Road A3
Brierie Avenue B3
Brierie Gardens B4
Brierie Hill Court B4
Brierie Hill Grove B4
Brierie Lane A4
Brieriehill Grove B4
Brieriehill Road A4
Broomfield D3
Burnlea Crescent A2
Chapel Road B1
Claymore Drive D4
Clippens Road E4
Cormorant Avenue D4
Craigburn Avenue D5
Craigburn Crescent D5
Craigburn Place D5
Craigends Road D5, E2, E4
Craigholme D2
Crawford Road D3
Cricketfield Lane B1
Crosslea Gardens B3
Crosslee Crescent C3
Crosslee Park C3
Crosslee Road A5
Crossways D2
Cunningham Gardens D3
Dunlin Crescent C3
Dunnet Drive B3
Earlsgate B3
Fields Lane B1
Fleming Road A2
Forties Road C4
Four Windings B2
Fulton Drive E4
Fulton Gardens E4
Glebe Gardens B2
Glenartney B2
Goldenlee View A4
Gryfebank Avenue E4
Gryfebank Close E3
Gryfebank Crescent E3
Gryfebank Way E3
Gryfebank D3
Gryfewood Crescent E3
Gryfewood Way E3
Hagart Road B2
Hewett Crescent C3
Hillfoot D4
Hillside E4
Houston Road C3
Houstonfield Quadrant A2
Houstonfield Road A2
Hutton Avenue C4
Kilallan Road A1
Kilmacolm Road B1
Kingslea Road B2
Kirk Road B1
Leeburn Avenue C3
Leeburn Gardens C3
Leman Drive D4
Leman Grove D4
Locher Avenue E3
Locher Crescent E3
Locher Gait E4
Locher Gardens E4
Locher Way E4
Locherburn Avenue D4
Locherburn Grove D4
Locherburn Place E4
Lyle's Land B1
Magnus Road C4
Main Street A1
Manse Crescent B2
Meadows, The D3
Mill Brae B4
Murchison Road C3
Netherburn Avenue E4
Netherburn Gardens E4
Neuk Avenue C3
Neuk Crescent C2
Neuk Way C3
Ninian Avenue C4
North Mains Farm Cottages E1
North Street B1
Northbank B1
Old Bridge of Weir Road A2
Old Schoolhouse Lane B1
Piper Avenue C4
Piper Road C4
Quarry Brae C2
Riverside D3
St Fillans Drive A2
Sandholes Road C5
South Mains Cottages E2
South Mound A2
South Street A2
Spiers Road B2
Strawberry Field Road B3
Trefoil Place A1
Viking Crescent D4
West Fulton E5
Whirlie Court C4
Whirlie Drive B3
Whirlie Road B4
Whirlie Way C4
Woodburn Place E5
Woodside D3

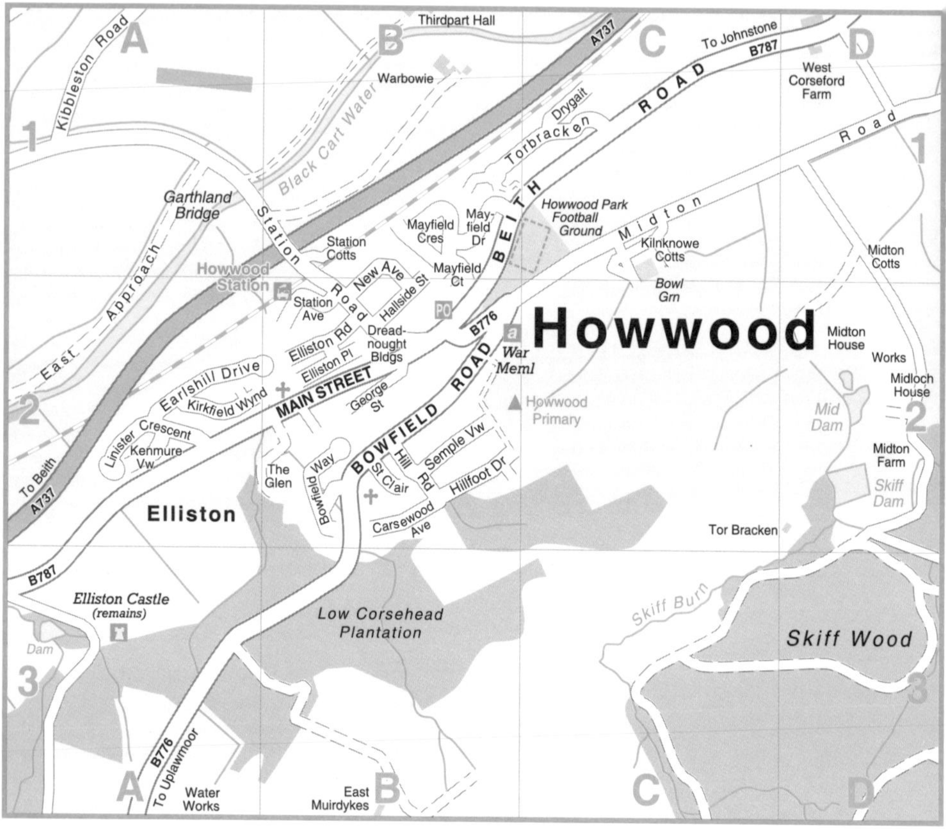

Thirdpart Hall
Kibbleston Road
Warbowie
A737
To Johnstone
B787
West Corseford Farm
Black Cart Water
Torbracken
Drygait
ROAD
Road
Garthland Bridge
Station
East Approach
Howwood Station
Station Cotts
Mayfield Cres
Mayfield Dr
Mayfield Ct
BEITH
Howwood Park Football Ground
Midton
Kilnknowe Cotts
Bowl Grn
Midton Cotts
Station Ave
Road
New Ave
Hallside St
PO
Dread-nought Bldgs
Elliston Rd
Elliston Pl
B776
Howwood
Midton House
Works
War Meml
Earlshill Drive
Kirkfield Wynd
MAIN STREET
George St
BOWFIELD ROAD
Howwood Primary
Midloch House
Mid Dam
Linister Crescent
Kenmure Vw
The Glen
Bowfield Way
Hill Rd
St Clair
Semple Vw
Hillfoot Dr
Midton Farm
Skiff Dam
To Beith
A737
Elliston
Carsewood Ave
Tor Bracken
B787
Elliston Castle (remains)
Dam
Low Corsehead Plantation
Skiff Burn
Skiff Wood
B776
To Uplawmoor
Water Works
East Muirdykes

## Index to Howwood

| | | | |
|---|---|---|---|
| Beith Road | B1 | Kirkfield Wynd | A2 |
| Bowfield Road | B2 | Linister Crescent | A2 |
| Bowfield Way | B2 | Main Street | B2 |
| Carsewood Avenue | B2 | Mayfield Court | B1 |
| Dreadnought Buildings | B2 | Mayfield Crescent | B1 |
| | | Mayfield Drive | B1 |
| Drygait | C1 | Midton Cottages | D1 |
| Earlshill Drive | A2 | Midton Road | B2 |
| East Approach | A2 | New Avenue | B2 |
| Elliston Place | B2 | St Clair | B2 |
| Elliston Road | B2 | Semple View | B2 |
| George Street | B2 | Station Avenue | B2 |
| Glen, The | B2 | Station Cottages | B1 |
| Hallside Street | B2 | Station Road | B1 |
| Hill Road | B2 | Torbracken | C1 |
| Hillfoot Drive | B2 | | |
| Kenmure View | A2 | | |
| Kibbleston Road | A1 | | |
| Kilnknowe Cottages | C1 | | |

## Index to Inverkip

| | | | |
|---|---|---|---|
| Aberdour Place | B4 | Cullen Place | B4 |
| Alexander Place | B2 | Daff Avenue | B2 |
| Alison Court | C2 | Duncan Place | B2 |
| Ardgowan Crescent | B3 | Dunlin Grove | D1 |
| Ardgowan Place | B3 | Dunnock Grove | D2 |
| Ardoch Drive | B3 | Findhorn Crescent | C3 |
| Bailey Grove | A1 | Findhorn Place | C3 |
| Baron Place | C3 | Findhorn Road | B4 |
| Beatock Place | B3 | Finnockbog Drive | B3 |
| Blaeberry Drive | A3 | Finnockbog Road | B3 |
| Boak Place | B2 | Forres Place | C4 |
| Boyd Avenue | C2 | Fran Terrace | B2 |
| Bridgend | C1 | Fraserburgh Place | B4 |
| Cameron Place | B2 | Glebe Road | C2 |
| Clyde View | B2 | Glen Crescent | C2 |
| Commoncraig Place | A3 | Harbour Square | A1 |
| Crawford Lane | C2 | Harbourside | A2 |
| Cromarty Grove | A1 | Hebrides Grove | A1 |
| Cullen Crescent | B4 | Hill Road | B3 |

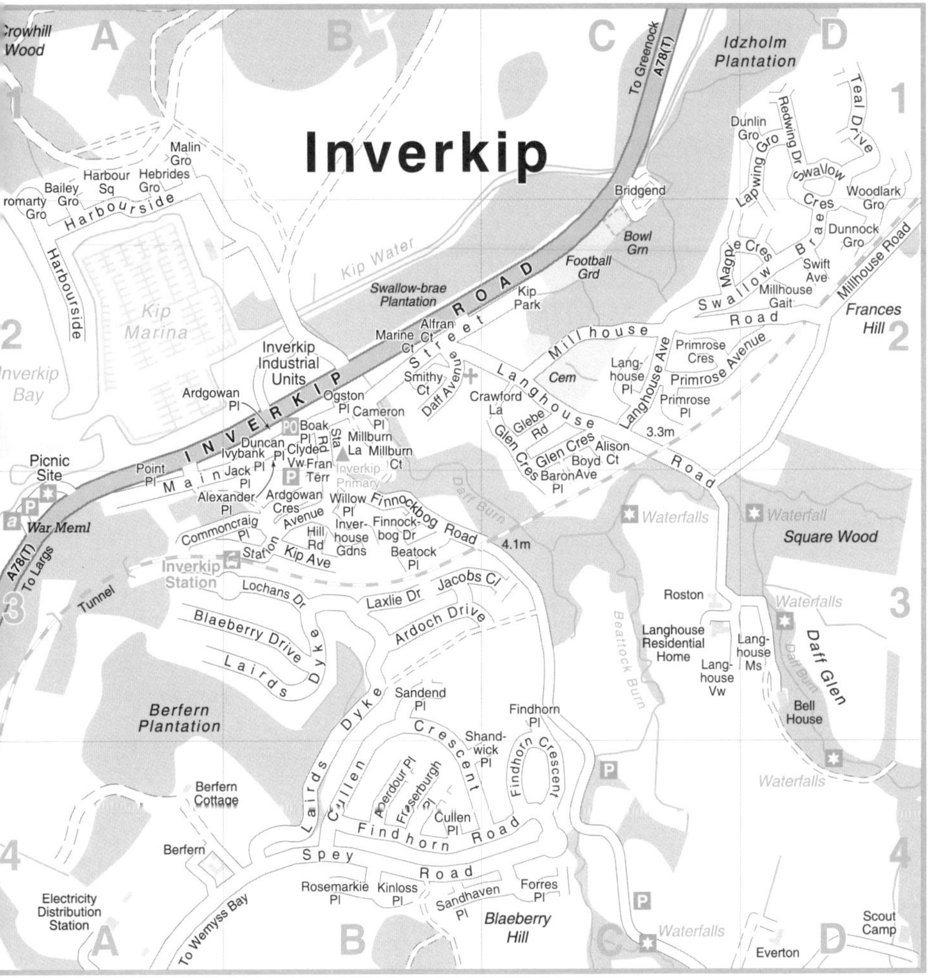

# Inverkip

| | | | | | | | |
|---|---|---|---|---|---|---|---|
| Inverhouse Gardens | B3 | Langhouse Road | C2 | Primrose Avenue | C2 | Swift Avenue | D2 |
| Inverkip Road | A2 | Langhouse View | C3 | Primrose Crescent | C2 | Teal Drive | D1 |
| Ivybank Place | B2 | Lapwing Grove | D1 | Primrose Place | C2 | Willow Place | B3 |
| Jack Place | B2 | Laxlie Drive | B3 | Redwing Drive | D1 | Woodlark Grove | D1 |
| Jacobs Close | B3 | Magpie Crescent | C2 | Rosemarkie Place | B4 | | |
| Kinloss Place | B4 | Main Street | B2 | Sandend Place | B3 | | |
| Kip Avenue | B3 | Malin Grove | A1 | Sandhaven Place | B4 | | |
| Kip Park | C2 | Marine Court | B2 | Shandwick Place | B4 | | |
| Lairds Dyke | B3, B4 | Millburn Court | B2 | Smithy Court | B2 | | |
| Langhouse Avenue | C2 | Millburn Lane | B2 | Spey Road | B4 | | |
| Langhouse Mews | D3 | Millhouse Gait | D2 | Station Avenue | B3 | | |
| Langhouse Place | C2 | Millhouse Road | C2 | Station Road | B2 | | |
| | | Ogston Place | B3 | Swallow Crescent | D1 | | |
| | | Point Place | A3 | Swallow Brae | D2 | | |

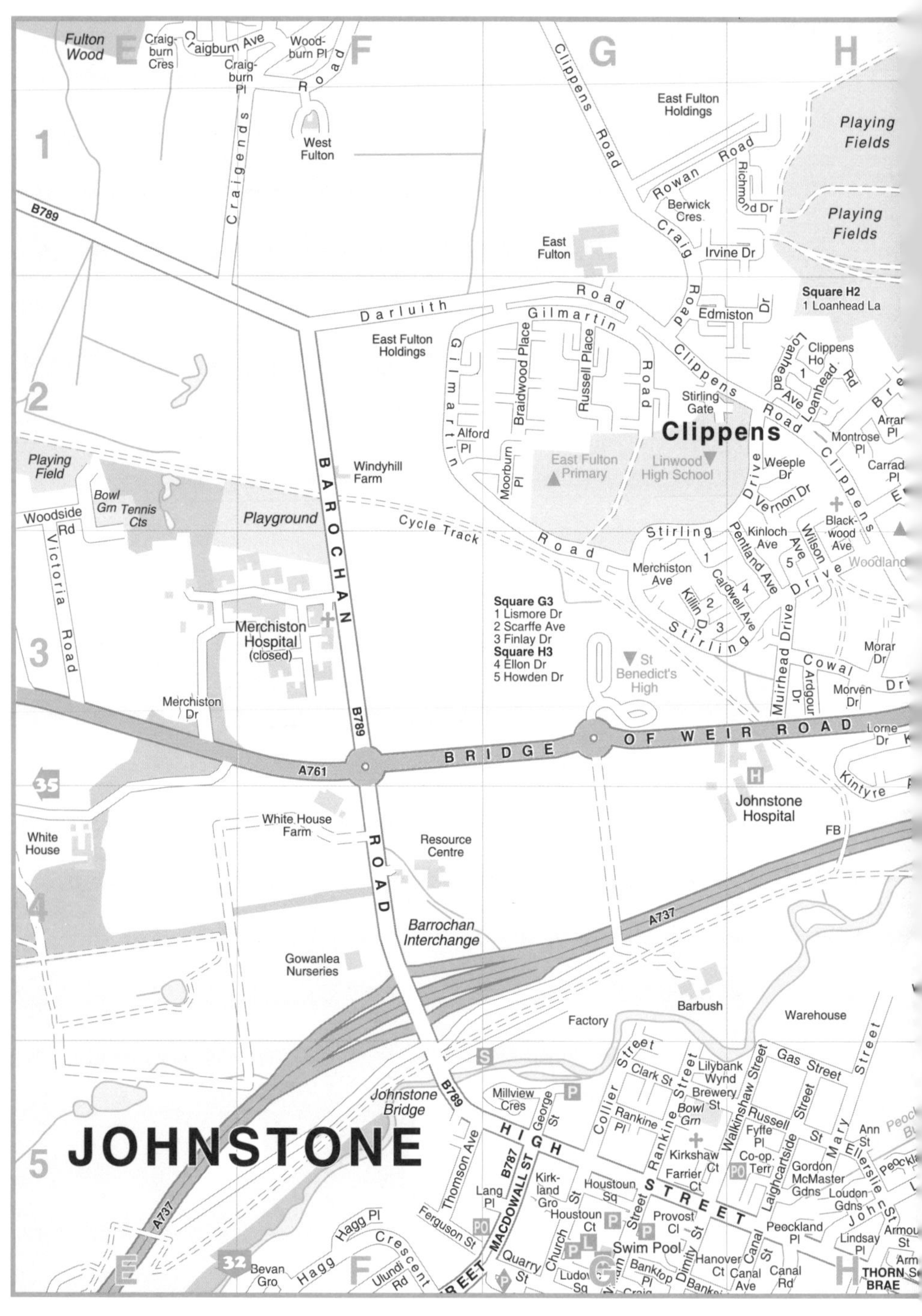
JOHNSTONE
Clippens
Square G3
1 Lismore Dr
2 Scarffe Ave
3 Finlay Dr
Square H3
4 Ellon Dr
5 Howden Dr
Square H2
1 Loanhead La
Fulton Wood
West Fulton
East Fulton
East Fulton Holdings
Windyhill Farm
Playground
Playing Field
Playing Fields
Bowl Grn Tennis Cts
Merchiston Hospital (closed)
White House Farm
White House
Resource Centre
Barrochan Interchange
Gowanlea Nurseries
Johnstone Hospital
Johnstone Bridge
East Fulton Primary
Linwood High School
St Benedict's High
Barbush
Factory
Warehouse
Swim Pool
BARROCHAN ROAD
BRIDGE OF WEIR ROAD
HIGH STREET
MACDOWALL ST
Cycle Track
A761
A737
B789
B787
FB
THORN BRAE

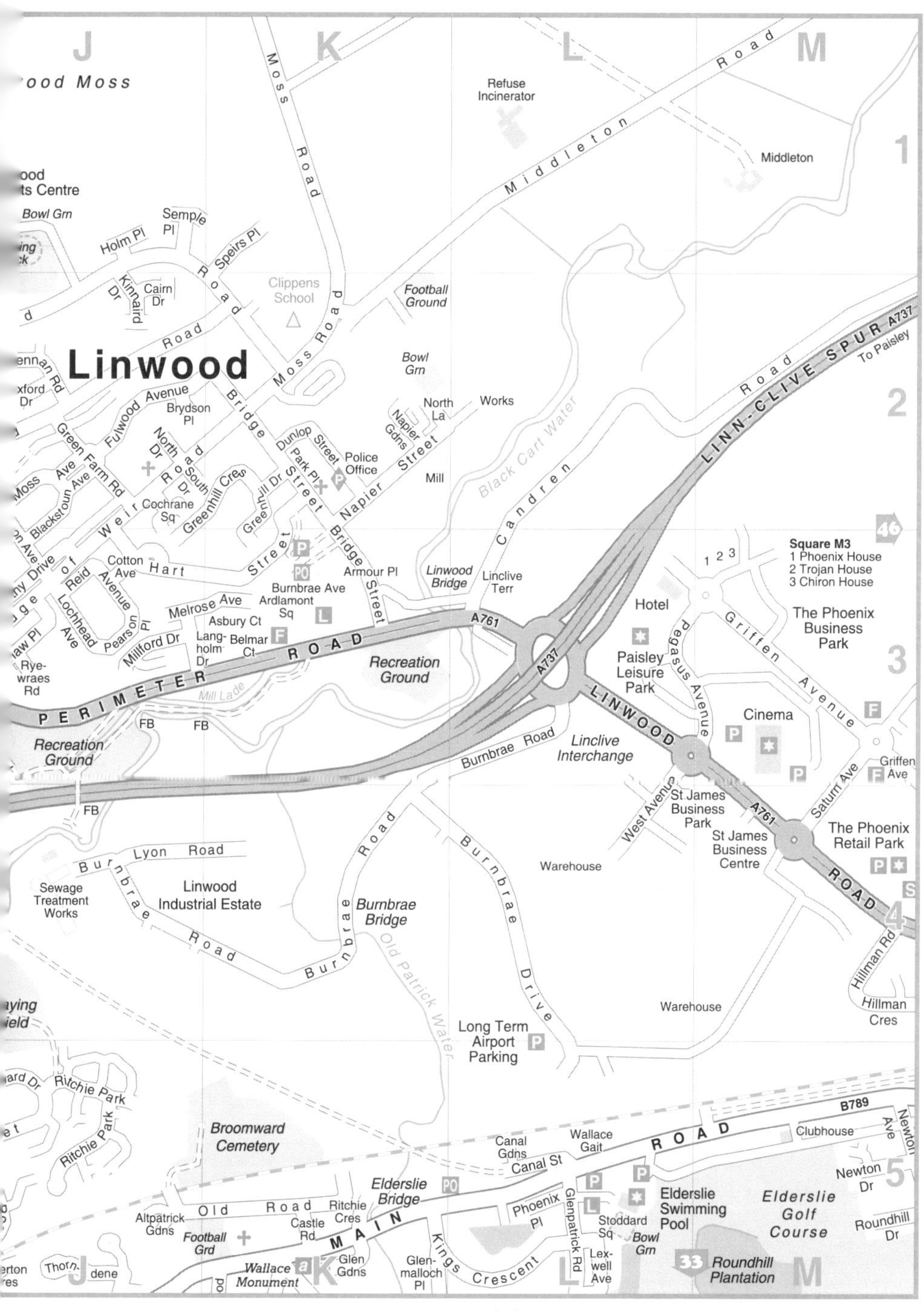


Index to street names can be found starting on page 69

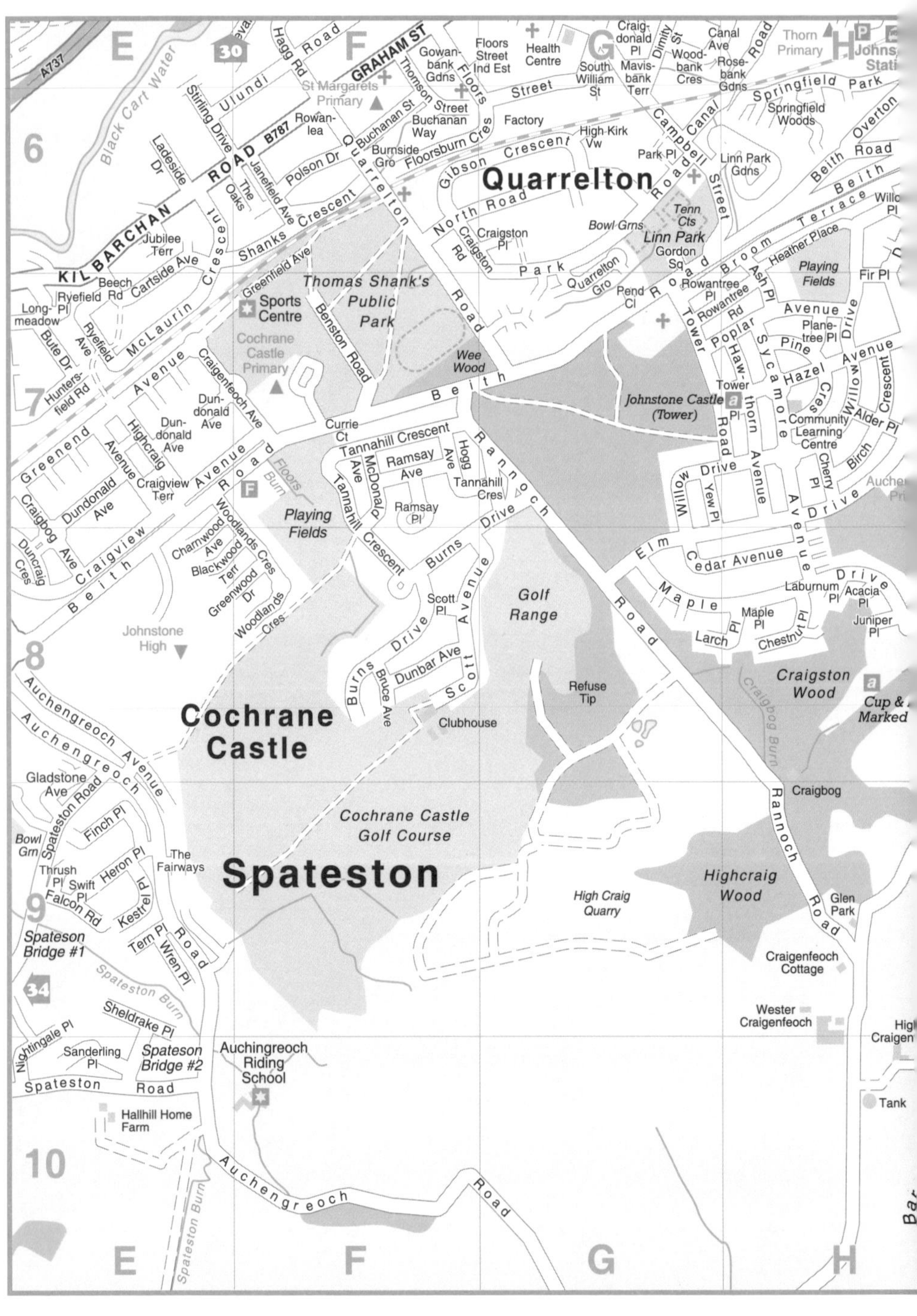
Quarrelton
Cochrane Castle
Spateston
Cochrane Castle Golf Course
Thomas Shank's Public Park
Sports Centre
Cochrane Castle Primary
Johnstone High
St Margarets Primary
Thorn Primary
Playing Fields
Golf Range
Refuse Tip
Clubhouse
High Craig Quarry
Highcraig Wood
Craigston Wood
Wee Wood
Johnstone Castle (Tower)
Linn Park
Tenn Cts
Bowl Grns
Auchingreoch Riding School
Hallhill Home Farm
Craigenfeoch Cottage
Wester Craigenfeoch
Craigbog
Glen Park
Tank
Health Centre
Floors Street Ind Est
Factory
Community Learning Centre
Springfield Woods
Spateson Bridge #1
Spateson Bridge #2
Cup &
Marked
KILBARCHAN ROAD B787
GRAHAM ST
A737
Black Cart Water
Spateston Burn
Craigbog Burn
Floors Burn
Beith Road
Rannoch Road
Auchengreoch Road
Auchengreoch Avenue
Spateston Road
Greenend Avenue
Craigview Avenue
Broom Road
Tower Road
Springfield Park
Overton Road
Beith Terrace
Campbell Street
Canal Street
Quarrelton Road
North Road
Gibson Crescent
Floorsburn Cres
Shanks Crescent
McLaurin Crescent
Tannahill Crescent
Burns Drive
Scott Avenue
Maple Drive
Elm Avenue
Cedar Avenue
Willow Drive
Sycamore Avenue
Hawthorn Avenue
Ulundi Road
Stirling Drive
Hagg Rd
Ladeside Dr
Janefield Ave
The Oaks
Polson Dr
Rowanlea
Buchanan St
Buchanan Way
Burnside Gro
Thomson Street
Gowanbank Gdns
Floors Street
Craigdonald Pl
Dimity St
South William St
Mavisbank Terr
Woodbank Cres
Canal Ave
Rosebank Gdns
High Kirk Vw
Park Pl
Linn Park Gdns
Craigston Pl
Craigston Rd
Park Quarrelton Gro
Gordon Sq
Pend Cl
Rowantree Pl
Rowantree Rd
Ash Pl
Heather Place
Fir Pl
Poplar Rd
Planetree Pl
Pine Pl
Hazel Cres
Willow Crescent
Alder Pl
Birch
Cherry Pl
Yew Pl
Laburnum Pl
Acacia Pl
Juniper Pl
Larch Pl
Maple Pl
Chestnut Pl
Greenfield Ave
Benston Road
Currie Ct
Ramsay Ave
Ramsay Pl
McDonald Ave
Hogg Ave
Tannahill Cres
Scott Pl
Dunbar Ave
Bruce Ave
Jubilee Terr
Cartside Ave
Beech Rd
Ryefield Pl
Ryefield Ave
Longmeadow
Bute Dr
Huntersfield Rd
Craigenfeoch Ave
Dundonald Ave
Highcraig Avenue
Craigview Terr
Craigbog Ave
Duncraig Cres
Charnwood Ave
Blackwood Terr
Greenwood Dr
Woodlands Cres
Gladstone Ave
Bowl Grn
Finch Pl
Heron Pl
Thrush Pl
Swift Pl
Falcon Rd
Kestrel Pl
Tern Pl
Wren Pl
The Fairways
Sheldrake Pl
Nightingale Pl
Sanderling Pl
30
34

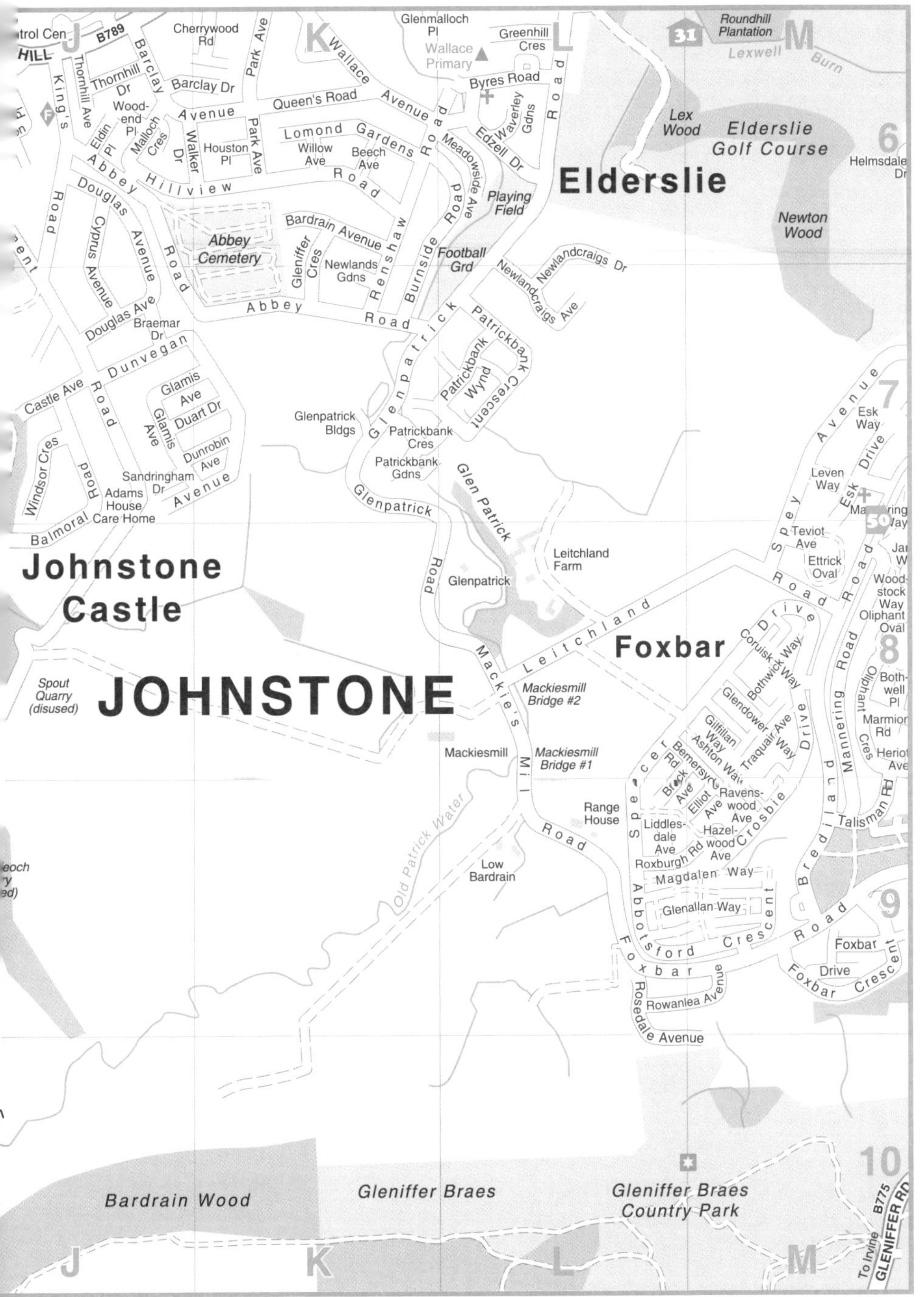


Index to street names can be found starting on page 69

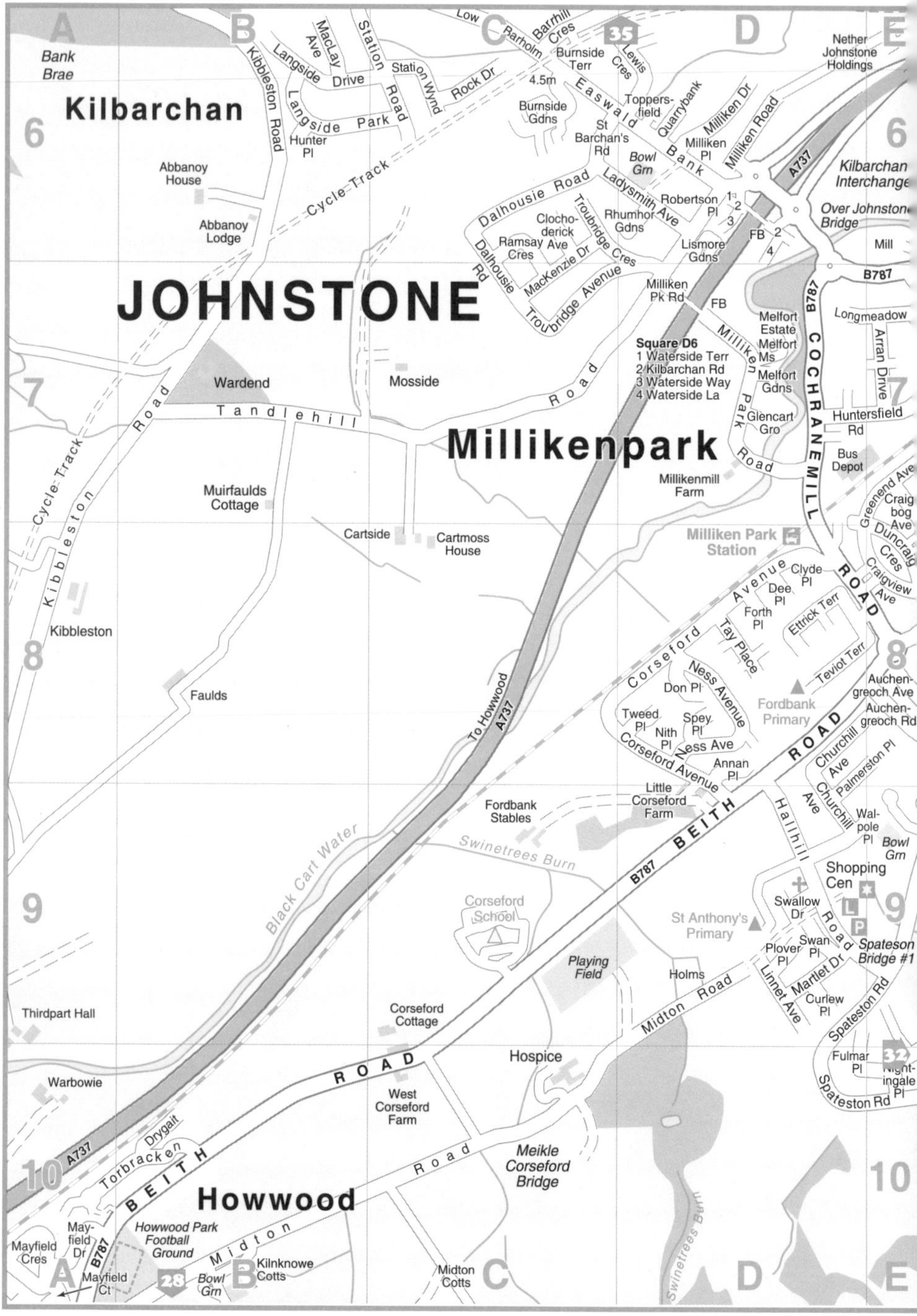

A B C D E
6 7 8 9 10

Kilbarchan
JOHNSTONE
Millikenpark
Howwood

Bank Brae
Kibbleston Road
Langside Drive
Langside Park
MacLay Ave
Station Road
Station Wynd
Rock Dr
Low Barholm
Barrhill Cres
Burnside Terr
Lewis Cres
4.5m
Burnside Gdns
Easwald Bank
Toppersfield
Quarrybank
Milliken Dr
Milliken Road
St Barchan's Rd
Bowl Grn
Milliken Pl
Hunter Pl
Abbanoy House
Abbanoy Lodge
Cycle Track
Dalhousie Road
Dalhousie Rd
Ladysmith Ave
Robertson Pl
Rhumhor Gdns
Clochoderick Ave
Ramsay Cres
Troubridge Cres
MacKenzie Dr
Troubridge Avenue
Lismore Gdns
Milliken Pk Rd
FB
A737
Kilbarchan Interchange
Over Johnstone Bridge
Mill
B787
Longmeadow
Arran Drive
Melfort Estate
Melfort Ms
Melfort Gdns
Milliken Park Road
Glencart Gro
COCHRANEMILL ROAD
Huntersfield Rd
Bus Depot
Square D6
1 Waterside Terr
2 Kilbarchan Rd
3 Waterside Way
4 Waterside La
Wardend
Mosside
Tandlehill Road
Millikenmill Farm
Muirfaulds Cottage
Cartside
Cartmoss House
Greenend Ave
Craigbog Ave
Duncraig Cres
Craigview Ave
Milliken Park Station
Clyde Pl
Dee Pl
Forth Pl
Ettrick Terr
Tay Place
Corseford Avenue
Kibbleston
Faulds
Ness Avenue
Don Pl
Teviot Terr
Auchengreoch Ave
Auchengreoch Rd
Fordbank Primary
Tweed Pl
Spey Pl
Nith Pl
Ness Ave
Annan Pl
Churchill Ave
Palmerston Pl
To Howwood
Little Corseford Farm
Fordbank Stables
BEITH ROAD
Hallhill
Walpole Pl
Bowl Grn
Shopping Cen
Black Cart Water
Swinetrees Burn
Corseford School
Swallow Dr
St Anthony's Primary
Spateson Bridge #1
Plover Pl
Swan Pl
Martlet Dr
Playing Field
Holms
Midton Road
Linnet Ave
Curlew Pl
Spateston Rd
Thirdpart Hall
Corseford Cottage
Hospice
Fulmar Pl
Nightingale Pl
Warbowie
West Corseford Farm
Meikle Corseford Bridge
Drygait
Torbracken
Mayfield Cres
Mayfield Dr
Mayfield Ct
Howwood Park Football Ground
Kilnknowe Cotts
Midton Cotts
Nether Johnstone Holdings
32
35
28

Index to street names can be found starting on page 69

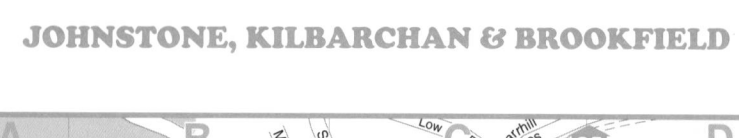

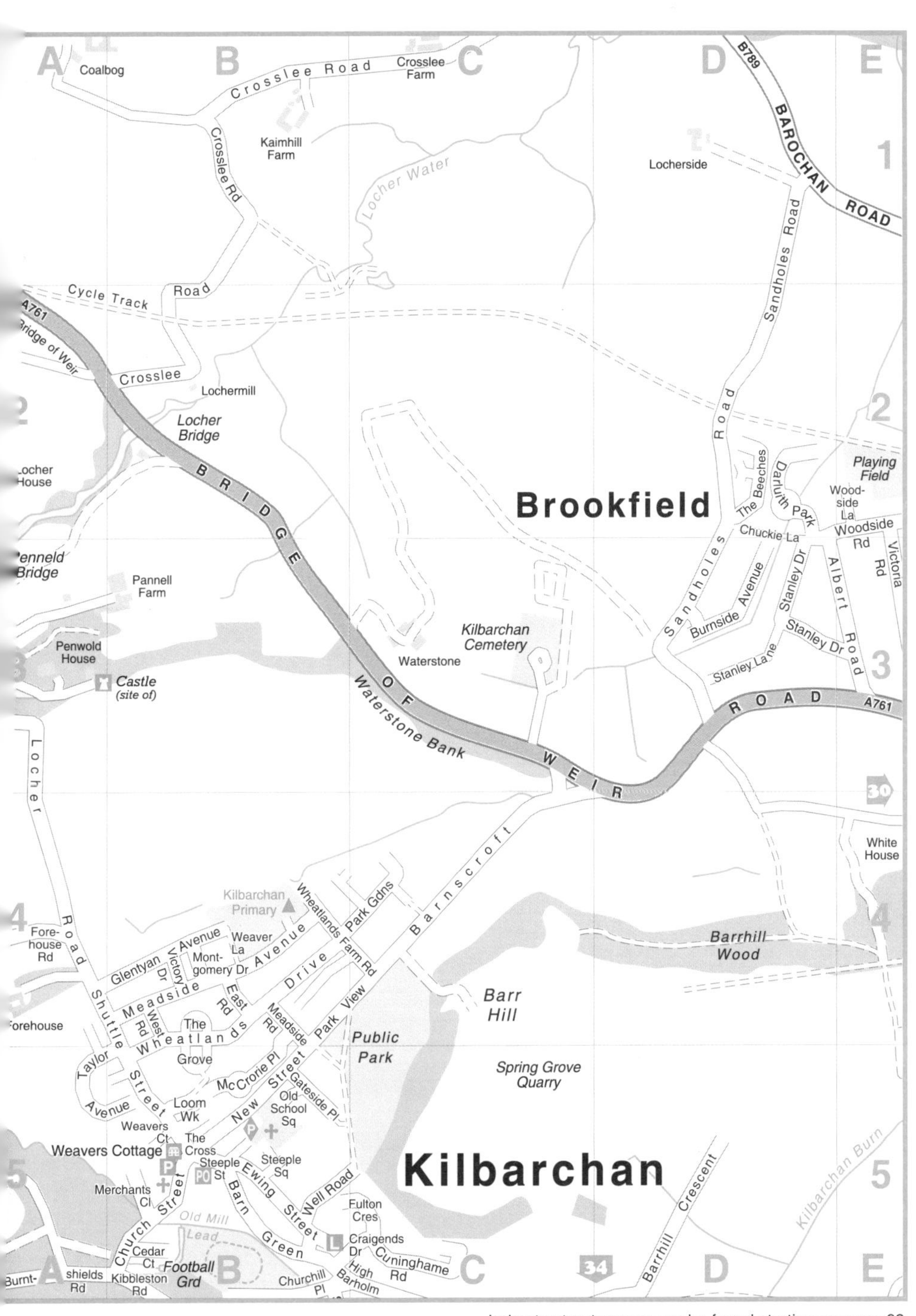


Index to street names can be found starting on page 69

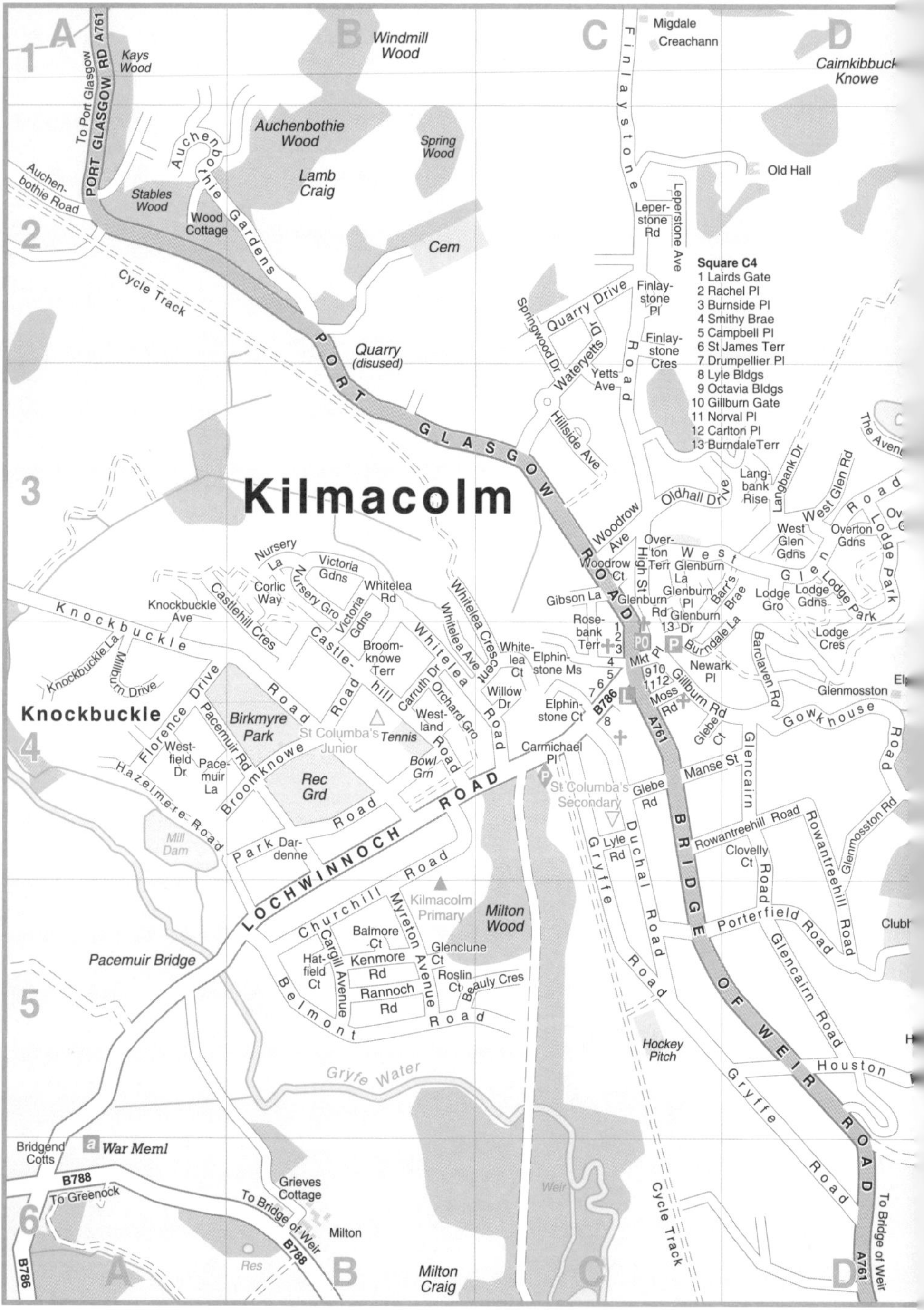

# Kilmacolm

**Square C4**
1 Lairds Gate
2 Rachel Pl
3 Burnside Pl
4 Smithy Brae
5 Campbell Pl
6 St James Terr
7 Drumpellier Pl
8 Lyle Bldgs
9 Octavia Bldgs
10 Gillburn Gate
11 Norval Pl
12 Carlton Pl
13 BurndaleTerr

A B C D
1 2 3 4 5 6

To Port Glasgow
PORT GLASGOW RD A761
Kays Wood
Windmill Wood
Migdale
Creachann
Cairnkibbuck Knowe
Auchenbothie Wood
Spring Wood
Auchenbothie Gardens
Lamb Craig
Old Hall
Auchen-bothie Road
Stables Wood
Wood Cottage
Cem
Finlaystone Road
Leperstone Rd
Leperstone Ave
Cycle Track
Quarry Drive
Springwood Dr
Wateryetts Dr
Finlaystone Pl
Finlaystone Cres
Yetts Ave
PORT GLASGOW ROAD
Quarry (disused)
Hillside Ave
The Avenue
Langbank Dr
West Glen Rd
Langbank Rise
Oldhall Drive
Woodrow Ave
Woodrow Ct
Overton Terr
High St
West Glen Road
West Glen Gdns
Overton Gdns
Lodge Park
Glenburn La
Glenburn Pl
Glenburn Rd
Glenburn Dr
Barr's Brae
Lodge Gro
Lodge Gdns
Lodge Cres
Burndale La
Newark Pl
Barclaven Rd
Glenmosston
Gowkhouse Road
Gibson La
Rosebank Terr
PO
Mkt Pl
Moss Rd
Gillburn Rd
Glebe Ct
Glencairn Road
Manse St
Glebe Rd
Elphinstone Ms
Elphinstone Ct
B786
A761
Carmichael Pl
St Columba's Secondary
Duchal Road
Lyle Rd
Gryffe Road
Rowantreehill Road
Clovelly Ct
Glenmosston Rd
Porterfield Road
Glencairn Road
Club
BRIDGE OF WEIR ROAD
Houston
Hockey Pitch
Cycle Track
To Bridge of Weir
Weir
Milton Craig
Nursery La
Victoria Gdns
Corlic Way
Nursery Gro
Whitelea Rd
Knockbuckle Ave
Castlehill Cres
Knockbuckle
Knockbuckle La
Millburn Drive
Castlehill Road
Broomknowe Terr
Whitelea Road
Whitelea Ave
Whitelea Crescent
Whitelea Ct
Willow Dr
Carruth Dr
Orchard Gro
Westland Road
Florence Drive
Pacemuir Rd
Birkmyre Park
St Columba's Junior
Tennis
Bowl Grn
West-field Dr
Pacemuir La
Broomknowe Road
Rec Grd
Hazelmere Road
Mill Dam
Park Dardenne
LOCHWINNOCH ROAD
Churchill Road
Kilmacolm Primary
Milton Wood
Myreton Avenue
Balmore Ct
Cargill Avenue
Glenclune Ct
Hatfield Ct
Kenmore Rd
Rannoch Rd
Roslin Ct
Beauly Cres
Belmont Road
Pacemuir Bridge
Gryfe Water
Bridgend Cotts
War Meml
B788
To Greenock
Grieves Cottage
To Bridge of Weir
Milton
Res
B786

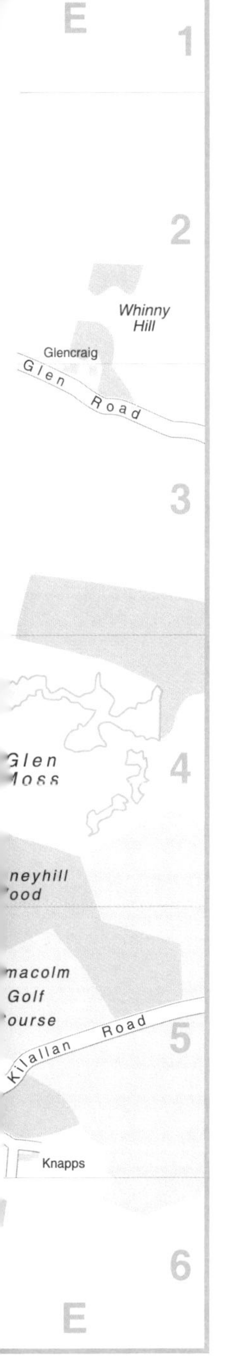

# Index to Kilmacolm

| Street | Grid |
|---|---|
| Auchenbothie Gardens | A2 |
| Auchenbothie Road | A2 |
| Avenue, The | D3 |
| Balmore Court | B5 |
| Barclaven Road | D4 |
| Barr's Brae | C3 |
| Beauly Crescent | B5 |
| Belmont Road | B5 |
| Bridge of Weir Road | C4 |
| Bridgend Cottages | A6 |
| Broomknowe Road | B4 |
| Broomknowe Terrace | B4 |
| Burndale Lane | C4 |
| Burndale Terrace (13) | C4 |
| Burnside Place (3) | C4 |
| Campbell Place (5) | C4 |
| Cargill Avenue | B5 |
| Carlton Place (12) | C4 |
| Carmichael Place | C4 |
| Carruth Drive | B4 |
| Castlehill Crescent | B4 |
| Castlehill Road | B4 |
| Churchill Road | B5 |
| Clovelly Court | D4 |
| Corlic Way | B3 |
| Dardenne | B4 |
| Drumpellier Place (7) | C4 |
| Duchal Road | C4 |
| Elphinstone Court | C4 |
| Elphinstone Mews | C4 |
| Finlaystone Crescent | C2 |
| Finlaystone Place | C2 |
| Finlaystone Road | C3 |
| Florence Drive | A4 |
| Gibson Lane | C3 |
| Gillburn Gate (10) | C4 |
| Gillburn Road | C4 |
| Glebe Court | C4 |
| Glebe Road | C4 |
| Glenburn Drive | C3 |
| Glenburn Lane | C3 |
| Glenburn Place | C3 |
| Glenburn Road | C3 |
| Glencairn Road | D4, D5 |
| Glenclune Court | B5 |
| Glenmosston Road | D4 |
| Gowkhouse Road | D4 |
| Gryffe Road | C4 |
| Hatfield Court | B5 |
| Hazelmere Road | A4 |
| High Street | C3 |
| Hillside Avenue | C3 |
| Houston Road | D5 |
| Kenmore Road | B5 |
| Kilallan Road | E5 |
| Knockbuckle Avenue | A4 |
| Knockbuckle Lane | A4 |
| Knockbuckle Road | B4 |
| Lairds Gate (1) | C4 |
| Langbank Drive | D3 |
| Langbank Rise | D3 |
| Leperstone Avenue | C2 |
| Leperstone Road | C2 |
| Lochwinnoch Road | B5 |
| Lodge Crescent | D4 |
| Lodge Gardens | D3 |
| Lodge Grove | D3 |
| Lodge Park | D3 |
| Lyle Buildings (8) | C4 |
| Lyle Road | C4 |
| Manse Street | D4 |
| Market Place | C4 |
| Millburn Drive | A4 |
| Moss Road | C4 |
| Myreton Avenue | B5 |
| Newark Place | C4 |
| Norval Place (11) | C4 |
| Nursery Grove | B3 |
| Nursery Lane | B3 |
| Octavia Buildings (9) | C4 |
| Old Hall Drive | C3 |
| Orchard Grove | B4 |
| Overton Gardens | D3 |
| Overton Grove | D3 |
| Overton Terrace | C3 |
| Pacemuir Lane | A4 |
| Pacemuir Road | A4 |
| Park Road | B4 |
| Port Glasgow Road | A2 |
| Porterfield Road | D5 |
| Quarry Drive | C2 |
| Rachel Place (2) | C4 |
| Rannoch Road | B5 |
| Rosebank Terrace | C4 |
| Roslin Court | B5 |
| Rowantreehill Road | D4 |
| St James Terrace (6) | C4 |
| Smithy Brae (4) | C4 |
| Springwood Drive | C2 |
| Victoria Gardens | B3 |
| Wateryetts Drive | C3 |
| West Glen Gardens | D3 |
| West Glen Road | C3, E3 |
| Westfield Drive | A4 |
| Westland | B4 |
| Whitelea Avenue | B4 |
| Whitelea Court | C4 |
| Whitelea Crescent | B3 |
| Whitelea Road | B4 |
| Willow Drive | C4 |
| Woodrow Avenue | C3 |
| Woodrow Court | C3 |
| Yetts Avenue | C3 |

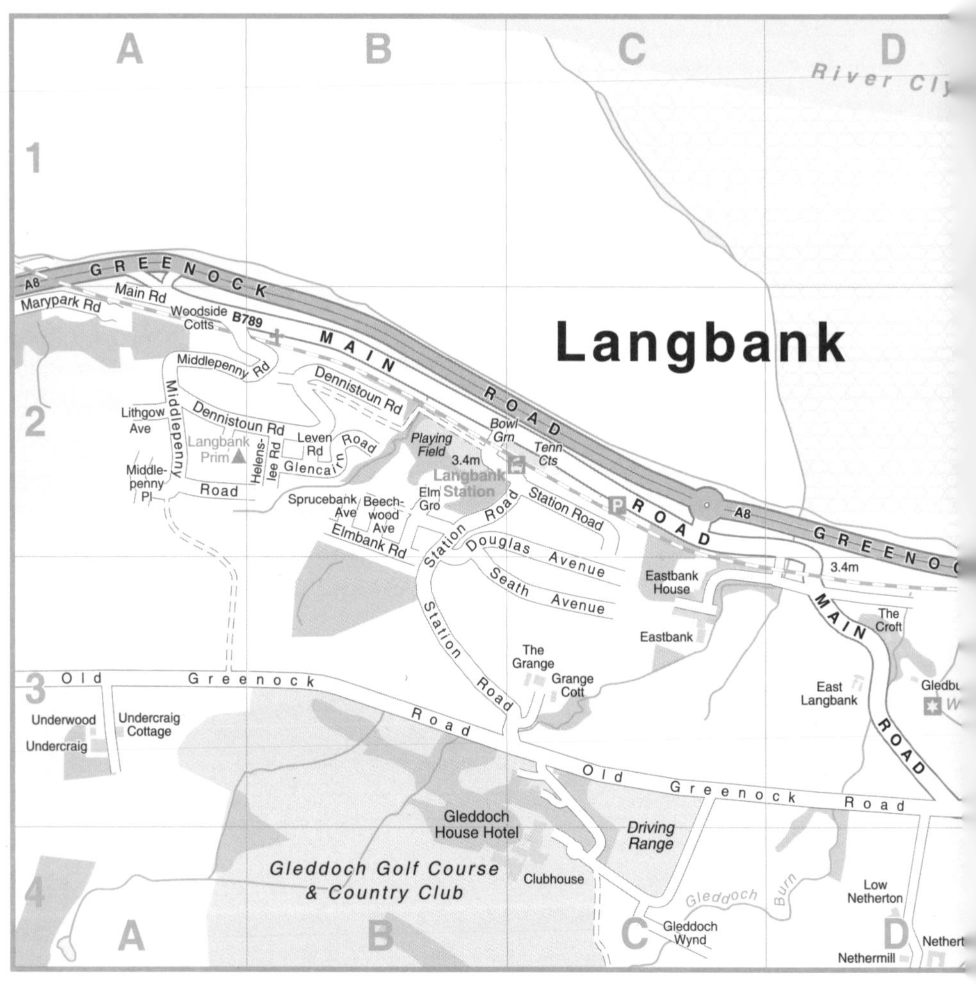

Langbank
River Cly
A8
GREENOCK MAIN ROAD
Main Rd
Marypark Rd
Woodside Cotts
B789
Middlepenny Rd
Dennistoun Rd
Dennistoun Rd
Lithgow Ave
Middlepenny
Langbank Prim
Leven Rd
Road
Helens-lee Rd
Glencairn
Middle-penny Pl
Road
Sprucebank Ave
Beech-wood Ave
Elm Gro
Playing Field
3.4m
Langbank Station
Bowl Grn
Tenn Cts
Station Road
Station Road
Elmbank Rd
Douglas Avenue
Seath Avenue
Station Road
Eastbank House
Eastbank
3.4m
The Croft
The Grange
Grange Cott
East Langbank
Gledbu
Old Greenock Road
Underwood
Undercraig Cottage
Undercraig
Old Greenock Road
Gleddoch House Hotel
Driving Range
Gleddoch Golf Course & Country Club
Clubhouse
Gleddoch Burn
Low Netherton
Gleddoch Wynd
Nethert
Nethermill
A B C D
1 2 3 4

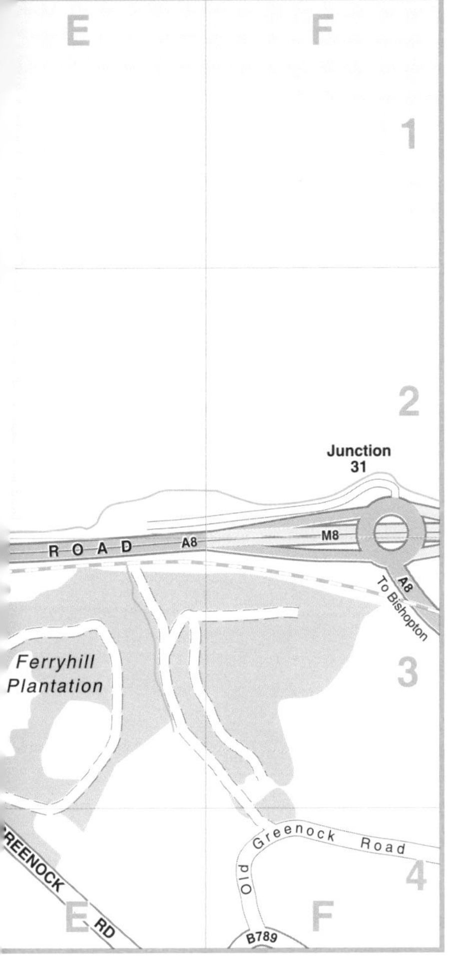

## Index to Langbank

| Street | Grid |
|---|---|
| Beech Wood Avenue | B2 |
| Dennistoun Road | B2 |
| Douglas Avenue | B2 |
| Elm Grove | B2 |
| Elmbank Road | B2 |
| Ferryhill Cottages | E3 |
| Gleddoch Wynd | C4 |
| Glencairn Road | B2 |
| Greenock Road | A1, D2 |
| Helenslee Road | B2 |
| Leven Road | B2 |
| Lithgow Avenue | A2 |
| Main Road | B2 |
| Marypark Road | A2 |
| Middlepenny Place | A2 |
| Middlepenny Road | A2 |
| Old Greenock Road | A3, C3, E4, F4 |
| Seath Avenue | B3 |
| Sprucebank Avenue | B2 |
| Station Road | B3, C2 |
| Woodside Cottages | A2 |

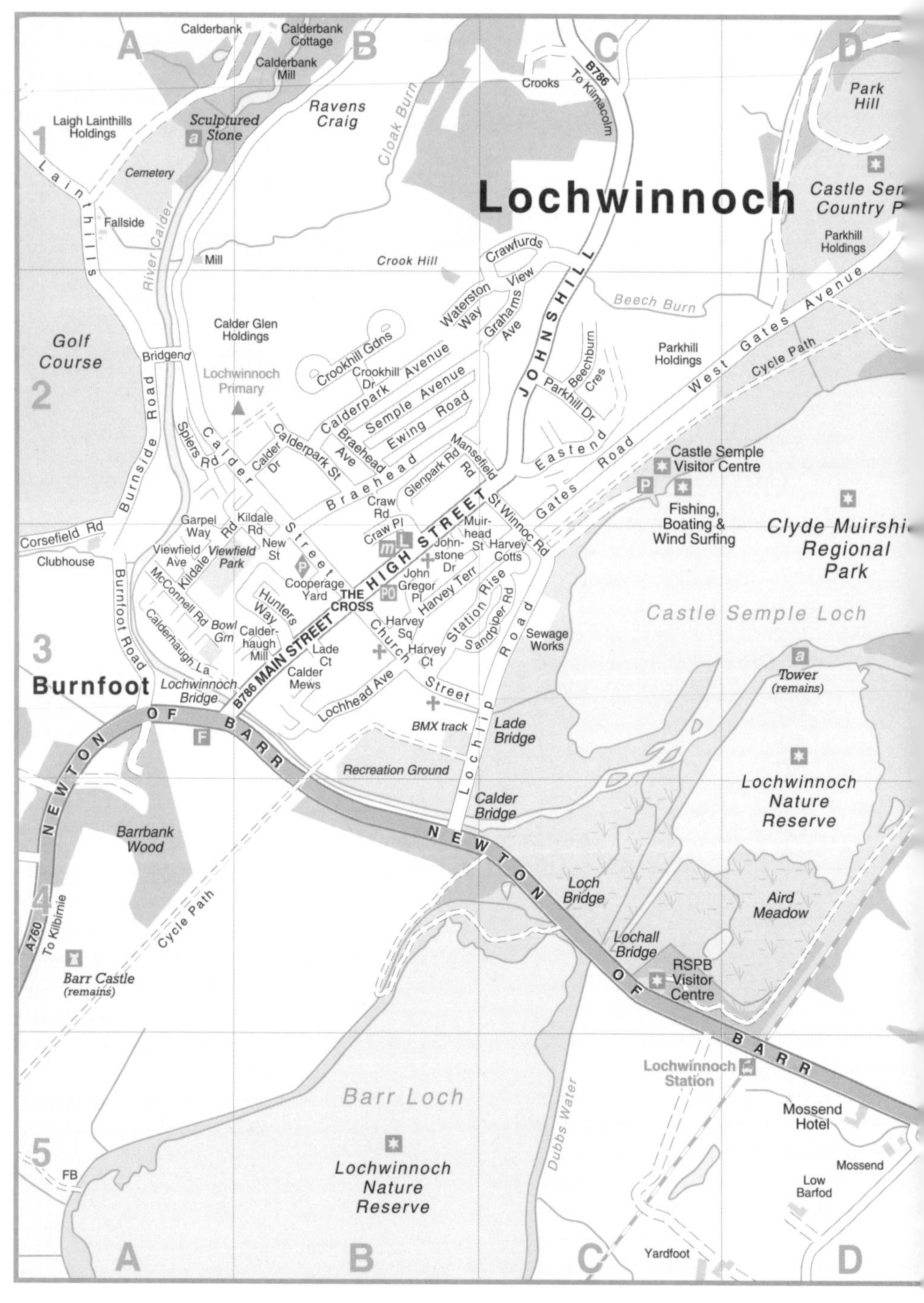
Lochwinnoch
Burnfoot
Calderbank
Calderbank Cottage
Calderbank Mill
Crooks
B786 To Kilmacolm
Park Hill
Laigh Lainthills Holdings
Sculptured Stone
Ravens Craig
Cloak Burn
Cemetery
Castle Semple Country Park
Lainthills
Fallside
River Calder
Mill
Crook Hill
Crawfurds
Parkhill Holdings
Waterston Way
View
Grahams Ave
Beech Burn
Johnshill
Calder Glen Holdings
Crookhill Gdns
Golf Course
Bridgend
Crookhill Dr
Calderpark Avenue
Semple Avenue
Ewing Road
Beechburn Cres
Parkhill Dr
West Gates Avenue
Cycle Path
Lochwinnoch Primary
Burnside Road
Spiers Rd
Calder Dr
Calderpark St
Braehead Ave
Braehead
Glenpark Rd
Mansefield Rd
Eastend
Gates Road
Castle Semple Visitor Centre
Fishing, Boating & Wind Surfing
Clyde Muirshi
Regional Park
Corsefield Rd
Garpel Way
Kildale Rd
New St
Craw Rd
Craw Pl
Muir-head St
Johnstone Dr
Harvey Cotts
St Winnoc Rd
Clubhouse
Viewfield Ave
Kildale
Viewfield Park
Street
High Street
Cooperage Yard
The Cross
John Gregor Pl
Harvey Terr
Station Rise
Sandpiper Rd
Road
Castle Semple Loch
Burnfoot Road
McConnell Rd
Bowl Grn
Hunters Way
Calder-haugh Mill
Harvey Sq
Harvey Ct
Church
Sewage Works
Calderhaugh La
B786 Main Street
Lade Ct
Calder Mews
Tower (remains)
Lochwinnoch Bridge
Lochhead Ave
Street
BMX track
Lade Bridge
Lochlip
Newton of Barr
Recreation Ground
Calder Bridge
Lochwinnoch Nature Reserve
Barrbank Wood
Loch Bridge
Aird Meadow
A760 To Kilbirnie
Cycle Path
Lochall Bridge
RSPB Visitor Centre
Barr Castle (remains)
Lochwinnoch Station
Barr Loch
Dubbs Water
Mossend Hotel
FB
Lochwinnoch Nature Reserve
Mossend
Low Barfod
Yardfoot
A
B
C
D
1
2
3
4
5

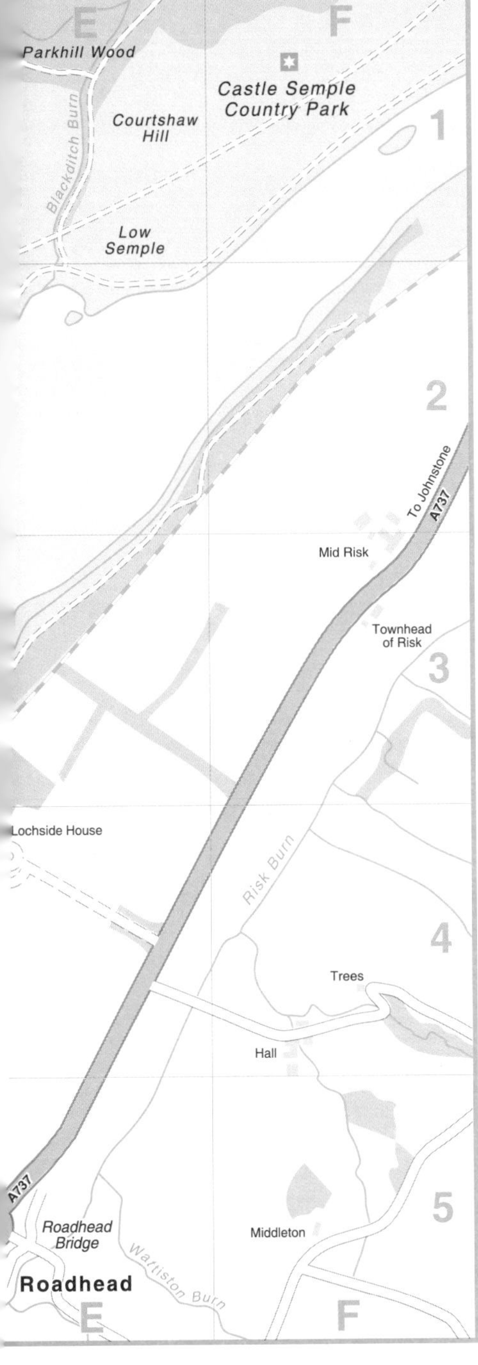

## Index to Lochwinnoch

Beechburn Crescent C2
Braehead B2
Braehead Avenue B2
Bridgend A2
Burnfoot Road A3
Burnside Road A2, A3
Calder Drive B2
Calder Mews B3
Calder Street A2
Calderhaugh Lane A3
Calderpark Avenue B2
Calderpark Street B2
Church Street B3
Cooperage Yard B3
Corsefield Road A3
Craw Place B3
Craw Road B2
Crawfurds View C1
Crookhill Drive B2
Crookhill Gardens B2
Cross, The B3
Eastend C2
Ewing Road B2
Garpel Way A3
Gates Road C2
Glenpark Road B2
Grahams Avenue C2
Harvey Cottages B3
Harvey Court B3
Harvey Square B3
Harvey Terrace B3
High Street B3
Hunters Way B3
John Gregor Place B3
Johnshill C2
Johnstone Drive B3
Kildale Road A3
Lade Court B3
Lainthills A1
Lochhead Avenue B3
Lochlip Road B4
McConnell Road A3
Main Street B3
Mansefield Road B2
Muirhead Street B3
New Street B3
Newton of Barr A4, B4
Parkhill Drive C2
St Winnoc Road C2
Sandpiper Road B3
Semple Avenue B2
Spiers Road A2
Station Rise B3
Viewfield Avenue A3
Waterston Way B2
West Gates Avenue C2

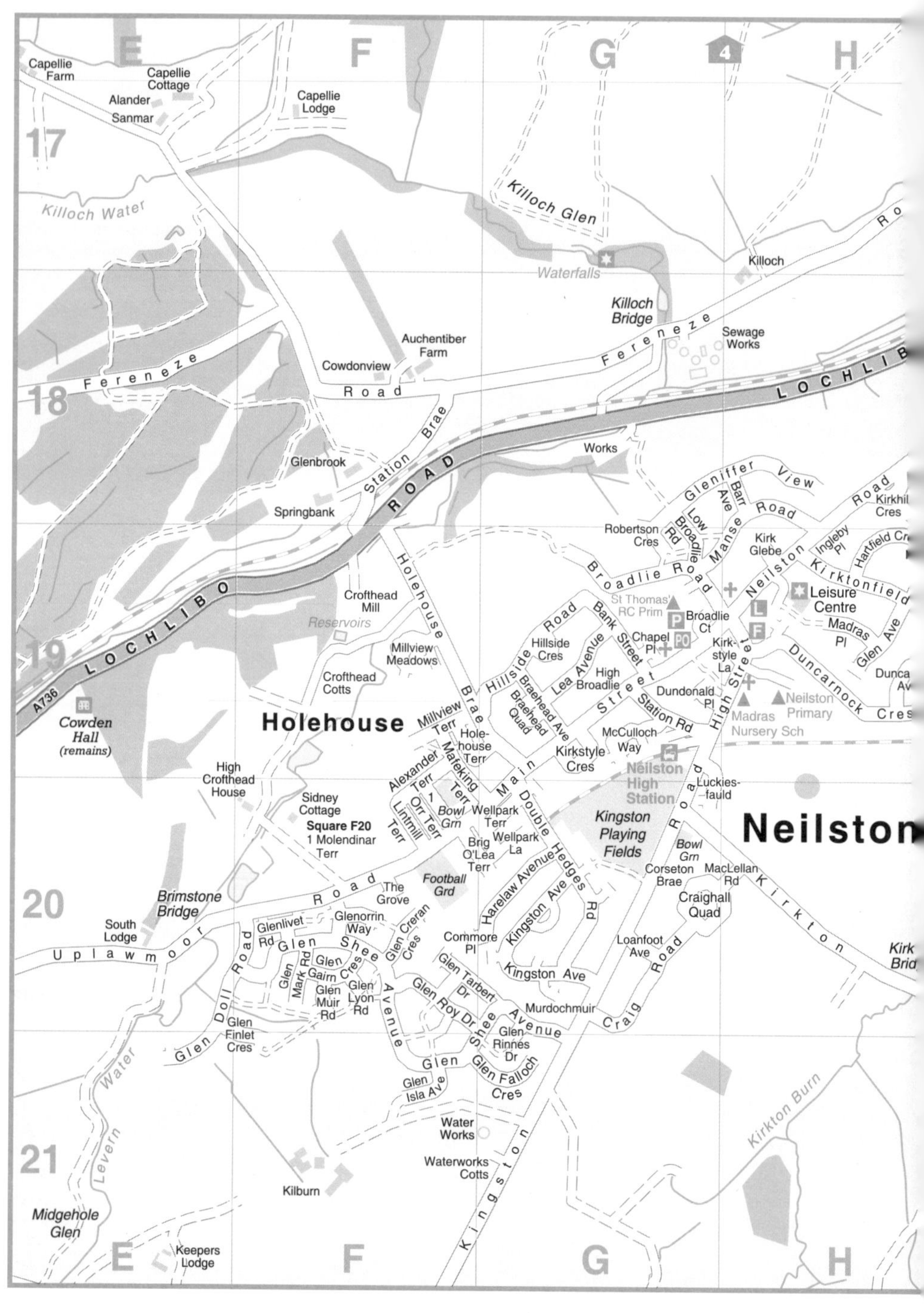

E
F
G
H
4
17
18
19
20
21
Capellie Farm
Capellie Cottage
Alander
Sanmar
Capellie Lodge
Killoch Water
Killoch Glen
Waterfalls
Killoch
Killoch Bridge
Sewage Works
Auchentiber Farm
Cowdonview
Fereneze Road
Fereneze
LOCHLIBO ROAD
A736
Station Brae
Glenbrook
Works
Springbank
Gleniffer View
Barr Ave
Low Broadlie Rd
Robertson Cres
Manse Road
Kirk Glebe
Road
Kirkhill Cres
Ingleby Pl
Hartfield Cres
Kirktonfield
Broadlie Road
Neilston
Leisure Centre
St Thomas' RC Prim
Broadlie Ct
Madras Pl
Glen Ave
Holehouse
Crofthead Mill
Reservoirs
Hillside Road
Bank Street
Chapel Pl
Hillside Cres
Lea Avenue
High Broadlie
Kirk-style La
Duncarnock Cres
Duncan Av
Millview Meadows
Crofthead Cotts
Dundonald Pl
High Street
Neilston Primary
Madras Nursery Sch
Cowden Hall (remains)
Holehouse
Millview Terr
Brae
Braehead Ave
Braehead Quad
Station Rd
McCulloch Way
Hole-house Terr
Mafeking Terr
Alexander Terr
Kirkstyle Cres
Main
Neilston High Station
Luckies-fauld
High Crofthead House
Sidney Cottage
Square F20
1 Molendinar Terr
1
Orr Terr
Lintmill Terr
Bowl Grn
Wellpark Terr
Wellpark La
Brig O'Lea Terr
Double Hedges Rd
Kingston Playing Fields
Neilston
Bowl Grn
Corseton Brae
MacLellan Rd
Kirkton
Craighall Quad
Football Grd
The Grove
Harelaw Avenue
Kingston Ave
Brimstone Bridge
South Lodge
Uplawmoor Road
Glenlivet Rd
Glenorrin Way
Glen Creran Cres
Commore Pl
Loanfoot Ave
Kirk Brid
Glen Shee Avenue
Glen Mark Rd
Gairn Cres
Glen Muir Rd
Glen Lyon Rd
Doll Road
Glen Tarbert Dr
Kingston Ave
Murdochmuir
Craig Road
Glen Finlet Cres
Glen
Glen Roy Dr
Glen Rinnes Dr
Glen Falloch Cres
Glen Isla Ave
Water Works
Waterworks Cotts
Kingston
Kirkton Burn
Levern Water
Kilburn
Midgehole Glen
Keepers Lodge

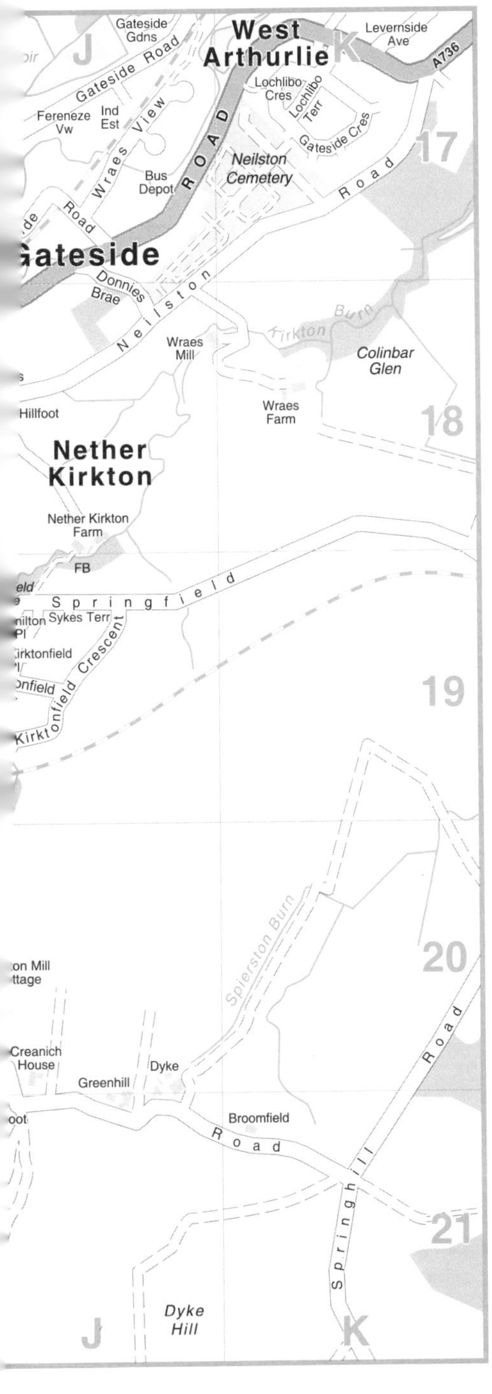

## Index to Neilston

Alexander Terrace F19
Bank Street G19
Barr Avenue H18
Braehead Avenue G19
Braehead Quadrant G19
Brig O'lea Terrace F20
Broadlie Court G19
Broadlie Road G19
Chapel Place G19
Cochran Avenue H19
Commore Place F20
Corseton Brae G20
Craig Road G20
Craighall Quadrant G20
Crofthead Cottages F19
Donnies Brae J18
Double Hedges Road G20
Duncarnock Avenue H19
Duncarnock Crescent H19
Dundonald Place G19
Fereneze Road E18
Gateside Gardens J17
Glen Avenue H19
Glen Creran Crescent F20
Glen Doll Road E20
Glen Falloch Crescent G21
Glen Finlet Crescent F21
Glen Gairn Crescent F20
Glen Isla Avenue F21
Glen Lyon Road F20
Glen Mark Road F20
Glen Muir Road F20
Glen Orrin Way F20
Glen Rinnes Drive G21
Glen Roy Drive F20
Glen Shee Avenue F20
Glen Tarbet Drive F20
Glenlivet Road F20
Gleniffer View G18
Grove, The F20
Hamilton Place J19
Harelaw Avenue G20
Hartfield Crescent H19
High Broadlie G19
High Street H19
Hillside Crescent G19
Hillside Road G19
Holehouse Brae F19
Holehouse Terrace F19
Ingleby Place H19
Kingston Avenue G20
Kingston Road G21
Kirk Glebe H19
Kirkhill Crescent H18
Kirkstyle Crescent G19
Kirkstyle Lane H19
Kirkton Road H20
Kirktonfield Crescent J19
Kirktonfield Drive J19
Kirktonfield Place J19
Kirtonfield Road H19
Lea Avenue G19
Lintmill Terrace F20
Loanfoot Avenue G20
Lochlibo Road E19
Low Broadlie Road G18
Luckiesfauld G20
McCulloch Way G19
McDonald Place H19
MacLelland Road H20
Madras Place H19
Mafeking Terrace F19
Main Street G19
Manse Road H19
Millview Meadows F19
Millview Terrace F19
Molendinar Terrace (1) F20
Murdochmuir G20
Neilston Road J18
Nether Kirkton Avenue J18
Nether Kirkton View H18
Nether Kirkton Way H18
Nether Kirkton Wynd H18
Orr Terrace F20
Procession Road G12
Robertson Crescent G19
Springfield Road J19
Springhill Road K21
Station Brae F18
Station Road G19
Sykes Terrace J19
Uplawmoor Road E20
Waterworks Cottages G21
Wellpark Lane G20
Wellpark Terrace G20

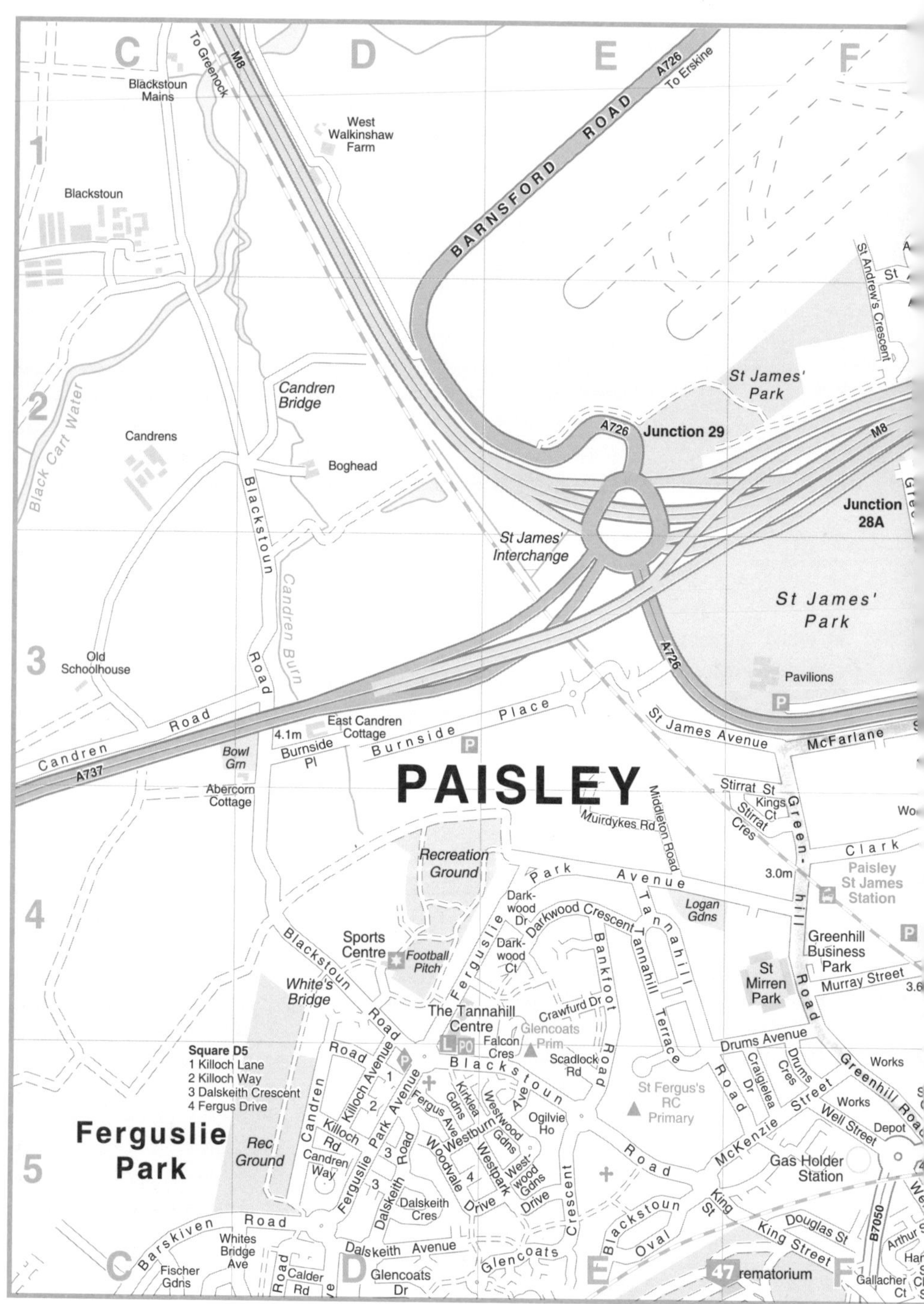
PAISLEY
Ferguslie Park
St James' Park
St James' Interchange
Junction 29
Junction 28A
BARNSFORD ROAD
A726
To Erskine
M8
To Greenock
A737
Blackstoun Mains
West Walkinshaw Farm
Blackstoun
Candren Bridge
Candrens
Boghead
Black Cart Water
Candren Burn
Old Schoolhouse
Candren Road
Blackstoun Road
East Candren Cottage
Burnside Place
Burnside Pl
Bowl Grn
Abercorn Cottage
Recreation Ground
Sports Centre
Football Pitch
White's Bridge
The Tannahill Centre
Glencoats Prim
Rec Ground
Pavilions
St James Avenue
McFarlane
Stirrat St
Kings Ct
Stirrat Cres
Middleton Road
Muirdykes Rd
Park Avenue
Clark
Paisley St James Station
Greenhill Business Park
St Mirren Park
Murray Street
Greenhill Road
Logan Gdns
Tannahill Terrace
Darkwood Crescent
Dark-wood Dr
Dark-wood Ct
Bankfoot Road
Crawfurd Dr
Falcon Cres
Scadlock Rd
Drums Avenue
Drums Cres
Craigielea Dr
St Fergus's RC Primary
Works
Well Street
Depot
McKenzie Street
Gas Holder Station
King St
King Street
Douglas St
B7050
Arthur
Gallacher Ct
Blackstoun Road
Blackstoun Avenue
Blackstoun Oval
Ogilvie Ho
Westwood Gdns
West-wood Gdns
Westpark Drive
Westburn Ave
Kirklea Gdns
Fergus Ave
Woodvale Drive
Ferguslie Park Avenue
Killoch Avenue
Killoch Rd
Candren Way
Candren Road
Dalskeith Road
Dalskeith Cres
Dalskeith Avenue
Glencoats Crescent
Glencoats Dr
Calder Rd
Barskiven Road
Whites Bridge Ave
Fischer Gdns
Crematorium
St Andrew's Crescent
St
4.1m
3.0m
47
Square D5
1 Killoch Lane
2 Killoch Way
3 Dalskeith Crescent
4 Fergus Drive

G H J K

1 2 3 4 5

Glasgow Airport
Passenger Terminal
Air Freight Terminal
Airlink Ind Estate
White Cart Water
Depot
Works
Moorpark
Knockhill Park
Wright Street
Bruce Rd
Ross Ave
Clydesdale Avenue
Fitzalan Rd
Wallace Rd
Kemp Ave
Somerled Ave
Methuen Road
Percy Road
Douglas Road
Sewage Works
Abbatoir
Sandyford Road
A741
Caledonia Way
Caledonia Way E
Caledonia Way W
Nevis Way
Argyll Ave
St Andrew's Dr
St Andrew's Drive
Campsie Drive
Abbotsinch Road
Arran Avenue
White Cart Rd
Hotel
Sanderling Road
Junction 28
Glasgow Airport Business Park
Marchburn Drive
Airlink Industrial Estate
Turner Rd
Abbotsinch Retail Park
Washington Rd
Junction 27
Renfrew Road
Phoenix Industrial Estate
Gateway Airlink Units
Osprey Ho
Vigilant Ho
Falcon Ho
Marchfield Avenue
Marchfield Dr
Abbotsburn Way
Wendour Way
Conval Way
Birkenshaw Way
Albany Way
Malvern Way
Broomdyke Way
Gockston
Osprey Crescent
Osprey View
Mosslands Road
Cromer Way
Dunard Way
Merksworth Way
Walkinshaw Way
Playing Fields
Inchinnan Road
New Harbour
Shortroods
Rec Ground
Tillet Oval
Gockston Road
Mossvale & St James's Prim
Mirrin Drive
Mirrin Wynd
Laighpark View
Fleming St
Nethercommon Ind Estate
New Inchinnan Rd
McLean Pl
Fullerton Street
Springbank Terr
Shortroods
Russell St
Galloway Ave
Galloway Terr
Mossvale Road
Mossvale Sq
Mossvale La
Mossvale Street
Greenock Rd
Laigh Park
Mirren Ct
Distillery
Warehouses
Abercorn Street
Harbour Road
Playing Field
Works
Reid Kerr College
Abercorn Ind Est
Renfrew Drive
Lennox Terrace
Montgomery Road
Gallowhill Ct
Glencairn Road
Bargarron Drive
Muir Terrace
Brewster Avenue
Carron Way
Priory Avenue
Dundonald Road
Knock Way
St Margarets Ave
Lochore Avenue
Play-ground
Arniston Way
Ellon Way
Ellon Gro
Mews La
Gallowhill
St Margaret's Ct
Bruce Road
Bruce Ave
Playing Fields
St Catherine's Primary
Moss Rd
Baron Rd
Belmont Rd
Netherhill Cres
Netherhill Road
Claud Rd
Schaw Rd
Byres Ave
Byres Crescent
Fitzalan Dr
Abbot St
Brabloch Cres
Brabloch Park
Arkleston Dr
Windsor Cres
Greenlaw Gdns
Greenlaw Cres
Barshaw Dr
Bowl Grn
Albion Gate
Caledonia Ct
Disability Resource Centre
Cartvale La
Sports Cen
Games Cts
Love Street
New Sneddon Street
McGown St
Depot
Works
Albion Street
Andrew St
Albion St
North St
Smith's La
Blythswood Dr
Wallace St
Carlile Pl
Fountain Ct
FB
Square H5
1 Back Sneddon St
2 New Sneddon St
3 County Sq
4 County Pl
Square H6
5 Causeyside St
Paisley Indoor Bowling Stadium
Greenlaw Ind Estate
Gallowhill Road
MacDowall Street
Caledonia St
Caledonia Ho Factory
Fountain Gardens
Back Sneddon St
Works
Black-law La
Cart La
Hamilton St
Store opens end of 2013
Square J5
6 Brick La
7 East Buchanan Ms
Whitehaugh
Wellington St
Glen Street
A726
Glen La
Moncrieff St
Sheriff Ct
Niddry St
Wallneuk Rd
Avenue
Mansionhouse Road
Greenlaw Drive
Cricket Grd
Hanover Ct
Underwood Road
St James' St
Kerr St
Westward Ho
Maxwell St
Harbour La
Christie La
North Croft St
Old Sneddon St
Weir St
Wallneuk
Bowl Grns
Garthland Cotts
Greenlaw Ho
Kelburne Gdns
Kelburne Oval
Kelburne Ct
2.5m
Stoney Brae
Paisley Gilmour Street Station
Central Rd
Abercorn Bridge
Incle Street
E Buchanan St
Cath
Garthland La
A761
Glasgow Road
Kilnside La
Paisley Grammar
Crossflat Cres
Williamsburgh Terr
Lacy St
Sutherland St
Uni of W Scotland
Underwood Halls
Hunter St
Graveyards
Moss St
Gilmour St
Meeting-house La
Central Way
Smithhills St
Lawn Street
Silk St
Coats Observatory
Oakshaw St East
Oakshaw Brae
Oakshaw-head
Oakshaw St West
Orr St
Orr Sq
Church Hill
School Wynd
The Cross
Dyers Wynd
Gauze St
Piazza Shop Cen
Civic Centre
Millar St
Christie St
Bank St
Lagoon Leisure Cen

Index to street names can be found starting on page 71

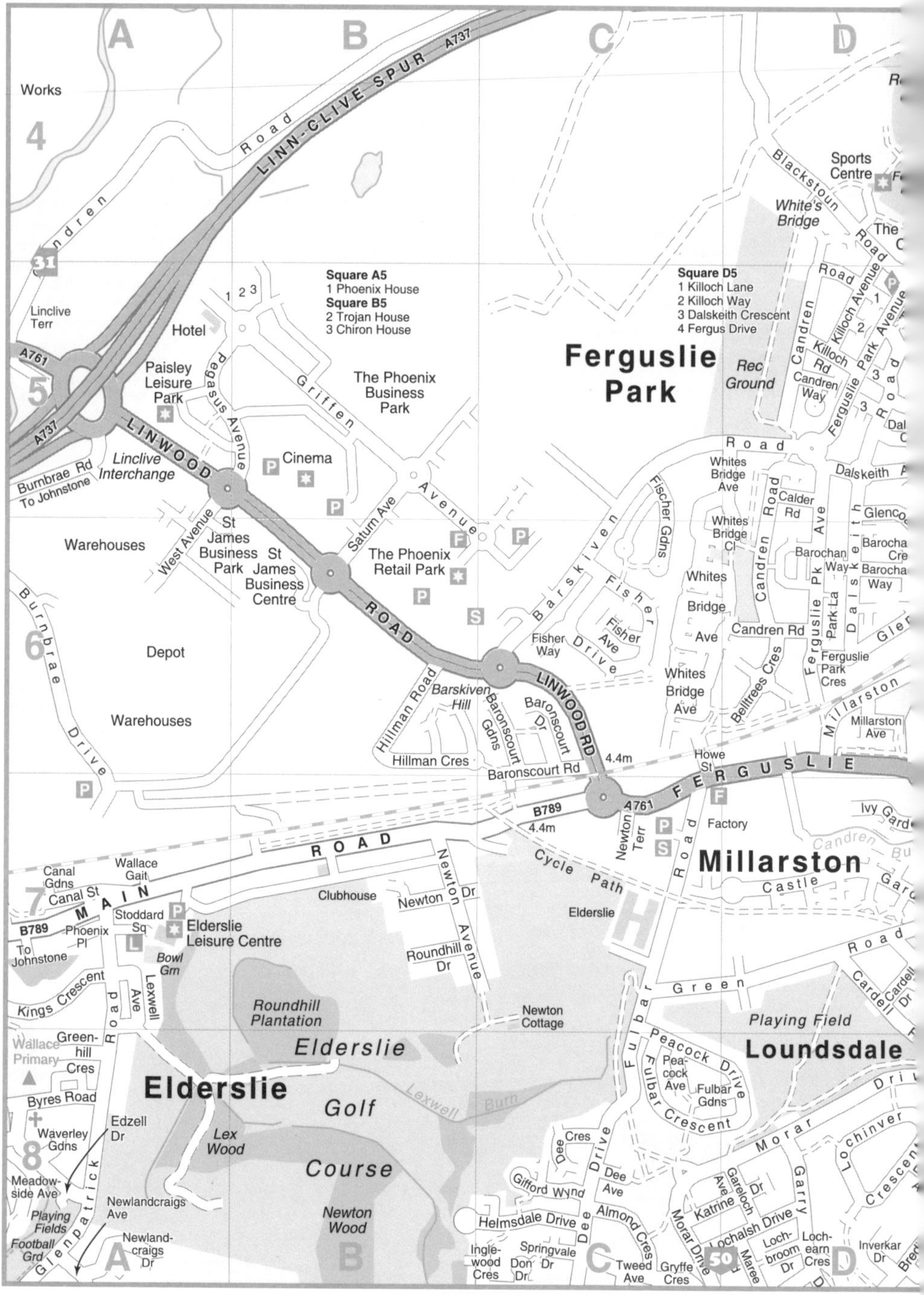

A B C D

4 5 6 7 8

Works

LINN-CLIVE SPUR A737

Road

Candren

31

Linclive Terr

A761

A737

Hotel

1 2 3

Paisley Leisure Park

Pegasus Avenue

LINWOOD ROAD

Linclive Interchange

Burnbrae Rd

To Johnstone

Warehouses

West Avenue

St James Business Park

St James Business Centre

Depot

Warehouses

Burnbrae Drive

**Square A5**
1 Phoenix House
**Square B5**
2 Trojan House
3 Chiron House

Griffen Avenue

The Phoenix Business Park

Cinema

Saturn Ave

The Phoenix Retail Park

Barskiven Road

Fisher Drive

Fisher Ave

Fisher Way

Barskiven Hill

Hillman Road

Hillman Cres

Baronscourt Gdns

Baronscourt Dr

Baronscourt Rd

LINWOOD RD

4.4m

B789

4.4m

A761

FERGUSLIE

Howe St

Factory

Newton Terr

Road

Millarston

Castle

Candren Burn

Ivy Gard

**Square D5**
1 Killoch Lane
2 Killoch Way
3 Dalskeith Crescent
4 Fergus Drive

Ferguslie Park

Rec Ground

Sports Centre

White's Bridge

Blackstoun Road

Road

Killoch Avenue

Killoch Rd

Candren Way

Candren Road

Ferguslie Park Avenue

Road

Dalskeith Road

Whites Bridge Ave

Fischer Gdns

Whites Bridge Cl

Calder Rd

Candren Road

Barochan Way

Barochan Cres

Barochan Way

Glencoe

Whites Bridge Ave

Candren Rd

Ferguslie Pk Ave

Ferguslie Park La

Dalskeith

Belltrees Cres

Ferguslie Park Cres

Millarston Ave

Millarston

Canal Gdns

Canal St

Wallace Gait

MAIN ROAD

B789

Phoenix Pl

To Johnstone

Stoddard Sq

Elderslie Leisure Centre

Bowl Grn

Clubhouse

Newton Dr

Newton Avenue

Roundhill Dr

Cycle Path

Elderslie

Kings Crescent

Lexwell Ave

Road

Roundhill Plantation

Newton Cottage

Elderslie

Wallace Primary

Green-hill Cres

Byres Road

Elderslie

Golf Course

Lexwell Burn

Edzell Dr

Waverley Gdns

Lex Wood

Meadow-side Ave

Playing Fields

Football Grd

Glenpatrick

Newlandcraigs Ave

Newland-craigs Dr

Newton Wood

Green Road

Cardell Dr

Cardell

Playing Field

Loundsdale

Fulbar Road

Peacock Drive

Pea-cock Ave

Fulbar Gdns

Fulbar Crescent

Morar Drive

Lochinver Crescent

Dee Cres

Dee Drive

Dee Ave

Gifford Wynd

Almond Cres

Helmsdale Drive

Ingle-wood Cres

Don Dr

Springvale Dr

Tweed Ave

Gryffe Cres

Morar Drive

Katrine Ave

Gareloch Dr

Garry

Lochalsh Drive

Maree

50

Loch-broom Dr

Loch-earn Cres

Inverkar Dr

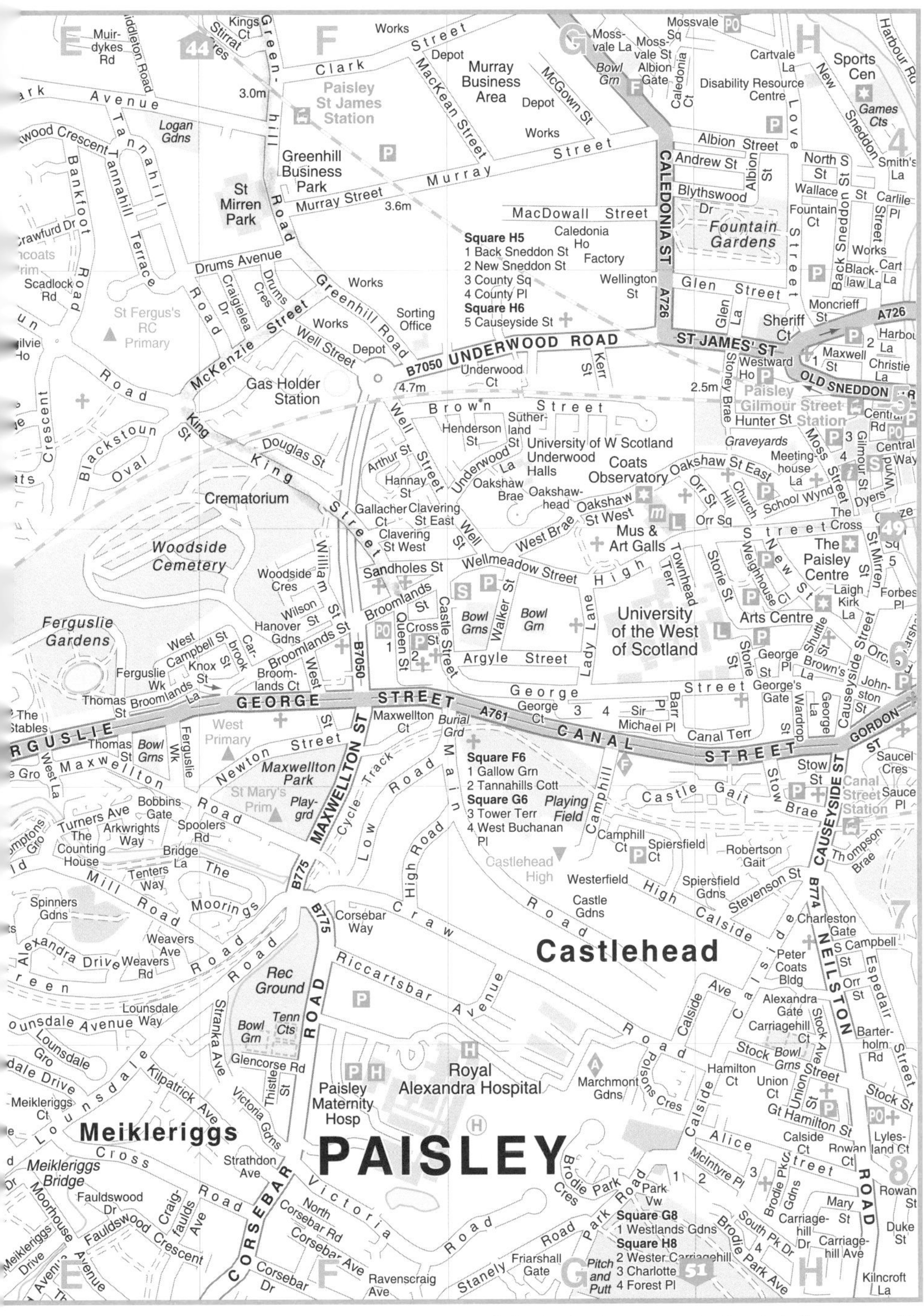
PAISLEY
Castlehead
Meikleriggs
Square H5
1 Back Sneddon St
2 New Sneddon St
3 County Sq
4 County Pl
Square H6
5 Causeyside St
Square F6
1 Gallow Grn
2 Tannahills Cott
Square G6
3 Tower Terr
4 West Buchanan Pl
Square G8
1 Westlands Gdns
Square H8
2 Wester Carriagehill
3 Charlotte
4 Forest Pl
University of the West of Scotland
Royal Alexandra Hospital
Paisley Maternity Hosp
Paisley St James Station
Paisley Gilmour Street Station
Canal Street Station
Greenhill Business Park
Murray Business Area
St Mirren Park
Fountain Gardens
Woodside Cemetery
Crematorium
Ferguslie Gardens
Maxwellton Park
Rec Ground
Gas Holder Station
The Paisley Centre
Arts Centre
Mus & Art Galls
Coats Observatory
Sports Cen
Disability Resource Centre
GEORGE STREET
CANAL STREET
UNDERWOOD ROAD
CALEDONIA ST
ST JAMES' ST
OLD SNEDDON
GORDON ST
CAUSEYSIDE ST
NEILSTON ROAD
MAXWELLTON ST
CORSEBAR ROAD
Index to street names can be found starting on page 71

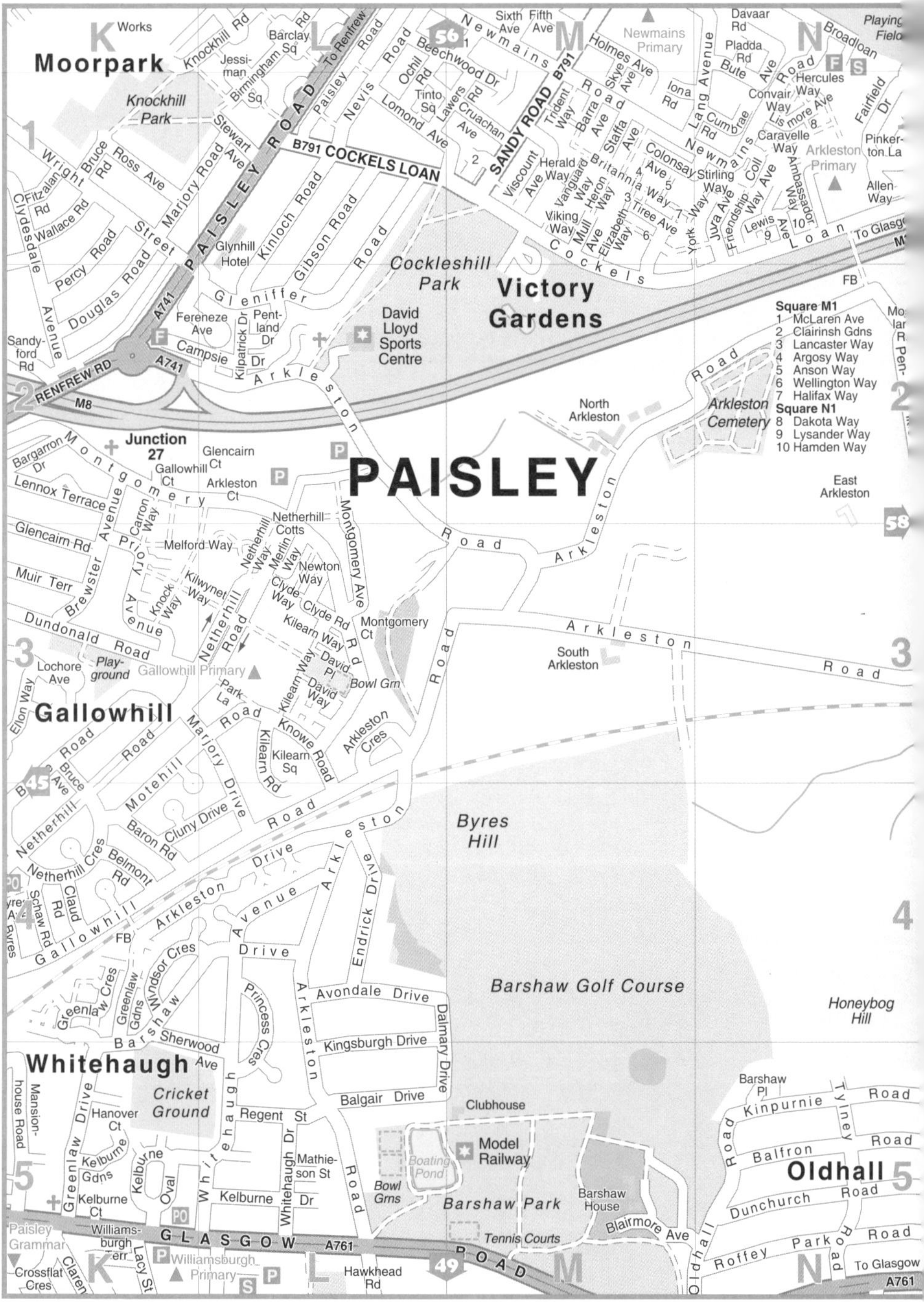

Moorpark

Knockhill Park

Victory Gardens

Cockleshill Park

David Lloyd Sports Centre

PAISLEY

Junction 27

North Arkleston

Arkleston Cemetery

**Square M1**
1 McLaren Ave
2 Clairinsh Gdns
3 Lancaster Way
4 Argosy Way
5 Anson Way
6 Wellington Way
7 Halifax Way

**Square N1**
8 Dakota Way
9 Lysander Way
10 Hamden Way

East Arkleston

South Arkleston

Gallowhill

Byres Hill

Barshaw Golf Course

Honeybog Hill

Whitehaugh

Cricket Ground

Model Railway

Barshaw Park

Barshaw House

Oldhall

Index to street names can be found starting on page 70

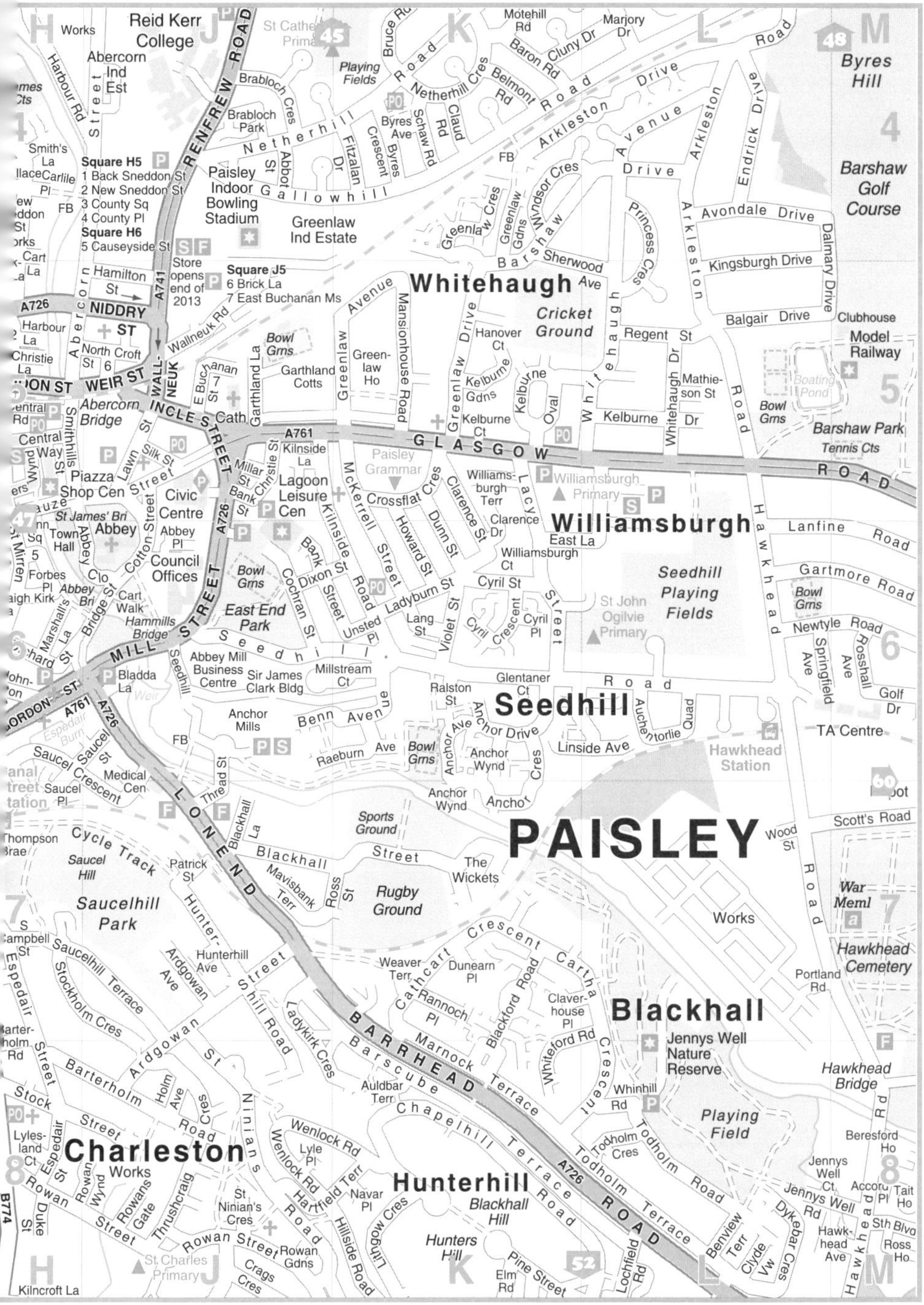
PAISLEY
Whitehaugh
Williamsburgh
Seedhill
Blackhall
Charleston
Hunterhill
Reid Kerr College
Abercorn Ind Est
Byres Hill
Barshaw Golf Course
Paisley Indoor Bowling Stadium
Greenlaw Ind Estate
Square H5
1 Back Sneddon St
2 New Sneddon St
3 County Sq
4 County Pl
Square H6
5 Causeyside St
Square J5
6 Brick La
7 East Buchanan Ms
Store opens end of 2013
Cricket Ground
Model Railway
Barshaw Park
Seedhill Playing Fields
East End Park
Council Offices
Civic Centre
Abbey
Town Hall
Lagoon Leisure Cen
Paisley Grammar
Williamsburgh Primary
St John Ogilvie Primary
Hawkhead Station
TA Centre
Sports Ground
Rugby Ground
Saucelhill Park
Cycle Track
Hawkhead Cemetery
War Meml
Jennys Well Nature Reserve
Hawkhead Bridge
Playing Field
Hunters Hill
Blackhall Hill
St Charles Primary
GLASGOW ROAD
BARRHEAD ROAD
RENFREW ROAD
LONEND
MILL STREET
INCLE STREET
NIDDRY ST
WEIR ST
A726
A761
A741
B774

Index to street names can be found starting on page 71

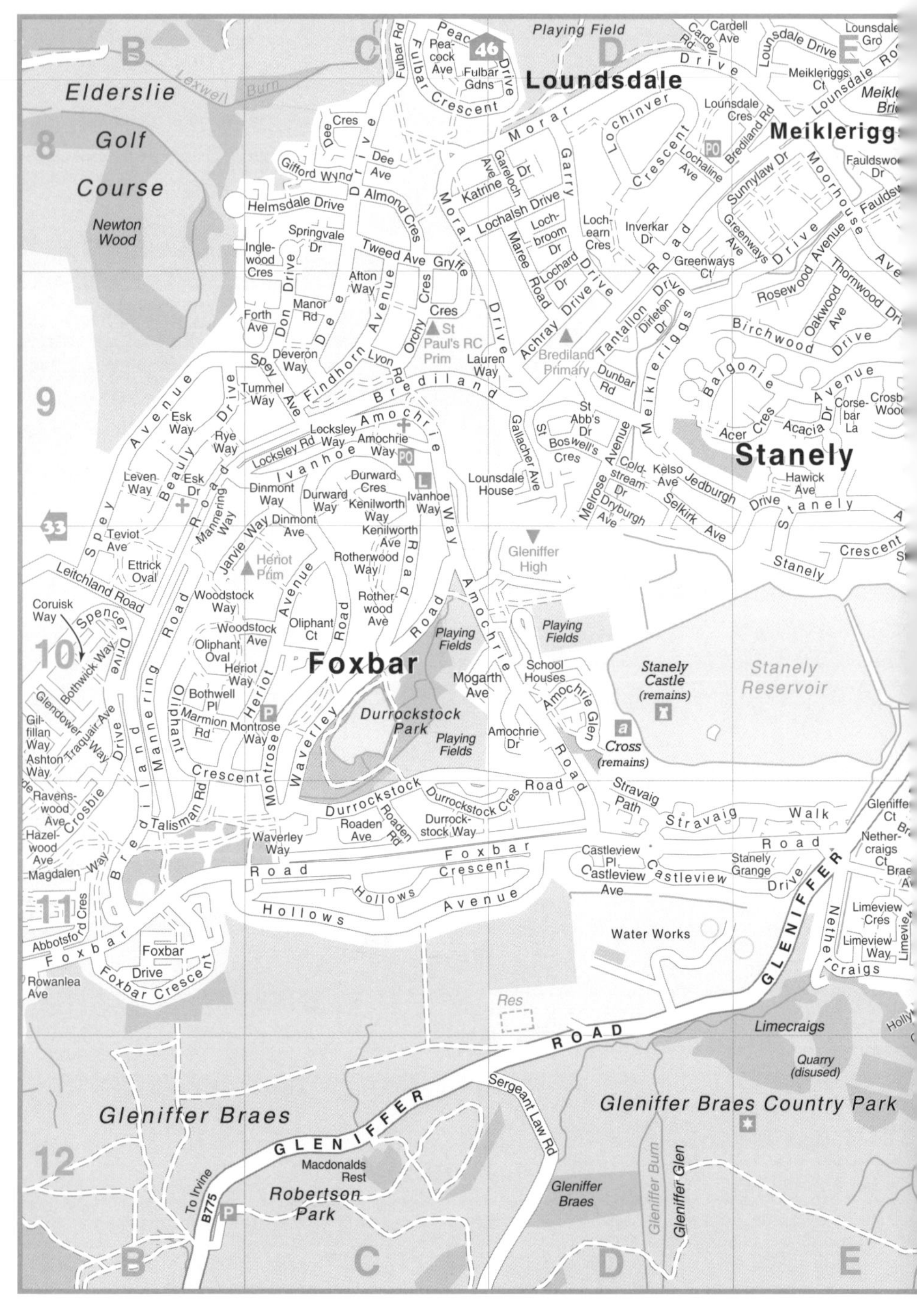

Loundsdale
Meikleriggs
Stanely
Foxbar
Elderslie Golf Course
Newton Wood
Durrockstock Park
Playing Fields
Stanely Castle (remains)
Stanely Reservoir
Cross (remains)
Water Works
Res
Limecraigs
Quarry (disused)
Gleniffer Braes Country Park
Gleniffer Braes
Macdonalds Rest
Robertson Park
Gleniffer Burn
Gleniffer Glen
To Irvine
B775
GLENIFFER ROAD
Foxbar Road
Bredilland Road
Amochrie Road
Amochrie Way
Ivanhoe Road
Mannering Road
Spey Avenue
Morar Drive
Lochinver Crescent
Meikleriggs Drive
Moorhouse Avenue
St Paul's RC Prim
Brediland Primary
Gleniffer High
Heriot Prim
Lounsdale House
School Houses
Playing Field
46
33

Index to street names can be found starting on page 71

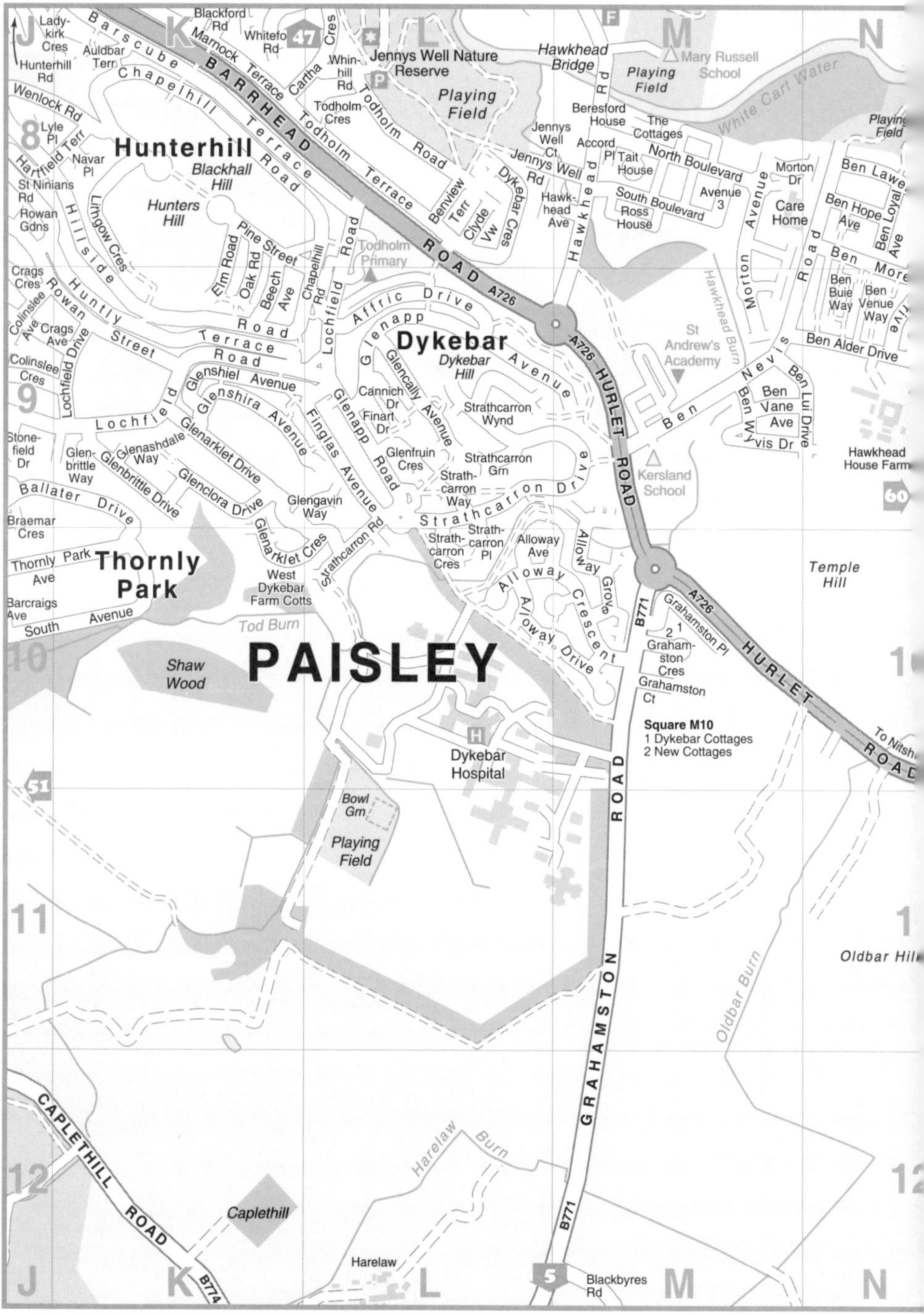

PAISLEY

Hunterhill
Blackhall Hill
Hunters Hill
Dykebar
Dykebar Hill
Thornly Park
Shaw Wood
Tod Burn
Dykebar Hospital
Bowl Grn
Playing Field
Caplethill
Harelaw
Harelaw Burn
Oldbar Burn
Oldbar Hill
Temple Hill
Hawkhead Bridge
Jennys Well Nature Reserve
Playing Field
Mary Russell School
White Cart Water
Todholm Primary
St Andrew's Academy
Hawkhead Burn
Kersland School
Hawkhead House Farm
Care Home
West Dykebar Farm Cotts

BARRHEAD ROAD A726
HURLET ROAD A726
GRAHAMSTON ROAD B771
CAPLETHILL ROAD B774
To Nitshill ROAD

Ladykirk Cres
Auldbar Terr
Hunterhill Rd
Barscube Terrace
Chapelhill Road
Blackford Rd
Whitefoord Rd
Marnock Terrace
Cartha Cres
Whinhill Rd
Todholm Cres
Todholm Road
Todholm Terrace
Wenlock Rd
Lyle Pl
Navar Pl
Hartfield Terr
St Ninians Rd
Rowan Gdns
Hillside
Lithgow Cres
Pine Street
Elm Road
Oak Rd
Beech Ave
Chapelhill Rd
Lochfield Road
Crags Cres
Rowan Street
Huntly Terrace
Colinslee Ave
Crags Ave
Colinslee Cres
Lochfield Drive
Glenshiel Avenue
Glenshira Avenue
Lochfield Road
Glenarklet Drive
Glenashdale Way
Stonefield Dr
Glenbrittle Way
Glenbrittle Drive
Glenclora Drive
Ballater Drive
Braemar Cres
Thornly Park Ave
Barcraigs Ave
South Avenue
Glenarklet Cres
Glengavin Way
Strathcarron Rd
Finglas Avenue
Glenapp Road
Glenapp Avenue
Glencally Avenue
Cannich Dr
Finart Dr
Glenfruin Cres
Affric Drive
Strathcarron Wynd
Strathcarron Grn
Strathcarron Way
Strathcarron Drive
Strathcarron Cres
Strathcarron Pl
Alloway Ave
Alloway Drive
Alloway Crescent
Alloway Grove
Benview Terr
Clyde Vw
Dykebar Cres
Hawkhead Ave
Hawkhead Rd
Jennys Well Rd
Jennys Well Ct
Beresford House
Accord Pl
Tait House
The Cottages
North Boulevard
South Boulevard
Ross House
Avenue 3
Morton Avenue
Morton Dr
Morton Road
Ben Lawers
Ben Hope Ave
Ben Loyal Ave
Ben More
Ben Buie Way
Ben Venue Way
Ben Alder Drive
Ben Nevis
Ben Lui Drive
Ben Vane Ave
Ben Wyvis Dr
Grahamston Pl
Grahamston Cres
Grahamston Ct
Blackbyres Rd

Square M10
1 Dykebar Cottages
2 New Cottages

J K L M N
8 9 10 11 12

47 51 60 5

Index to street names can be found starting on page 71

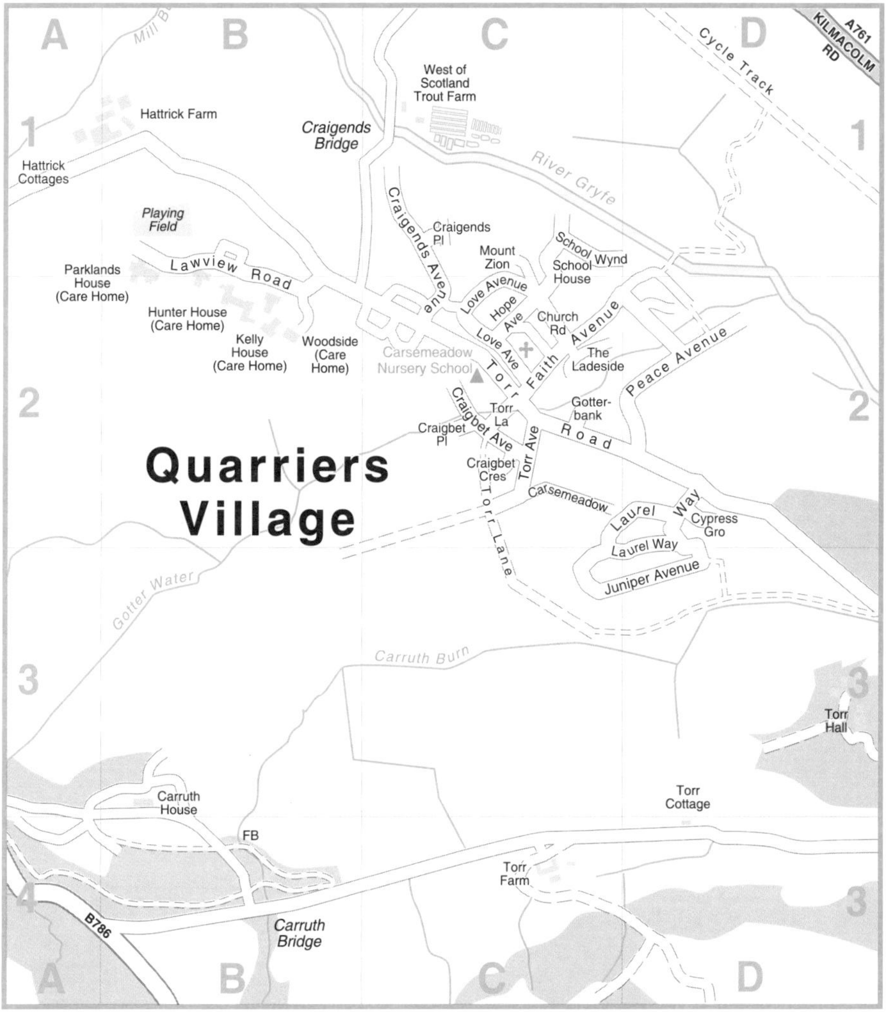

# Quarriers Village

A B C D
1 2 3 4
Mill Burn
Hattrick Farm
Hattrick Cottages
Craigends Bridge
West of Scotland Trout Farm
Cycle Track
A761 KILMACOLM RD
River Gryfe
Playing Field
Lawview Road
Parklands House (Care Home)
Hunter House (Care Home)
Kelly House (Care Home)
Woodside (Care Home)
Carsemeadow Nursery School
Craigends Avenue
Craigends Pl
Mount Zion
School Wynd
School House
Love Avenue
Hope Ave
Church Rd
Avenue
Love Ave
Faith
The Ladeside
Peace Avenue
Torr Road
Gotter-bank
Torr La
Craigbet Pl
Craigbet Ave
Torr Ave
Craigbet Cres
Carsemeadow
Torr Lane
Laurel Way
Cypress Gro
Juniper Avenue
Gotter Water
Carruth Burn
Torr Hall
Torr Cottage
Carruth House
FB
Torr Farm
B786
Carruth Bridge

## Index to Quarriers Village

Carsemeadow C2
Church Road C2
Craigbet Avenue C2
Craigbet Crescent C2
Craigbet Place C2
Craigends Avenue C1
Craigends Place C1
Cypress Grove D2
Faith Avenue C2
Hattrick Cottages A1
Hope Avenue C2
Gotterbank C2
Juniper Avenue C3
Kilmacolm Road D1
Ladeside, The C2
Laurel Way C2, C3
Lawview Road B1
Love Avenue C2
Mount Zion C1
Peace Avenue D2
School House C1
School Wynd C1
Torr Avenue C2
Torr Lane C2
Torr Road C2

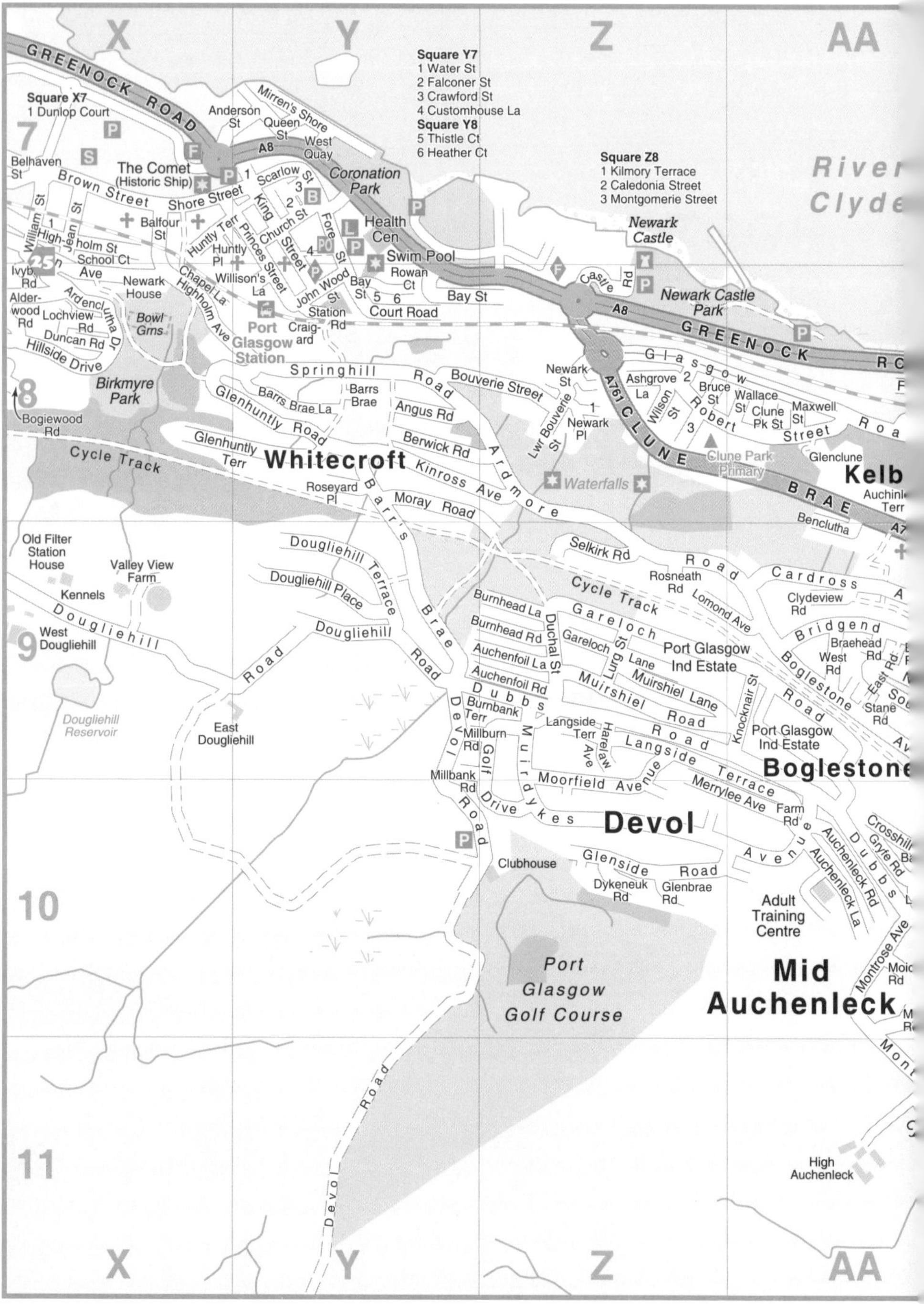
X
Y
Z
AA
7
8
9
10
11
Square X7
1 Dunlop Court
Square Y7
1 Water St
2 Falconer St
3 Crawford St
4 Customhouse La
Square Y8
5 Thistle Ct
6 Heather Ct
Square Z8
1 Kilmory Terrace
2 Caledonia Street
3 Montgomerie Street
River Clyde
GREENOCK ROAD
A8
Anderson St
Mirren's Shore
Queen St
West Quay
Coronation Park
Belhaven St
The Comet (Historic Ship)
Brown Street
Shore Street
Scarlow St
King Street
Church St
Fore St
Health Cen
Swim Pool
Rowan Ct
Bay St
Court Road
Station Rd
Craig-ard
Port Glasgow Station
John Wood St
Willison's La
Princes Street
Huntly Terr
Huntly Pl
Balfour St
William St
High-holm St
Jean St
School Ct
Ivybank Rd
Ave
Newark House
Chapel La
Highholm Ave
Ardenclutha Dr
Alder-wood Rd
Lochview Rd
Duncan Rd
Hillside Drive
Bowl Grns
Birkmyre Park
Bogiewood Rd
Springhill Road
Barrs Brae
Barrs Brae La
Glenhuntly Road
Glenhuntly Terr
Whitecroft
Angus Rd
Berwick Rd
Kinross Ave
Ardmore Road
Bouverie Street
Lwr Bouverie St
Newark St
Newark Pl
Roseyard Pl
Moray Road
Barr's Brae
Cycle Track
Newark Castle
Castle Rd
Newark Castle Park
Glasgow Road
A761 CLUNE BRAE
Ashgrove La
Wilson St
Robert St
Bruce St
Wallace St
Clune Pk St
Maxwell St
Street
Clune Park Primary
Glenclune
Kelb
Auchinleck Terr
Benclutha
Waterfalls
Old Filter Station House
Valley View Farm
Kennels
Dougliehill Road
West Dougliehill
Dougliehill Terrace
Dougliehill Place
Dougliehill Reservoir
East Dougliehill
Selkirk Rd
Rosneath Rd
Lomond Ave
Cardross Road
Clydeview Rd
Bridgend Road
Braehead Rd
West Rd
East Rd
Stane Rd
Boglestone Road
Burnhead La
Burnhead Rd
Duchal St
Gareloch Road
Gareloch Lane
Lurg St
Port Glasgow Ind Estate
Muirshiel Lane
Auchenfoil La
Auchenfoil Rd
Muirshiel Road
Knocknair St
Dubbs Road
Burnbank Terr
Millburn Rd
Devol Road
Golf Drive
Muirdykes
Langside Terr
Harelaw Ave
Langside Terrace
Boglestone
Millbank Rd
Moorfield Avenue
Merrylee Ave
Farm Rd
Devol
Glenside Road
Clubhouse
Dykeneuk Rd
Glenbrae Rd
Avenue
Auchenleck Rd
Auchenleck La
Crosshill
Gryfe Rd
Adult Training Centre
Port Glasgow Golf Course
Mid Auchenleck
Montrose Ave
Moidart Rd
High Auchenleck

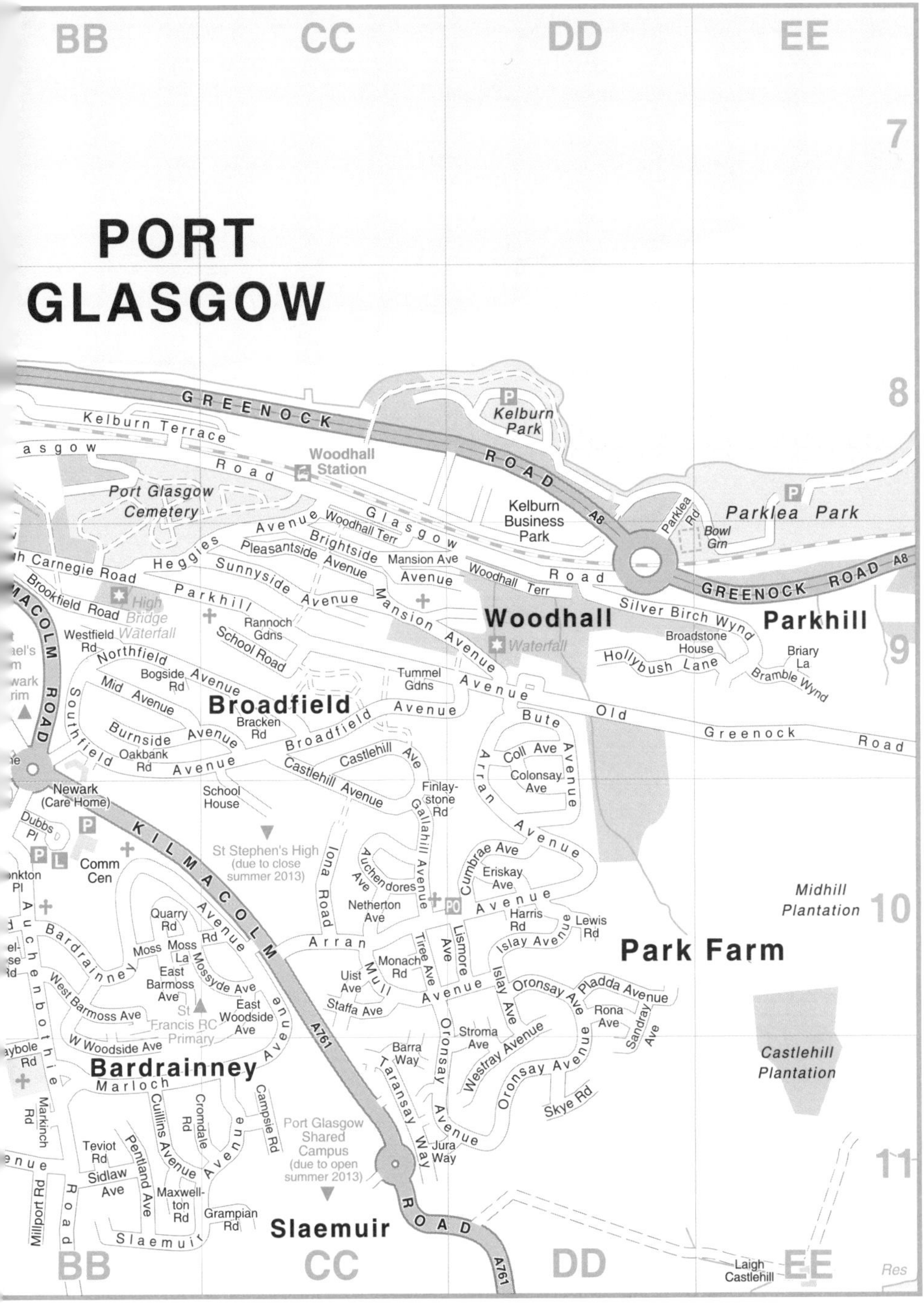

BB CC DD EE

7 8 9 10 11

# PORT GLASGOW

GREENOCK ROAD
A8
Kelburn Terrace
Glasgow Road
Woodhall Station
Kelburn Park
Kelburn Business Park
Parklea Park
Parklea Rd
Bowl Grn
Port Glasgow Cemetery
Avenue
Woodhall Terr
Brightside Avenue
Pleasantside Avenue
Mansion Ave
Avenue
Heggies
Sunnyside Avenue
Carnegie Road
Brookfield Road
High Bridge Waterfall
Parkhill
Rannoch Gdns
School Road
Mansion Avenue
Woodhall
Waterfall
Silver Birch Wynd
Parkhill
Broadstone House
Hollybush Lane
Briary La
Bramble Wynd
Westfield Rd
Northfield Avenue
Bogside Rd
Mid Avenue
Broadfield
Bracken Rd
Tummel Gdns
Avenue
Old Greenock Road
Bute Avenue
Coll Ave
Colonsay Ave
Arran Avenue
Burnside Avenue
Broadfield Avenue
Castlehill Ave
Castlehill Avenue
Southfield Avenue
Oakbank Rd
KILMACOLM ROAD
Newark (Care Home)
School House
Finlaystone Rd
Gallahill Avenue
Dubbs Pl
Comm Cen
St Stephen's High (due to close summer 2013)
Iona Road
Auchendores Ave
Cumbrae Ave
Eriskay Ave
Netherton Ave
PO
Avenue
Harris Rd
Lewis Rd
Islay Avenue
Midhill Plantation
Monkton Pl
Auchenbothie Road
Quarry Rd
Moss Rd
Moss La
Mossyde Ave
Bardrainney Avenue
Arran
Mull Avenue
Monach Rd
Tiree Ave
Lismore Ave
Park Farm
East Barmoss Ave
East Woodside Ave
Uist Ave
Staffa Ave
Islay Ave
Oronsay Ave
Pladda Avenue
Rona Ave
Sandray Ave
West Barmoss Ave
St Francis RC Primary
W Woodside Ave
A761
Barra Way
Stroma Ave
Westray Avenue
Oronsay Avenue
Castlehill Plantation
Bardrainney
Marloch Avenue
Cullins Avenue
Crombdale Rd
Campsie Rd
Taransay Way
Skye Rd
Markinch Rd
Teviot Rd
Pentland Ave
Sidlaw Ave
Maxwellton Rd
Port Glasgow Shared Campus (due to open summer 2013)
Jura Way
Millport Rd
Grampian Rd
Slaemuir
Laigh Castlehill
Res

Index to street names can be found starting on page 65

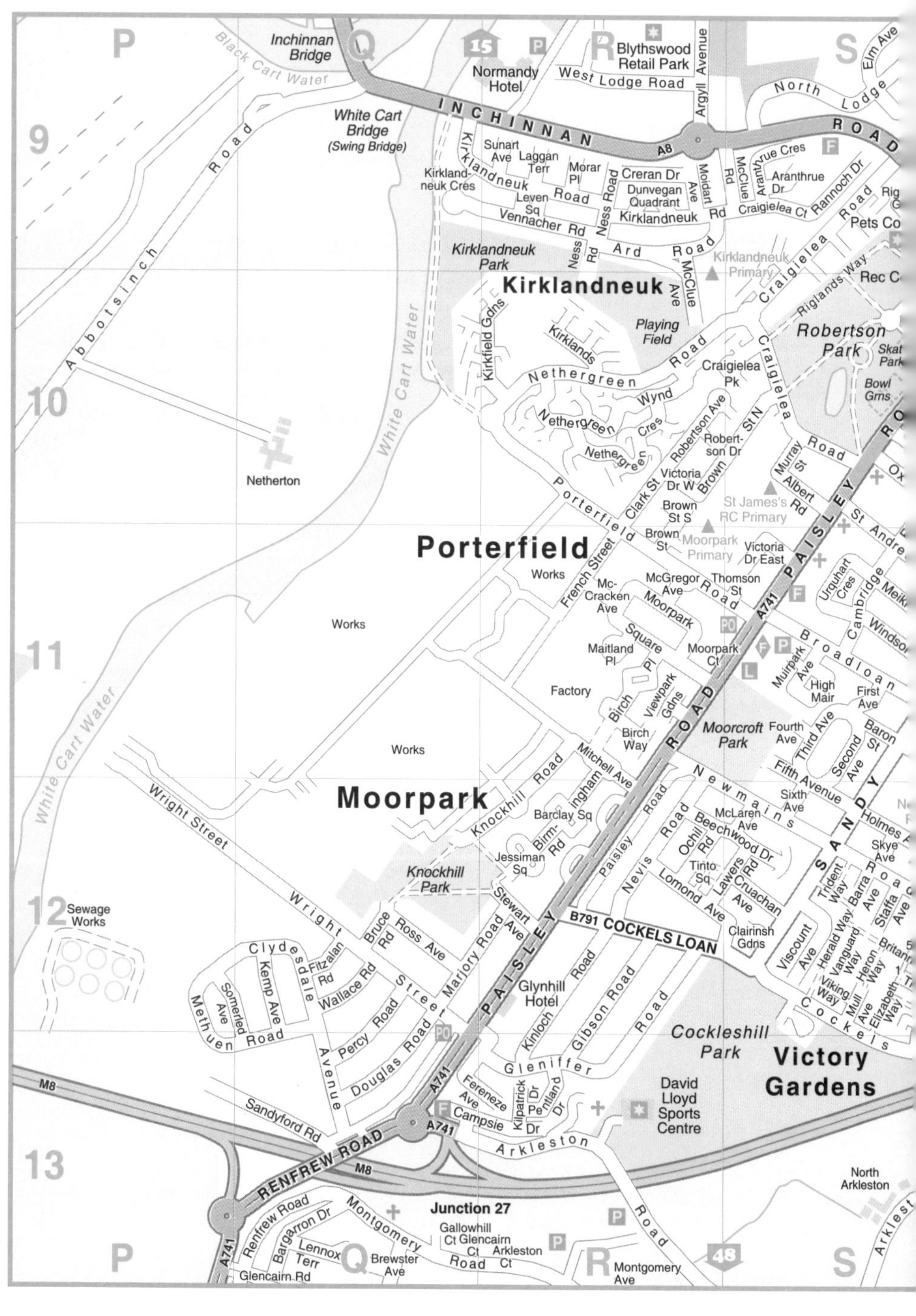

Inchinnan Bridge
Black Cart Water
Normandy Hotel
Blythswood Retail Park
West Lodge Road
Argyll Avenue
North Lodge Road
Elm Ave
INCHINNAN ROAD
A8
White Cart Bridge
(Swing Bridge)
Sunart Ave
Laggan Terr
Morar Pl
Creran Dr
Kirklandneuk Cres
Kirklandneuk Road
Leven Sq
Dunvegan Quadrant
Moidart Ave
McClue Rd
Aranthrue Cres
Aranthrue Dr
Rannoch Dr
Ness Road
Kirklandneuk Rd
Craigielea Ct
Vennacher Rd
Ness Rd
Ard Road
McClue Ave
Kirklandneuk Park
Kirklandneuk Primary
Craigielea Road
Riglands Way
Pets Co
Rec C
Kirklandneuk
Playing Field
Robertson Park
Skat Park
Bowl Grns
Abbotsinch Road
Kirkfield Gdns
Kirklands
Nethergreen Road
Craigielea Pk
Wynd
Nethergreen Cres
Nethergreen
Robertson Ave
Robertson Dr
St N
Murray St
Road
Albert Rd
White Cart Water
Netherton
Victoria Dr W
Brown St S
Clark St
St James's RC Primary
St Andrews
Porterfield Road
Brown St
Moorpark Primary
Victoria Dr East
PAISLEY ROAD
Porterfield
French Street
Works
Mc-Cracken Ave
McGregor Ave
Thomson St
Road
Urquhart Cres
Cambridge
Meik
Moorpark Square
A741
Broadloan
Windsor
Maitland Pl
Moorpark Ct
Muirpark Ave
High Mair
First Ave
Factory
Birch Pl
Viewpark Gdns
Birch Way
Moorcroft Park
Fourth Ave
Third Ave
Second Ave
Baron St
Works
Mitchell Ave
Fifth Avenue
Newmains
Sixth Ave
Knockhill Road
McLaren Ave
SANDY
Holmes
Moorpark
Barclay Sq
Birmingham Rd
Paisley Road
Beechwood Dr
Ochil Rd
Skye Ave
Wright Street
Jessiman Sq
Nevis Road
Tinto Sq
Lawers Rd
Cruachan Ave
Trident Way
Barra Ave
Knockhill Park
Lomond Ave
Staffa Ave
Sewage Works
Stewart Ave
B791 COCKELS LOAN
Clairinsh Gdns
Herald Way
Vanguard Way
Britannia
Bruce Rd
Ross Ave
Marjory Road
Viscount Ave
Heron Way
Clydesdale
Fitzalan Rd
Wallace Rd
Kemp Ave
Street
Glynhill Hotel
Viking Way
Mull Ave
Elizabeth Way
Somerled Ave
Methuen Road
Percy Road
Kinloch Road
Gibson Road
Road
Cockles
Cockleshill Park
Victory Gardens
M8
Avenue
Douglas Road
Gleniffer
Fereneze Ave
Kilpatrick Dr
Pentland Dr
Pe Dr
David Lloyd Sports Centre
Sandyford Rd
A741
Campsie Dr
RENFREW ROAD
Arkleston
13
M8
North Arkleston
Junction 27
Renfrew Road
Bargarron Dr
Montgomery Road
Gallowhill Ct
Glencairn Ct
Arkleston Ct
Road
Lennox Terr
Brewster Ave
Montgomery Ave
48
Arkleston
Glencairn Rd
A741
15
P
Q
R
S
9
10
11
12

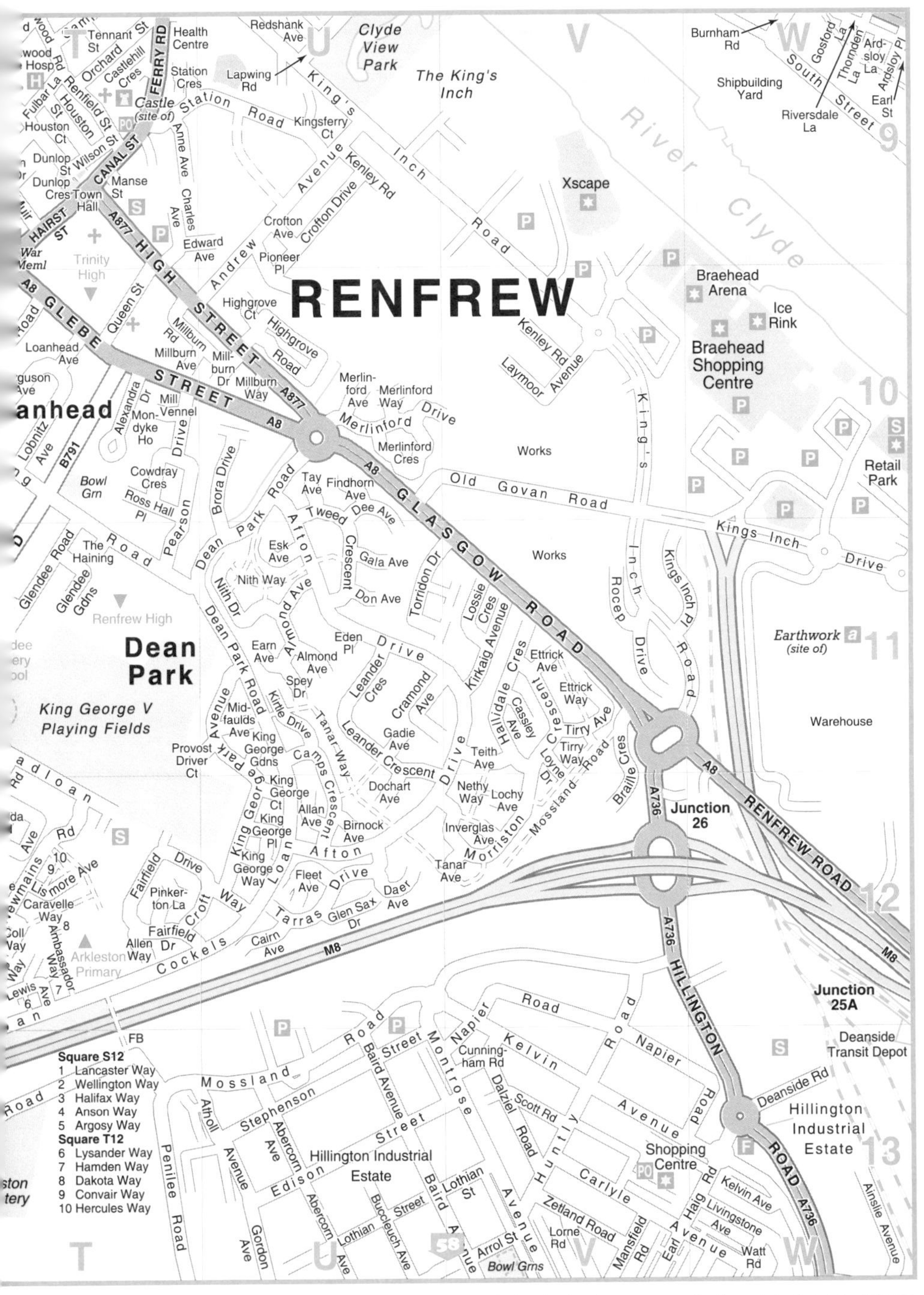


Index to street names can be found starting on page 74

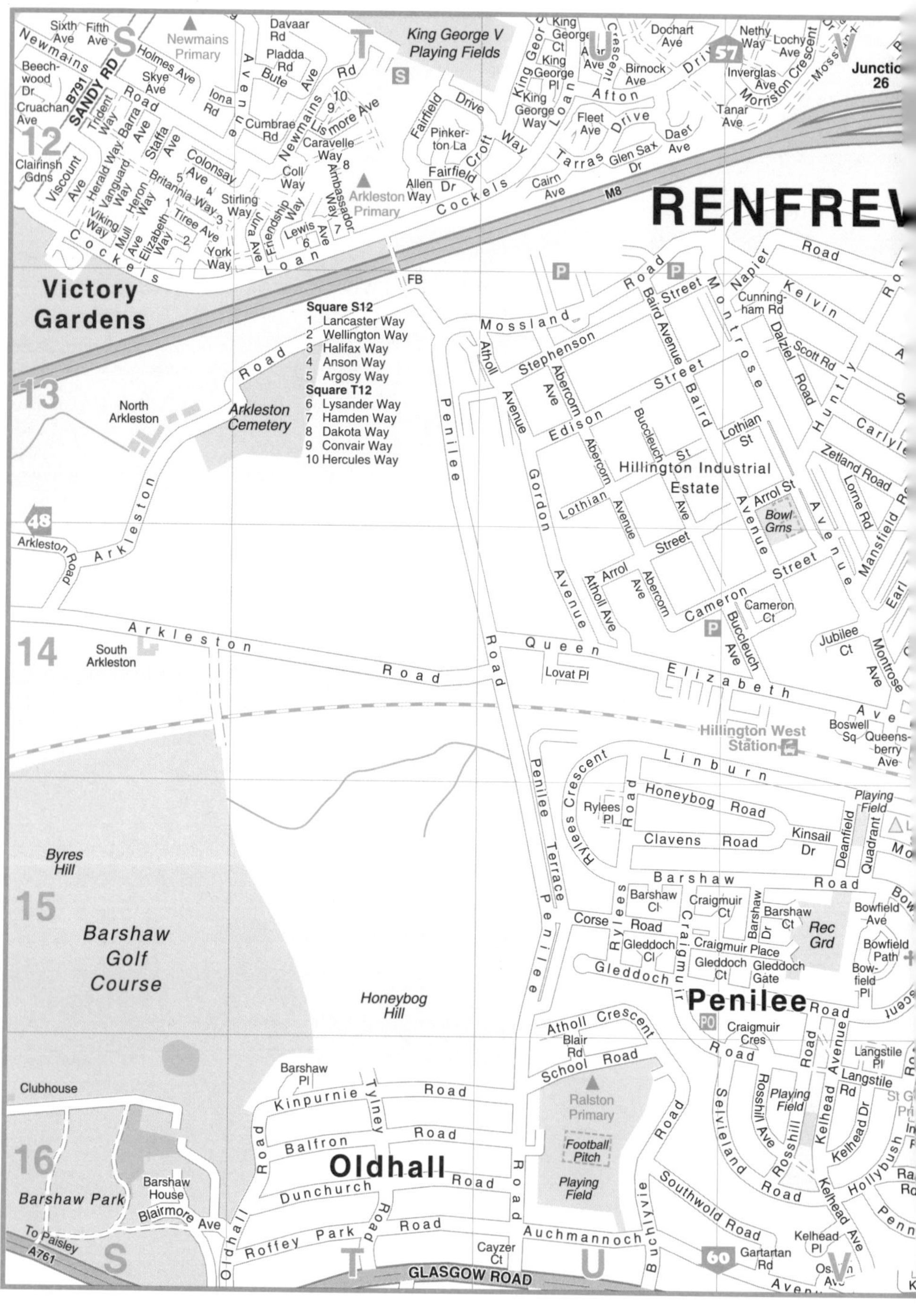

RENFREW
Victory Gardens
Oldhall
Penilee
Hillington Industrial Estate
Arkleston Cemetery
Barshaw Golf Course
Barshaw Park
Barshaw House
Clubhouse
Byres Hill
Honeybog Hill
King George V Playing Fields
North Arkleston
South Arkleston
Hillington West Station
Newmains Primary
Arkleston Primary
Ralston Primary
Football Pitch
Playing Field
Rec Grd
Bowl Grns
GLASGOW ROAD
To Paisley A761
SANDY RD B791
M8
Junction 26
FB
Square S12
1 Lancaster Way
2 Wellington Way
3 Halifax Way
4 Anson Way
5 Argosy Way
Square T12
6 Lysander Way
7 Hamden Way
8 Dakota Way
9 Convair Way
10 Hercules Way
Arkleston Road
Penilee Road
Penilee Terrace
Queen Elizabeth Ave
Mossland Road
Stephenson Street
Edison Street
Gordon Avenue
Atholl Avenue
Baird Street
Baird Avenue
Montrose Avenue
Napier Street
Kelvin Road
Dalziel Road
Scott Rd
Huntly Road
Cunningham Rd
Lothian Street
Lothian St
Buccleuch St
Buccleuch Ave
Abercorn Ave
Abercorn Avenue
Arrol Ave
Arrol St
Atholl Ave
Cameron Street
Cameron Ct
Lovat Pl
Jubilee Ct
Montrose Ave
Zetland Road
Lorne Rd
Mansfield Rd
Carlyle
Boswell Sq
Queensberry Ave
Linburn Road
Honeybog Road
Clavens Road
Kinsail Dr
Deanfield Quadrant
Rylees Crescent
Rylees Pl
Rylees Road
Barshaw Road
Barshaw Ct
Barshaw Dr
Craigmuir Ct
Craigmuir Place
Craigmuir Road
Craigmuir Cres
Corse Road
Gleddoch Road
Gleddoch Ct
Gleddoch Cl
Gleddoch Gate
Bowfield Ave
Bowfield Path
Bowfield Pl
Atholl Crescent
Blair Rd
School Road
Kinpurnie Road
Tylney Road
Balfron Road
Dunchurch Road
Roffey Park Road
Oldhall Road
Barshaw Pl
Blairmore Ave
Cayzer Ct
Auchmannoch Road
Buchlyvie Road
Southwold Road
Selvieland Road
Rosshill Ave
Rosshill Road
Kelhead Avenue
Kelhead Dr
Kelhead Pl
Kelhead Ave
Langstile Pl
Langstile Rd
Hollybush Road
Gartartan Rd
Newmains Road
Newmains Rd
Sixth Ave
Fifth Ave
Holmes Ave
Skye Ave
Beechwood Dr
Cruachan Ave
Trident Way
Barra Ave
Staffa Ave
Iona Rd
Davaar Rd
Pladda Rd
Bute Ave
Cumbrae Rd
Lismore Ave
Caravelle Way
Ambassador Way
Coll Way
Colonsay Ave
Clairinsh Gdns
Viscount Ave
Herald Way
Vanguard Way
Heron Way
Britannia Way
Stirling Way
Tiree Ave
Viking Way
Mull Ave
Elizabeth Way
York Way
Jura Ave
Friendship Way
Lewis Ave
Cockels Loan
Fairfield Drive
Fairfield Dr
Pinkerton La
Croft Way
Allen Way
Cairn Ave
Tarras Drive
Glen Sax Dr
Daer Ave
Fleet Ave
Afton Drive
King George Way
King George Pl
King George Ct
Birnock Ave
Crescent
Dochart Ave
Nethy Way
Lochy Ave
Inverglas Ave
Morriston Crescent
Tanar Ave

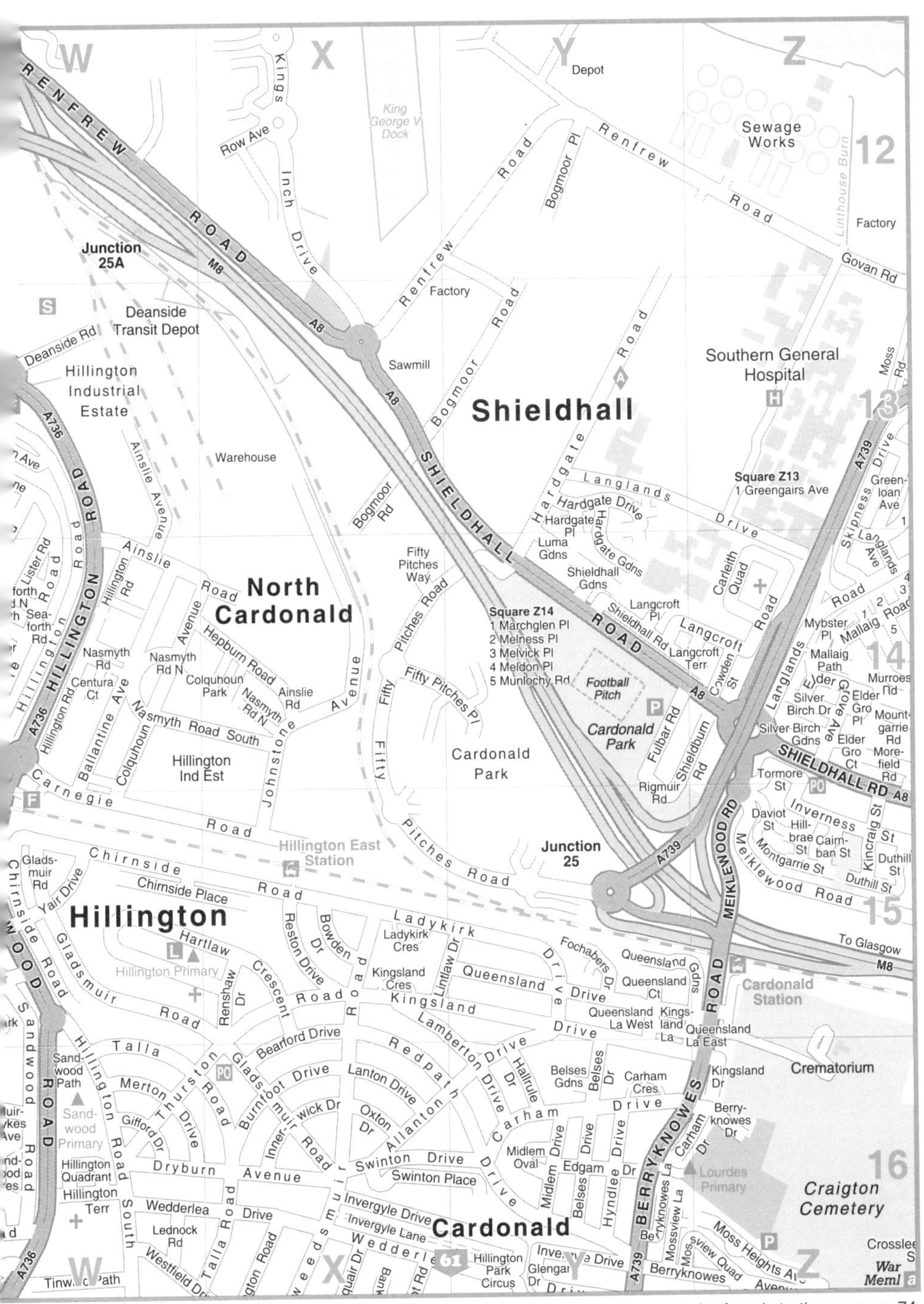


Index to street names can be found starting on page 74

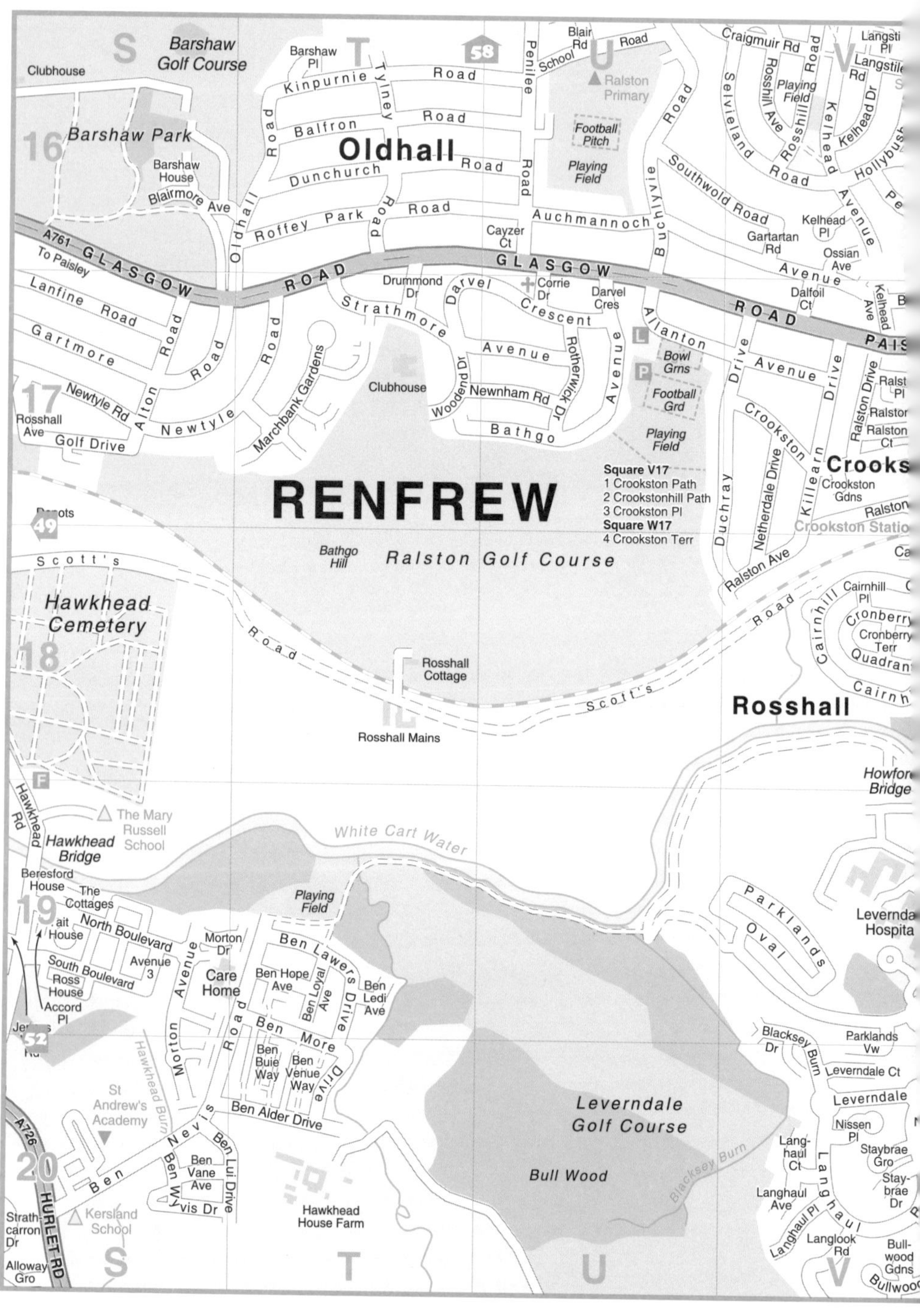

RENFREW
Oldhall
Rosshall
Crooks
Barshaw Golf Course
Barshaw Park
Barshaw House
Clubhouse
Hawkhead Cemetery
Ralston Golf Course
Bathgo Hill
Leverndale Golf Course
Bull Wood
White Cart Water
Blacksey Burn
Hawkhead Burn
Hawkhead Bridge
Howford Bridge
The Mary Russell School
Ralston Primary
St Andrew's Academy
Kersland School
Hawkhead House Farm
Rosshall Cottage
Rosshall Mains
Care Home
Playing Field
Football Pitch
Football Grd
Bowl Grns
Crookston Statio
Leverndale Hospita
A761 GLASGOW ROAD
To Paisley
PAISLEY ROAD
A726 HURLET RD
Scott's Road
Square V17
1 Crookston Path
2 Crookstonhill Path
3 Crookston Pl
Square W17
4 Crookston Terr
Kinpurnie Road
Balfron Road
Dunchurch Road
Roffey Park Road
Tyiney Road
Penilee Road
Auchmannoch Avenue
Oldhall Road
Blairmore Ave
Barshaw Pl
Cayzer Ct
Blair Rd
School Road
Buchlyvie Road
Southwold Road
Selvieland Road
Craigmuir Rd
Rosshill Ave
Rosshill Road
Kelhead Dr
Kelhead Avenue
Kelhead Pl
Kelhead Ave
Langstile Pl
Langstile Rd
Hollybush Road
Gartartan Rd
Ossian Ave
Dalfoil Ct
Lanfine Road
Gartmore Road
Newtyle Rd
Newtyle Road
Alton Road
Rosshall Ave
Golf Drive
Marchbank Gardens
Strathmore Avenue
Drummond Dr
Darvel Crescent
Corrie Dr
Darvel Cres
Woodend Dr
Newnham Rd
Rotherwick Dr
Bathgo Avenue
Allanton Avenue
Crookston Drive
Netherdale Drive
Killearn Drive
Duchray
Ralston Drive
Ralston Pl
Ralston Ct
Ralston Ave
Crookston Gdns
Cairnhill Pl
Cairnhill
Cronberry
Cronberry Terr
Quadrant
Parklands Oval
Parklands Vw
Blacksey Dr
Leverndale Ct
Leverndale
Nissen Pl
Staybrae Gro
Staybrae Dr
Langhaul Ct
Langhaul Ave
Langhaul Pl
Langhaul
Langlook Rd
Bullwood Gdns
Hawkhead Rd
Beresford House
The Cottages
North Boulevard
Avenue 3
South Boulevard
Ross House
Accord Pl
Morton Avenue
Morton Dr
Ben Lawers Drive
Ben Hope Ave
Ben Loyal Ave
Ben Ledi Ave
Ben More Drive
Ben Buie Way
Ben Venue Way
Ben Alder Drive
Ben Nevis Road
Ben Vane Ave
Ben Lui Drive
Strathcarron Dr
Alloway Gro
Langstile
49
52
58
16
17
18
19
20
S
T
U
V

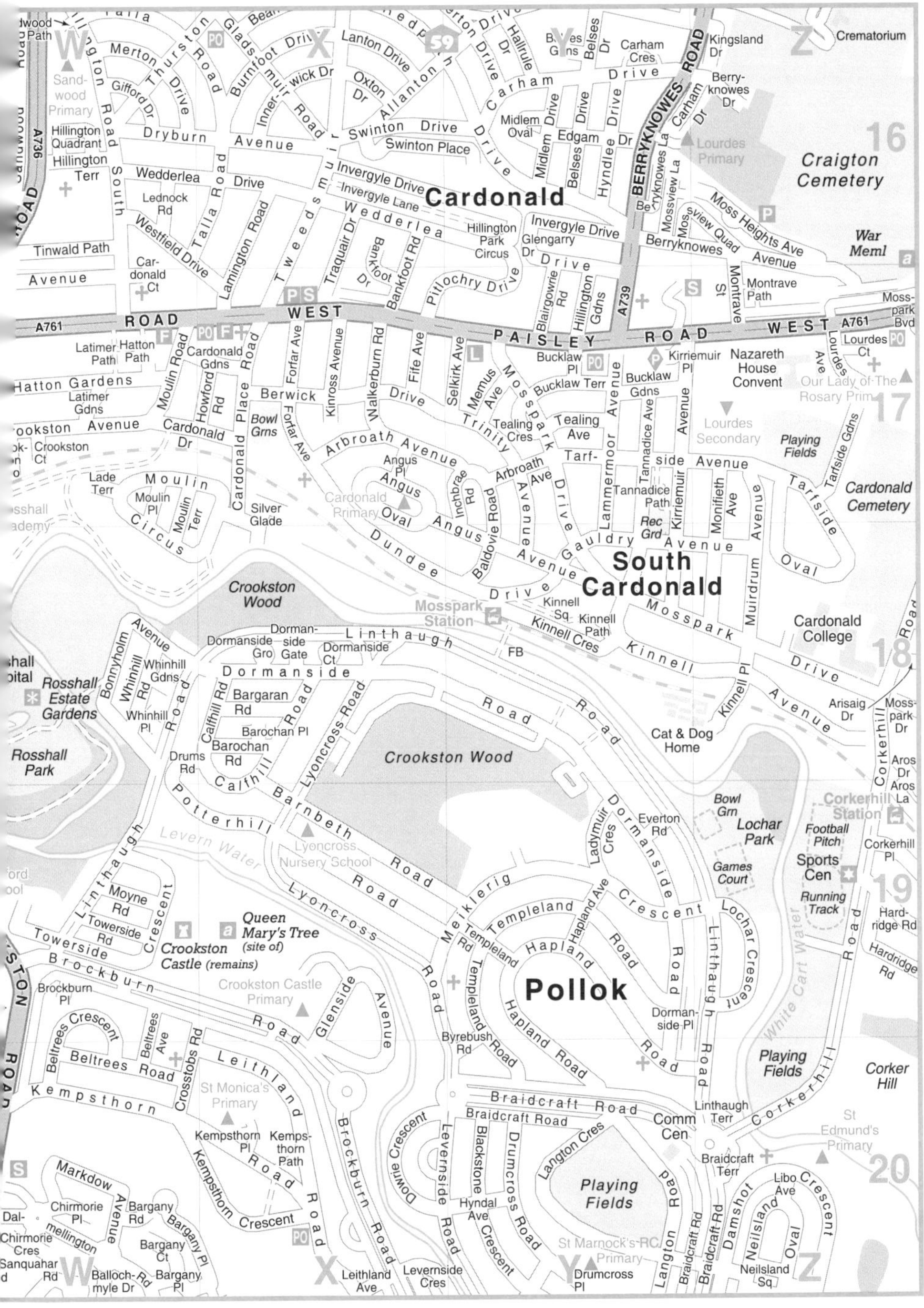


Index to street names can be found starting on page 74

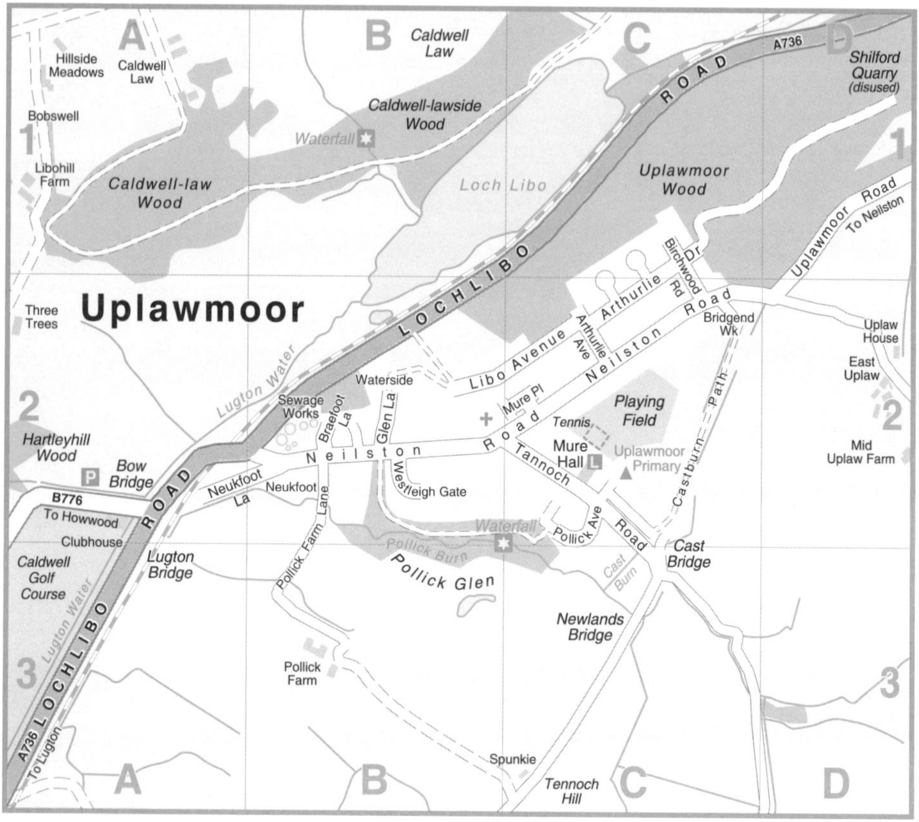

Caldwell Law
Hillside Meadows
Caldwell Law
Bobswell
Caldwell-lawside Wood
Waterfall
Libohill Farm
Caldwell-law Wood
Loch Libo
Uplawmoor Wood
Shilford Quarry (disused)
A736
LOCHLIBO ROAD
Uplawmoor Road
To Neilston
Three Trees
Uplawmoor
Birchwood Rd
Dr
Arthurlie
Arthurlie Ave
Neilston Road
Bridgend Wk
Uplaw House
East Uplaw
Libo Avenue
Waterside
Lugton Water
Sewage Works
Braefoot La
Glen La
Mure Pl
Playing Field
Tennis
Mure Hall
Uplawmoor Primary
Castburn Path
Mid Uplaw Farm
Hartleyhill Wood
Bow Bridge
B776
To Howwood
Clubhouse
Neukfoot La
Neukfoot
Westleigh Gate
Tannoch Road
Pollick Ave
Waterfall
Pollick Burn
Cast Bridge
Caldwell Golf Course
Lugton Bridge
Pollick Farm Lane
Pollick Glen
Cast Burn
Newlands Bridge
Pollick Farm
A736 To Lugton
Spunkie
Tennoch Hill

## Index to Uplawmoor

| | |
|---|---|
| Arthurlie Avenue | C2 |
| Arthurlie Drive | C2 |
| Birchwood Road | C1 |
| Braefoot Lane | B2 |
| Bridgend Walk | C2 |
| Castburn Path | C2 |
| Glen Lane | B2 |
| Libo Avenue | B2 |
| Lochlibo Road | A3, B2 |
| Mure Place | C2 |
| Neilston Road | B2, C2 |
| Neukfoot | B2 |
| Neukfoot Lane | A2 |
| Pollick Avenue | C2 |
| Pollick Farm Lane | B3 |
| Tannoch Road | C2 |
| Uplawmoor Road | D1 |
| Waterside | B2 |
| Westleigh Gate | B2 |

## Index to Wemyss Bay

| | |
|---|---|
| Ardgowan Road | B2 |
| Ascog Place | B2 |
| Beech Walk | B3 |
| Broom Road | B2 |
| Brueacre Drive | B1, B2 |
| Brueacre Place | B1 |
| Brueacre Road | B2 |
| Burns Drive | B2 |
| Carron Road | B2 |
| Castle Road | A2 |
| Castle Wemyss Drive | B2 |
| Castle Wemyss Place | A2 |
| Cedar Walk | B3 |
| Cliff Terrace Road | B3 |
| Elm Walk | B3 |
| Etive Road | B2 |
| Fir Avenue | B3 |
| Forbes Place | B3 |
| Greenock Road | B4 |
| Hawthorn Way | B3 |
| Hazel Walk | B3 |
| Innellan Road | B2 |
| Katrine Road | B3 |
| Kilchattan Place | B2 |
| Kishorn Road | B3 |
| Kyles, The | B3 |
| Larch Walk | B3 |
| Leapmoor Drive | A2 |
| Leven Road | B3 |
| Linnhe Road | B2 |
| Lomond Road | B3 |
| Maple Avenue | B3 |
| Melfort Road | B3 |
| Morar Road | B3 |
| Mount Stuart Drive | C2 |
| Oak Avenue | B3 |
| Poplar Way | B3 |
| Rannoch Road | B3 |
| Ryan Road | B3 |
| Sanda | B5 |
| Shore Road | B5 |
| Station Cottages | B5 |
| Striven Road | B3 |
| Sunart Road | B2 |
| Toward | B4 |
| Toward Road | B2 |
| Tummel Road | B3 |
| Undercliff Court | A3 |
| Undercliff Road | A3 |
| Wallace Road | B3 |
| Wemyss Bay Road | B4 |
| Weymss Court | A2 |
| Weymss Point | B3 |
| Whiting Road | B2 |

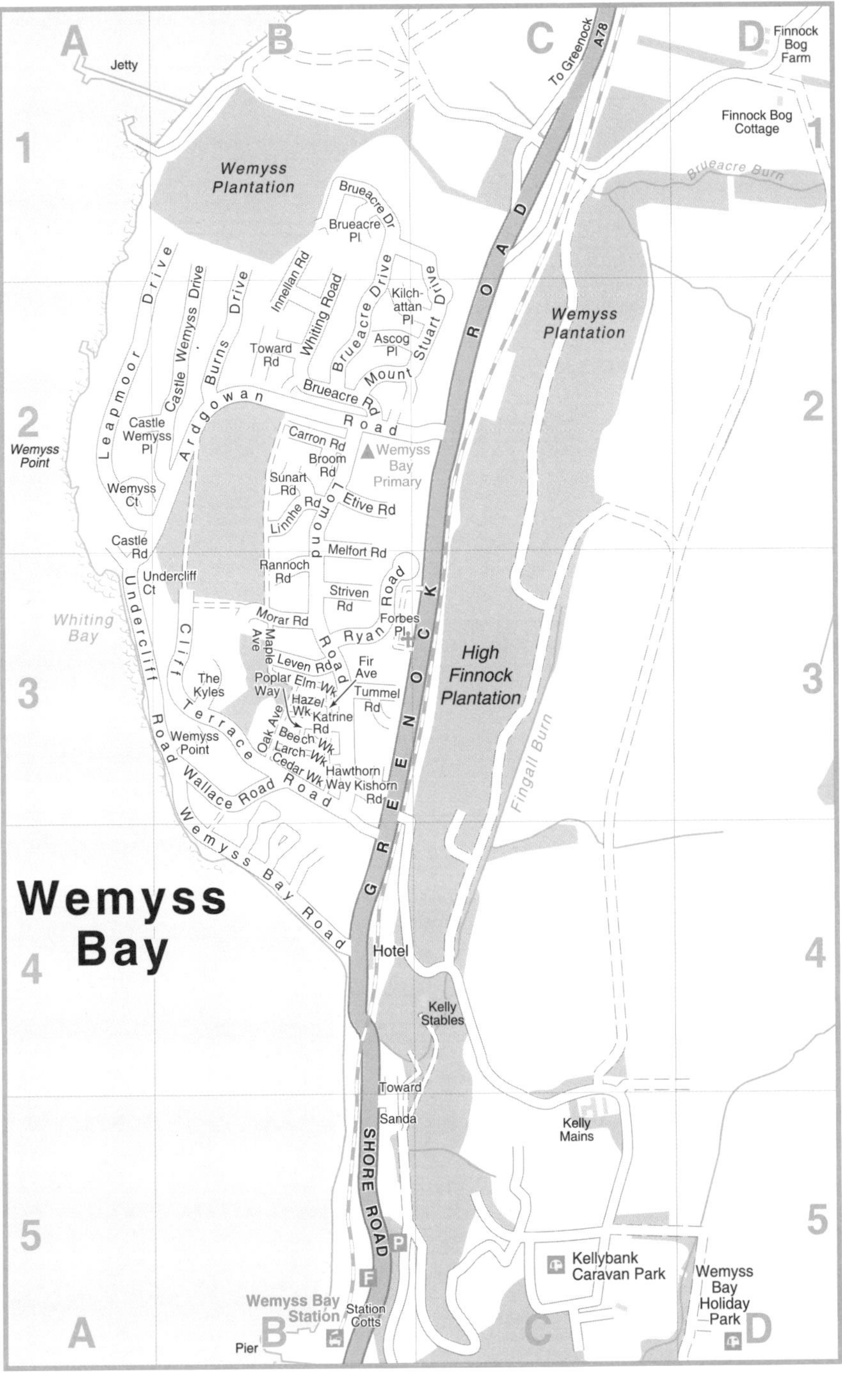
Wemyss Bay
A
B
C
D
1
2
3
4
5
Jetty
Wemyss Plantation
Brueacre Dr
Brueacre Pl
Finnock Bog Farm
Finnock Bog Cottage
Brueacre Burn
To Greenock
A78
GREENOCK ROAD
Leapmoor Drive
Castle Wemyss Drive
Burns Drive
Innellan Rd
Whiting Road
Brueacre Drive
Kilchattan Pl
Stuart Drive
Ascog Pl
Toward Rd
Mount
Brueacre Rd
Ardgowan Road
Castle Wemyss Pl
Wemyss Point
Carron Rd
Broom Rd
Wemyss Bay Primary
Sunart Rd
Lomond Road
Etive Rd
Linnhe Rd
Wemyss Ct
Castle Rd
Melfort Rd
Rannoch Rd
Undercliff Ct
Striven Rd
Ryan Road
Forbes Pl
Morar Rd
Whiting Bay
Undercliff Road
Cliff Terrace
Maple Ave
Leven Rd
Fir Ave
High Finnock Plantation
The Kyles
Poplar Way
Elm Wk
Tummel Rd
Hazel Wk
Katrine Rd
Oak Ave
Beech Wk
Larch Wk
Cedar Wk
Hawthorn Way
Kishorn Rd
Fingall Burn
Wallace Road
Wemyss Bay Road
Hotel
Kelly Stables
Toward
Sanda
SHORE ROAD
Kelly Mains
Kellybank Caravan Park
Wemyss Bay Holiday Park
Wemyss Bay Station
Station Cotts
Pier
P
F

All index entries are given as street name followed by page number and grid reference

**Index to Bishopton & Erskine**

Abbotsinch Road 15 Q9
Agamemnon Street 13 P3
Allands Avenue 14 L8
Allison Avenue 12 H3
Almond Drive 8 D3
Anderson Road 8 C1
Ard Road 15 R9
Argyll Avenue 15 R9
Arnish 14 L6
Arran Avenue 13 N2
Auckland Place 13 M1
Auld Street 13 N2
Aytoun Drive 12 H2
Baird Drive 12 H2
Ballater Drive 14 M6
Balmedie 12 J3
Balmoral Crescent 15 N6
Balmoral Drive 9 E4
Banchory Avenue 14 M6
Bargarran Road 12 H2
Barhill Road 12 J4, J2
Barnsford Avenue 14 K9
Barnsford Road 12 K10
Barnsford Road 14 J8
Beardmore Cottages 15 N7
Beardmore Place 13 N2
Beardmore Street 13 M2, N2
Beardmore Way 13 M3, N3
Beatty Street 13 N2
Benbow Road 13 P3
Birkhall Avenue 14 M6
Blantyre Court 12 J2
Blantyre Drive 8 C1
Blythswood Road 15 T8
Boquhanran Road 13 P3
Bourne Court 14 M6
Bourne Crescent 14 M6
Braemar Avenue 13 P1
Braemar Road 14 M6
Bridge Street 13 N2
Bridgend 8 C2
Bridgewater Place 12 K3
Brisbane Road 8 D2
Brisbane Street 13 M1
Brook Street 13 P1
Broom Avenue 14 K6
Broomhill Crescent 14 K6
Broomlands Avenue 13 M5
Broomlands Court 14 M6
Broomlands Crescent 13 M5
Broomlands Gardens 13 M5
Broomlands Way 13 N5
Broomlea Crescent 14 L6
Broompark Drive 14 M6
Brown Street South 15 R10
Brownsfield Crescent 14 K8
Brownsfield Road 14 K8
Bruce Road 8 D2
Buchanan Avenue 8 D1
Buckie 12 J2
Bulldale Court 15 U8
Bulldale Place 15 U8
Bulldale Road 15 U8
Bulldale Street 15 U8
Burnhaven 12 J3
Burns Avenue 8 D2
Burns Street 13 N2
Burnside Court 13 N1
Bute Road 13 M2
Cable Depot Road 13 P3
Cairns Road 8 C1
Caledonia Street 13 N3
Cameron Avenue 8 D1
Campbell Avenue 8 D1
Campbell Street 15 T8
Camphill Gardens 9 E2
Campsie Drive 13 N2
Canberra Avenue 13 M1
Cardon Square 15 U8
Carrick Road 9 E3
Carron Drive 9 E3
Cartside Avenue 14 K9
Castle Court 13 N2
Castle Crescent 8 D3
Castle Grove 13 N2
Castle Street 13 N2
Cawdor Crescent 8 D3
Cedar Avenue 13 M1
Centreway 12 K3
Chartwell Road 8 D2
Chisholm Avenue 9 E2
Churchill Drive 8 D2
Clark Street 13 P1
Clark Street 15 R10
Clyde Gate 13 P3
Clyde Street 15 T8
Clyde Street 15 T8
Craigends Drive 12 H4
Craighead Road 8 D3
Craigiehall Avenue 14 J6
Craigiehall Crescent 14 J6
Craigiehall Way 14 J6
Creran Drive 15 R9
Crescent Court 13 N2
Crescent, The 13 N2
Crossgates 8 B2
Cullen 12 J2
Dalmuir Court 13 N2
Dargavel Avenue 8 D2
Dargavel Road 9 F4
Darroch Drive 12 H2
Darwin Place 13 M1
Delhi Avenue 13 L1
Devon Drive 9 E2
Dickens Avenue 13 P1
Douglas Crescent 12 H2
Drumcross Road 9 F2
Dumbarton Road 13 L1, M1
Dun Cann 14 L6
Dunglass Road 9 E3
Dunholme Park 13 M2
Dunn Street 13 N2
Dunsmore Road 8 C1
Dunswin Avenue 13 N2
Dunswin Court 13 N2
Duntocher Road 13 N2
Dunvegan Quadrant 15 R9
Durban Avenue 13 L1
Ellinger Court 13 N1
Elm Avenue 15 S8
Elm Avenue 15 T8
Erskine Ferry Road 8 C1
Erskine Ferry Road 9 F1
Etive Drive 9 E3
Ettrick Drive 9 E3
Farm Road 13 M2
Fern Avenue 14 K6
Ferry Road 15 T8
Findhorn 12 J3
Findochty 12 J2
Fishers Road 15 S8
Fleming Road 8 D2
Florish Road 13 N5
Flures Avenue 13 N5
Flures Crescent 13 N5
Flures Drive 13 N5
Flures Place 13 N5
Fountain Avenue 14 K9
Fountain Crescent 14 L8
Fountain Drive 14 L9
Fraser Avenue 8 D1
Freeland Drive 14 L7
Freeland Road 14 K6
Freelands Court (1) 13 L1
Freelands Place (4) 13 L1
Freelands Road (3) 13 L1
French Street 13 N2
Garnie Avenue 13 M5
Garnie Crescent 13 M4
Garnie Lane 13 M5
Garnie Oval 13 M4
Garnie Place 13 M4
Garnieland Road 13 M4
Gladstone Street 13 P3
Gledstane Road 8 D3
Glen Road 8 C1
Glendevon Cottages 13 P2
Glendevon Place 13 P2
Glenmoss Avenue 12 H4
Golf Road 8 D1
Golf View 13 P1
Gordon Avenue 8 D1
Greenhead Road 14 L6
Greenock Road 15 Q9
Greenock Road (Bishopton) 8 B1, D3
Greenock Road (Inchinnan) 14 K7, M7
Grove, The 8 C2
Hamilton Crescent (Bishopton) 8 B2
Hamilton Crescent (Inchinnan) 15 T8
Hamilton Drive 12 H2
Hawthorn Avenue 13 N5
Hawthorn Crescent 13 N5
Hawthorn Road 13 N5
Hawthorn Way 13 N5
Hay Avenue 9 E2
High Parksail 13 L5
Holmpark 8 D2
Holms Crescent 12 H3
Hopeman 12 J2
Houston Road 14 J9
Inchinnan Drive 12 K10
Inchinnan Drive 14 L9
Inchinnan Road 15 Q9
India Drive 14 L8
Ingliston Drive 8 B2
Inverarish 14 L6
Inverbervie 12 J3
Jellicoe Street 13 N2
Johnshaven 12 J3
Kilpatrick Drive 12 K3
King's Inch Road 15 T8
Kingston Grove 9 E2
Kingston Place 13 M1
Kingston Road 8 D3
Kingston Road 9 E1
Kingswood Road 8 B1
Kirkfield Gardens 15 R10
Kirklandneuk Crescent 15 R10
Kirklandneuk Road 15 R9
Kirklands 15 R10
Kirkton 12 J2
Kirkton Cottages 9 F1
Lachlan Crescent 9 G4
Ladyacres 14 M7
Ladyacres Way 14 M7
Ladymuir Circle 12 H4
LagganTerrace 15 R9
Laighpark Avenue 8 D2
Lamont Avenue 9 E2
Lang Avenue 9 E2
Lapwing Crescent 15 U8
Lapwing Road
Laurel Avenue
Laxford Road
Leathen Place
Lennox Avenue
Lennox Place
Leslie Avenue
Leven Place
Leven Square
Libo Place
Lilac Avenue
Linburn Road
Linnhe Place
Littleholm Place
Littleston Gardens
Lochy Place
Lomond Place
Lomond Way
London Street
London Street
Low Parksail
Loyal Avenue
Loyal Place
Lubnaig Drive
Luckingsford Avenue 1
Luckingsford Drive
Luckingsford Road
Lyle Crescent
Lyon Road
McClue Avenue 15
McDuff
Mains Drive 1
Mains Hill 1
Mains River 1
Mains Wood 1
Mainscroft 1
Mainshill Avenue 1
Mainshill Gardens 1
Mar Avenue
Maxwell Drive 1
Maxwell Road
Maxwell Street 1
Meadow Lane 1
Meadows Avenue 1
Meadows Drive 1
Meadowside Street 1
Methven Street 1
Millfield Avenue 12
Millfield Crescent 1
Millfield Drive 1
Millfield Gardens 1
Millfield Hill 12
Millfield Lane 12
Millfield Meadows 12
Millfield Place 12
Millfield View 12
Millfield Walk 12
Millfield Wynd 12
Moidart Avenue 15
Morar Crescent 9
Morar Place 15
Morven Gait 13
Moss Drive 14
Mountblow Road 13
Mulberry Square 15
Myrtle Road 13
Nairn Place 13
Nairn Street 13
Napier Court (2) 13
Neil Street 15
Ness Road 15
Nethergreen Crescent 15 R
Nethergreen Road 15 R
Newburgh 12
Newmains Avenue 14

ɔt Drive 13 L4
ı Road 8 C2
Court 14 L6
Barr Avenue 12 J2
odge Road 15 T8
Porton Road 9 E1
y Avenue 12 G1
rry Road 12 J1
eenock Road 8 A1
eenock Road 14 M6
14 L6
14 L6
Crescent 13 M1
un Court 13 N2
un Drive 13 P1
un Road 13 N1, P1
ank 12 K4
rae 13 L5
ourt 13 N1
rescent 14 M6
rive 12 K4, K5
rive 13 L5
ate 12 K5
lade 13 L5
reen 12 K5
Grove 13 L5
Hill 12 K4
Moor 12 K5
Ridge 12 K5
Road 13 P2, P1
nuir)
Road 14 M6
kine)
Top 13 L4
Way 14 L6
Winding 13 L5
Wood 13 L4
all Road 13 P1
ich 13 L5
ail 14 L6
ail Drive 13 L5
ale Avenue 13 M5
ale Crescent 13 M5
ale Drive 13 M5
ale Gardens 13 M5
ale Place 13 M5
ale Way 13 M5
on Street 13 N2
norran 14 L6
an 12 J2
Road 13 M1
r Avenue 8 D3
r Crescent 8 D3
r Drive 13 P1
rfield Road 15 R10
ssie 12 J3
ethen 12 J3
n Place 8 C1
oy 12 J3
es Park 12 G1
ns Drive 9 E2
enside Crescent 12 H4
say Street 13 P2
ieburn 12 J3
ieglen 12 J3
iehill 12 J3
ielee Avenue 12 K3
ielee Road 12 J3
iewood 12 J3
ay 12 J2
shank Avenue 15 U8
wood Crescent 9 E2
ent Place 13 N1
ent Street 13 N1
shaw Road 8 D2
Street 13 P1

Ritchieston 8 D1
River Drive 14 M8
Roberts Street 13 N2
Robertson Avenue 15 R10
Rossland Crescent 8 C2
Rossland Gardens 8 C2
Rossland Place 9 E4
Rossland View 8 C2
Rowan Drive 13 P1
Royal Inch Crescent 15 T8
Ryatlinn 12 H4
St Annes Avenue 13 M5
St Annes Wynd 13 M5
St Stephen's Court 13 P2
Sachelcourt Avenue 8 D3
Sandend 12 J2
Sandielands Avenue 13 M5
Sconser 14 L6
Scott Street 13 N1
Second Avenue 13 P2
Sempill Avenue 12 H3
Semple Avenue 8 D2
Shaftesbury Street 13 P3
Shakespeare Avenue 13 P2, P1
Shaw Avenue 9 E2
Shaw Court 12 H2, J2
Shilton Lane 12 G1
Simons Crescent 15 T8
Singer Road 13 P2
Somerled Avenue 13 P12
South Street 14 K9
South View 13 P2
Southbar Road 14 J6
Southbar Steading 12 H5
Station Road 8 D3
Stevenson Street 13 P1
Stewart Street 13 N2
Stuart Road 8 D1
Suisnish 14 L6
Sunart Avenue 15 R9
Swan Street 13 P2
Swindon Street 13 N2
Sydney Street 13 M1
Teviot Drive 9 E3
Tianavaig 14 L6
Torran Drive 13 N5
Trafalgar Street 13 P2
Trovaig 14 L6
Turnhill Avenue 14 K6
Turnhill Crescent 14 K6
Turnhill Drive 14 K6
Turnhill Gardens 14 K6
Turnyland Meadows 14 K6
Turnyland Way 12 K5
Umachan 14 L6
Valetta Place 13 M2
Vancouver Place 13 M1
Vennacher Road 15 R9
Victoria Drive West 15 R10
Walkinshaw Road 14 L10
Wallace Avenue 8 D2
Wellington Place 13 M1
Wells Street 13 P2
West Court 13 N1
West Lodge Road 15 R9
West Porton Place 8 B1
Westlands 12 K3
Whimbrel Way 15 U8
Whimbrel Wynd 15 U8
Whitehills 12 J3
Willow Court 13 P1
Wraisland Crescent 8 B1
Wrightlands Crescent 13 N5
Yarrow Crescent 9 E3

## Index to Gourock, Greenock & Port Glasgow

Abbot Lane 22 L6
Abbot Street 22 L6
Aberfoyle Road 23 R7
Adam Street (Gourock) 17 H2
Adam Street (Greenock) 23 R6
Adelaide Street 17 G1
Aileymill Gardens 20 G7
Ailsa Road 17 E3
Albert Road 17 F2
Alderbank Road 24 W8
Alderbrae Road 24 W8
Alderwood Crescent 24 W8
Alderwood Road 24 W8
Allan Place 23 R7
Alpine Grove 24 U6
Alva Terrace 18 J2
Anderson Street 25 Y7
Angus Road (Larkfield) 17 F5
Angus Road (Port Glasgow) 25 Y8
Ann Street 19 P4
Antigua Street 23 Q5
Ardbeg Lane 23 S7
Ardbeg Road 23 S7
Arden Road 23 T8
Ardenclutha Drive 25 X8
Ardgowan Square 19 N3
Ardgowan Street (Greenock) 19 M3
Ardgowan Street (Lilybank) 24 W7
Ardmore Place 22 N6
Ardmore Road (Greenock) 23 S8
Ardmore Road (Port Glasgow) 25 Z8
Ardyne Place 16 B4
Argyle Road 17 H3
Argyle Street 19 P3
Armadale Court 22 P5
Armadale Place 22 P5
Arran Avenue 55 DD9
Arran Road 17 F3
Arrol Gardens 23 T7
Arthur Street (5) 23 R5
Ashburn Gardens 17 E2
Ashburn Gate 17 E2
Ashgrove Avenue 17 E2
Ashgrove Lane 25 Z8
Ashton Place 17 E2
Ashton Road 17 E2
Ashton Terrace 17 E2
Athole Lane 20 F6
Athole Terrace 20 F6
Auchenbothie Road 55 BB10
Auchendarroch Street 23 S6
Auchendores Avenue 55 CC10
Auchenfoil Lane 54 Z9
Auchenfoil Road 54 Z9
Auchenleck Lane 54 AA10
Auchenleck Road 54 AA10
Auchinleck Terrace 25 AA8
Auchmead Road 17 G5
Auchmountain Road (Cartsdyke) 23 S6
Auchmountain Road (Strone) 23 T8
Auchmountain View 23 R7
Auchneagh Avenue 21 K5
Auchneagh Crescent 21 K5
Auchneagh Farm Lane 18 J4

Auchneagh Farm Road 18 K4
Auchneagh Road 21 K5
Avonmouth Place 17 H4
Ayr Lane 20 G6
Ayr Terrace 20 G6
Bagatelle Court 19 M2
Baker Street 23 Q6
Balclutha Court 19 M3
Balfour Street 25 X7
Balfron Road 23 S8
Balloch Road 23 R7
Ballochyle Place 16 A4
Balmoral Gardens 19 N3
Balmoral Place 16 A4
Balmore Road 23 R8
Banff Place 17 E4
Banff Road 17 E5, F4
Bank Street 22 P5
Bannockburn Street 21 L6
Bardrainney Avenue 55 BB10
Barmouth Avenue 17 H4
Barnhill Street 23 S6
Barra Way 55 CC11
Barrhill Road 17 F2
Barrs Brae 25 Y8
Barrs Brae Lane 25 Y8
Barscube Avenue 54 AA10
Bath Street 17 G1
Battery Park Avenue 18 K1
Battery Park Drive 18 K1
Bawhirley Road 23 R6
Baxter Street 23 T6
Bay Street 25 Y8
Bay View Road 17 H2
Bearhope Street 19 P4
Bedford Street 19 M2
Beech Place 17 E3
Beith Road 22 N7
Belhaven Street 25 X7
Bell Street 24 U7
Belleaire Drive 18 L2
Belleisle Place 16 C3
Belville Avenue 23 S6
Belville Drive 23 R6
Belville Street 23 R6, S6
Benclutha 54 AA9
Benmore Lane 20 G6
Bentinck Street 19 M2
Benview Avenue 55 BB9
Benview Road 54 AA9
Berryyards Road 22 P6
Berwick Place 17 F5
Berwick Road (Larkfield) 17 E5
Berwick Road (Lilybank) 25 Y8
Binnie Lane 17 G2
Binnie Street 17 G1
Birkmyre Avenue 24 W7
Blair Gardens 16 B4
Blairbeg Place 16 A4
Blairmore Crescent 23 S7
Blairmore Place 16 A4
Blairmore Road 23 R7
Bogiewood Road 25 X8
Bogle Street 23 Q5
Boglestone Avenue 54 AA9
Bogside Road 55 BB9
Bogstone Lane 24 V7
Border Street 23 S6
Bournemouth Road 17 G4
Bouverie Street 25 Y8
Bow Road 18 L4
Bow Road 21 K5
Brachelston Street 22 M5
Bracken Road 55 CC9
Brae View 18 L4
Braehead Road 54 AA9

Braemar Gardens 19 N3
Braeside Lane 20 F6
Braeside Road 20 F6
Bramble Wynd 55 EE9
Brambling Road 21 J5
Branchton Road 21 H6
Briar Place 17 F3
Briary Lane 55 EE9
Bridge Road 54 AA9
Bridgend Avenue 54 AA9
Bridgend Road 23 S6, S7
Brightside Avenue 55 CC9
Brisbane Street 19 M2, N3
Britannia House 23 R5
Broadfield Avenue 55 CC9
Broadford Terrace (4) 17 G5
Broadstone Avenue 24 W7
Broadstone Gardens 24 W7
Broadstone House 55 DD9
Brodick Drive 16 B4
Brookfield Road 55 BB9
Broomberry Drive 17 G1
Broomhill Court 22 N5
Broomhill Street 22 N5
Broomhill Way 22 N5
Brougham Street 19 N2
Brown Street (Bridgend) 23 T6
Brown Street (Lilybank) 25 X7
Bruce Street (Port Glasgow) 25 Z8
Bruce Street (Greenock) 19 N4
Brymner Street (3) 19 Q4
Buccleugh Street (7) 19 P4
Buchanan Street 21 K5
Burgh Walk 17 G1
Burnbank Terrace 54 Y9
Burnhead Lane 54 Z9
Burnhead Road 54 Z9
Burnhead Street 23 R7
Burns Road 17 F5, 20 F6
Burns Square 17 F5
Burnside Avenue 55 BB9
Burnside Road 17 H3
Bute Avenue 55 DD9
Bute Street 17 F3
Caddlehill Street 19 M4
Caird Avenue 18 L2
Cairncurran Court 22 N6
Caithness Road 17 E5
Caledonia Crescent 17 H2
Caledonia Crescent 18 J2
Caledonia Drive 24 W7
Caledonia Gardens 17 H2
Caledonia Street (2) 25 Z8
Cambridge Avenue 18 J3
Cambridge Road 17 F5
Cameron Court 16 B3
Campbell Court 19 N2
Campbell Street 19 M3, N2
Campsie Road 55 CC11
Canmore Crescent 21 J5
Captain Street 22 N5
Cardross Avenue 54 AA9
Cardross Crescent 23 S7
Cardross Place 23 S7
Cardwell Court 17 G2
Cardwell Road 17 H2
Carmichael Street 19 M3
Carnock Street 23 Q5
Carnoustie Avenue 16 C3
Carrick Lane 20 G6
Carrick Terrace 20 F6
Cartsburn Street 23 Q6, R6
Cartsdyke Avenue 23 S5
Cartsdyke Court 23 T6
Carwood Court 23 S6

Carwood Street 23 S6
Castle Brae 17 G1
Castle Gardens (2) 17 G1
Castle Levan Manor 16 B4
Castle Mansions (1) 17 G1
Castle Road (Garvock) 23 S7
Castle Road (Port Glasgow) 25 Z8
Castlehill Avenue 55 CC9
Cathcart Buildings 23 Q5
Cathcart Square 19 P4
Cathcart Street 19 Q4
Cawdor Crescent 21 J5
Cawdor Place 21 J5
Cedar Crescent 24 U7
Cedar Place 17 F3
Chalmers Lane 24 V7
Chalmers Street 17 H2
Chapel Lane 25 X8
Chapel Street 17 H2
Chapelton Street 24 W7
Charles Place (1) 19 P4
Chester Road 17 G5
Chromars Place 22 N6
Church Street (Gourock) 17 G1
Church Street (Lilybank) 25 Y7
Clachaig Place 16 A4
Clarence Street 19 P3
Cloch Brae 16 C3
Cloch Road 16 A4, C3
Clune Brae 25 Z8, AA8
Clune Park Street 25 AA8
Clyde Road 17 H2
Clyde Square (5) 19 P4
Clyde Wynd 22 N6
Clydeview Apartments 55 BB9
Clydeview Road (Greenock) 23 Q7
Clydeview Road (Port Glasgow) 54 AA9
Clynder Road 23 S7
Cobham Street 24 U7
Coll Avenue 55 DD9
Collingwood Terrace 17 H3
Colonsay Avenue 55 DD10
Columba Street 22 M5
Container Way 19 P3
Corlic Street 23 R7
Cornhaddock Street 22 M5
Court Road 25 Y8
Cove Road 17 H2
Cowal Crescent 16 D3
Cowal Place 17 E3
Cowal View 16 C3, D3
Cragburn Gate 17 E2
Craig-ard 25 Y8
Craigieknowes Street 23 S6
Craigmuschat Road 17 G2
Craigs, The 18 L2
Cranach Apartments 19 N3
Crawberry Road 23 Q7
Crawford Street (3) 25 Y7
Crawfurd Street 19 P3
Crawhin Gardens 22 M6
Crescent Street 23 R6
Crisswell Close 20 E7
Crisswell Crescent 20 E7
Cromdale Road 55 BB11
Cross Shore Street (1) 19 Q4
Crosshill Gardens 54 AA10
Crosshill Place 55 BB10
Crosshill Road 54 AA10
Crown Street (6) 19 P4
Cuillins Avenue 55 BB11
Culzean Drive 16 B4

Cumberland Road 17 G4
Cumberland Walk 17 G5
Cumbrae Avenue 55 DD10
Cumbrae Place 17 F3
Cupar Drive 21 H6
Curlew Crescent 21 K5
Curlew Lane 21 K5
Customhouse Lane (4) 25 Y7
Customhouse Place (4) 19 Q4
Customhouse Way 19 P3
Dalmally Street 24 V7
Dalmoak Road 23 S8
Dalriada Road 20 F6
Dalrymple Street 19 P3, Q4
Dardanelles (1) 19 N4
Darndaff Road 23 Q6
Darroch Avenue 17 G2
Darroch Drive 17 G2
Dartmouth Avenue 17 G4
Davaar Road 20 E6
Davey Street 18 K4
Davidson Drive 17 G2
Delfie Drive 21 K5
Dellingburn Street (1) 23 Q5
Dempster Court 22 P5
Dempster Street 22 M5, P5
Denholm Gardens 19 M4
Denholm Street 19 M3
Denholm Terrace 19 M4
Devol Avenue 24 W8
Devol Road 54 Y9, Y11
Devon Road 17 F5
Dingwall Drive 21 H6
Divert Road 17 E3
Divert Walk 17 E3
Dock Breast 19 Q4
Don Street 18 L4
Dornoch Grove 21 J6
Dorset Road 17 G5
Dougliehill Place 54 Y9
Dougliehill Road 54 X9, Y9
Dougliehill Terrace 54 Y9
Doune Gardens 16 B4
Dresling Road 22 N6
Drumfrochar Place 22 P6
Drumfrochar Road 22 M6, N5
Drumillan Hill 20 E7
Drummond Street 21 22 L5
Drums Terrace 18 K1
Drumshantie Road 17 G3
Drumshantie Terrace 17 G2
Drumslea 18 L1
Dubbs Place 55 BB10
Dubbs Road 54 Z9
Duchal Street 54 Z9
Duff Street 19 Q4
Duncan Road 25 X8
Duncan Street 22 N5
Dungourney Drive 18 L2
Dunlop Court (1) 25 X7
Dunlop Street 21 22 L6
Dunn Street 22 N5
Dunnet Place 21 H6
Dunrobin Drive 16 B3
Dunvegan Avenue 16 A4, B4
Durham Road 17 G4
Duthie Road 18 J3
Dykeneuk Road 54 Z10
Earnhill Gardens 17 F4
Earnhill Lane 17 E4
Earnhill Place 17 F4
Earnhill Road 17 E5, F4
East Barmoss Avenue 55 BB10
East Blackhall Street 23 Q5
East Breast (2) 19 Q4

East Crawford Street
East Hamilton Street
East India Breast (6)
East Road
East Shaw Street
East Stewart Street (4)
East Street
East William Street
East Woodside Avenue 5
Eastern View
Edinburgh Drive
Eldon Court
Eldon Place
Eldon Street 18
Elliot Court
Elm Terrace
Empress Court (3)
Endrick Road
Eriskay Avenue 55
Esplanade (Gourock)
Esplanade (Greenock)
Esplanade (Greenock)
Essex Road
Exmouth Place
Fairrie Street
Falcon Crescent
Falcon Lane
Falconer Street (2)
Falmouth Drive
Fancy Farm Place
Fancy Farm Road
Farm Road (Levan)
Farm Road (Port Glasgow) 54
Farquhar Road
Faulds Park Road 16
Fearnan Place
Fergus Drive
Fergus Place
Fergus Road
Fife Drive
Fife Road
Finbraken Drive
Finch Road
Finlaystone Road 55
Finnart Crescent
Finnart Road
Finnart Street 18 L2,
Finneston Lane
Finneston Street
Finneston Way
Finnie Terrace
Fintry Road
Fir Street
Fir Terrace
Firth Crescent
Flatterton Lane
Flatterton Road 20 D
Fletcher Avenue
Florence Street
Fore Street
Forfar Road
Forsyth Grove
Forsyth Street
Forsyth Street
Fort Matilda Place
Fort Matilda Terrace
Fox Street
Fox Street 1
Fullerton Lane 2
Fyfe Park Road 25
Fyfe Park Terrace 55
Fyfe Shore Road 25
Gabriel Street 2
Gael Street 2

ill Avenue 55 CC10
treet 23 S6
och Close 23 Q7
och Lane 54 Z9
och Road 23 Q6
enock)
och Road 54 Z9
Glasgow)
ld Street 23 S6
l Drive 22 M6
e Avenue 17 H3
ock Drive 22 M6
side Avenue 21 K5
side Gardens 21 K5
side Grove 21 K5
ge Road 17 G3
ge Square 19 N4
gian Court 19 N3
ill Road 24 U7
n Street 24 U7
our Street 23 S6
is Drive 18 J4
is Place 18 J4
gow Road 25 Z8
gow Road 55 BB8
Avenue (Lilybank) 24 X7
Avenue (Gourock) 17 H3
Douglas Place 22 L6
Douglas Road 22 L7
Douglas Way 22 M6
Fruin Road 22 L6
Kinglas Avenue 22 M7
Kinglas Road 22 L7
Luss Road (1) 22 L7
Luss Way (2) 22 M7
Street 19 M2
bervie Place 16 D3
brae Road 23 R7
eenock)
brae Road 54 Z10
rt Glasgow)
burn Street 24 W7
cairn Road 20 F6
clune 25 AA8
eagles Drive 16 C3
huntly Road 25 X8
huntly Terrace 25 X8
inver Road 17 H5
park Court 19 M2
eenock)
park Court 24 W7
ybank)
park Drive 24 W7
park House 24 W7
nside Road 54 Z10
view Terrace 22 M5
Drive 54 Z9
Place 18 L2
Road 17 E3
spie Drive 21 H6
don Street 22 N5
nam Street 18 L4
mpian Road 55 CC11
nt Street 23 S6
y Street 23 R6
enbank Mews 19 M4
enock Road 24 V7
oshill)
enock Road 25 X7
lybank)
enock Road 55 EE9
arkhill)
enock Road 25 Z8
rt Glasgow)
nville Road 17 H3
y Place 19 P3

Grieve Road 18 K4
Grieve Road 21 K5
Grosvenor Lane 23 T6
Grosvenor Road 23 T6
Gryfe Road 54 AA10
Haig Street 19 P3
Hamilton Gate (3) 19 P4
Hamilton Way (4) 19 P4
Harelaw Avenue 54 Z9
Harrier Way 21 K5
Harris Road 55 DD10
Harwood Court 19 N2
Hastie Street (2) 19 N4
Hawick Court 23 R6
Hawthorne Place 16 D3
Hay Street 22 P5
Hazel Terrace 17 E3
Heather Court (6) 25 Y8
Heggies Avenue 55 BB9
Helen Gardens 24 W7
Henderson Terrace 17 G3
Heritage Court 19 N2
Heron Road 18 J4
Hibernia Street 22 M5
High Carnegie Road 55 BB9
High Street 19 P4
Highholm Avenue 25 X8
Highholm Street 25 X7
Highland Mary Place (2) 19 P4
Hill Street 23 Q5
Hillend Drive 23 S6
Hillend Place 23 S6
Hillside Drive 25 X8
Hillside Road 17 F2
(Gourock)
Hillside Road 23 R7
(Greenock)
Hilltop Crescent 17 H3
Hilltop Road 17 G3
Hole Farm Road 21 L6
Hollybush Lane 55 DD9
Holmscroft Avenue 22 N5
Holmscroft Street 19 N4
Holmscroft Way 22 N5
Holt Court 23 R5
Hood Street 19 P3
Hope Street 22 P5
Hopeton Street (3) 17 G1
Houston Street 19 N3
Hunters Place 19 P4
Huntly Drive 21 H6
Huntly Place 25 X7
Huntly Terrace 25 X7
Inchgreen Gardens 24 V6
Inchgreen Street 24 V7
Ingleston Park 23 Q6
Ingleston Street 23 Q6
Inverkip Road 20 E8, G6
Inverkip Road 21 L5
Inverkip Street 19 N4
Iona Crescent 17 E3
Iona Road 55 CC10
Iona Street 21 L5
Iona Walk 17 E3
Irwin Street 24 U7
Islay Avenue 55 DD10
Ivy Crescent 17 G3
Ivybank Crescent 24 W8
Ivybank Road 25 X8
Jacobs Drive 17 F2
Jamaica Court 19 P3
Jamaica Lane 19 N3
Jamaica Street 19 N3
James Watt Way 23 S5
Jardine Terrace 19 N2
Jean Armour Lane 20 G6

Jean Armour Terrace 20 G6
Jean Street 25 X7
John Campbell Court 17 H2
John Campbell Street 17 H2
John Street (Gourock) 17 G2
John Street (Greenock) 23 R6
John Wilson Street 23 T7
John Wood Street 25 Y8
Johnston Street 19 M2
Johnston Terrace 19 M2
Juno Lane 20 F6
Juno Terrace 20 F6
Jupiter Lane 20 F6
Jupiter Terrace 20 F6
Jura Street 21 L5
Jura Way 55 CC11
Katrine Road 23 Q6
Keir Hardie Street 24 U7
Kelburn Terrace 55 BB8
Kelly Street 19 M4, N4
Kempock Place 17 G1
Kempock Street 17 F1
Kenilworth Crescent 22 M6
Kenmore Drive 21 J5
Kenmore Place 21 J5
Kennedy's Lane 23 R6
Ker Street (2) 19 P3
Kestrel Crescent 18 J4
Kestrel Place 18 J4
Kilblain Court 19 P4
Kilblain Street 19 P4
Kilbrannan Drive 21 K6
Kilcreggan View 23 S7
Killearn Road 23 R7
Killellan Place 16 B5
Killin Place 21 J5
Killochend Drive 22 N6
Kilmacolm Place 23 S8
Kilmacolm Road 23 R6
(Greenock)
Kilmacolm Road 54 AA9
(Port Glasgow)
Kilmacolm Road 55 BB10
(Port Glasgow)
Kilmory Terrace (1) 25 Z8
Kilmun Road 23 Q6
Kincaid Court 23 S5
Kincaid Street 18 K1
King Street (Gourock) 17 G2
King Street (Greenock) 19 P4
King Street (Lilybank) 25 Y7
Kingston Crescent 24 W7
Kingsway 17 F3
Kinloch Lane 20 G6
Kinloch Terrace 20 G6
Kinross Avenue 25 Y8
Kintyre Terrace 20 F6
Kirkwall Road 21 H6
Kirn Drive 17 E3, F3
Knockdhu Place 16 B4
Knocknair Street 54 AA9
Knowe Road 23 R5
Kylemore Lane 20 G6
Kylemore Terrace 20 F6
Laburnum Place (3) 24 V7
Laburnum Street 24 V7
Ladyburn Street 23 T6
Laird Street 19 P3
Langside Terrace 54 Z9
Lansbury Street 24 U7
Larkfield Grove 17 H5
Larkfield Road 17 G3, H4
Laverock Avenue 22 M6
Lawers Place 21 J5
Leitch Street 24 U6
Lemmon Street 22 M5

Leperstone Avenue 54 AA10
Levan Point 16 B4
Levan Wood 16 B4
Levanne Gardens 16 B3
Levanne Place 16 B3
Leven Place 23 S8
Leven Road 23 R7, S8
Lewis Road 21 L5
(Cowdenknowes)
Lewis Road 55 DD10
(Port Glasgow)
Lilybank Road 24 V7
Lime Street 22 N5
Lincoln Road 17 F5
Lindon Mansions 19 M3
Linnet Road 21 K5
Lismore Avenue 55 DD10
Lithgow Way 24 W6
Lochview Avenue 18 J2
Lochview Road 25 X8
Lomond Avenue 54 Z9
Lomond Road 23 Q6
Lothian Road 17 F5
Lower Bouverie Street 25 Z8
Lower Mary Street 24 W7
Lurg Street 54 Z9
Luss Avenue 23 R8
Luss Place 23 R8
Lyle Grove 18 K2
Lyle Place 18 J2
Lyle Road 18 J1, K2
Lyle Street 22 P5
Lyle Street 23 Q5
Lylefoot Crescent 18 K1, K2
Lylefoot Place 18 K2
Lynedoch Court 23 Q5
Lynedoch Street 22 P6
Lynedoch Street 23 Q5
Lynmouth Place 17 G4
MacBeth Road 18 J4
MacDougall Street 23 T5
MacGillivary Avenue 24 U6
MacGowan Way 24 U6
MacGregor Road 24 U6
MacKenzie Street 23 T6
MacMillan Drive 17 F3
McCallum Crescent 17 G2
McLeod Street 23 T6
McNab Place 23 T6
McPhail Street 23 T6
McPherson Drive 17 F3
Mackie Avenue 24 V8
Maclehose Court 19 N2
Madeira Lane 19 M2
Madeira Street 19 M2
Main Street 23 R5
Mallaig Road 55 BB10
Mallaig Terrace (2) 17 G5
Mallard Crescent 18 J3
Mallard Lane 18 J3
Manor Crescent 17 H2
Manor Crescent 18 J2
Mansion Avenue 55 CC9
Maple Road 21 K6
Margaret Street 17 H2
(Gourock)
Margaret Street 19 M3, N2
(Greenock)
Markinch Road 55 BB11
Marloch Avenue 55 BB11
Mars Road 20 E7
Mary Street 21 L5
(Cowdenknowes)
Mary Street (Lilybank) 24 W7
Mathie Crescent 17 G3
Mauchline Lane 20 G6

Mauchline Terrace 20 G6
Mavis Road 18 J4
Maxwell Street 25 AA8
Maxwellton Road 55 BB11
Maybole Road 55 BB11
Mearns Street 22 P4
Mearns Terrace 22 P5
Melrose Court (7) 23 R5
Melrose Road 55 BB10
Mercury Lane 20 F6
Merino Road 22 M6
Merlin Avenue 18 J3
Merlin Lane 18 J4
Merrylee Avenue 54 Z10
Methil Road 54 AA11
Mews Lane 18 L1
Mid Avenue 55 BB9
Mill Street 22 N5
Millar Street 23 R7
Millbank Road 54 Y9
Millburn Road 54 Y9
Millport Road 55 BB11
Milton Road 54 AA11
Minard Road 54 AA10
Minerva Lane 20 F6
Minerva Terrace 20 F6
Minto Street 22 M5
Mirrens Shore 25 Y7
Mitchell Street 24 V7
Moffat Street 23 S6
Moidart Road 54 AA10
Monach Road 55 CC10
Monkton Place 55 BB10
Montgomerie Street (3) 25 Z8
Montrose Avenue 54 AA10
Moorfield Avenue 54 Z9
Moorfield Lane 17 E3
Moorfield Road 17 E2
Moorfoot Drive 17 E3
Morar Road 54 AA10
Moray Road 25 Y8
Morris Street 23 S6
Moss Lane 55 BB10
Moss Road 55 BB10
Mossyde Avenue 55 CC10
Mount Pleasant Street 22 N5
Muirdykes Avenue 54 Z9
Muirshiel Lane 54 Z9
Muirshiel Road 54 Z9
Mull Avenue 55 CC10
Munro Street 21 J5
Murdieston Street 19 M4
Murdieston Street 22 M5
Muriel Blue Court (2) 17 H2
Murray Place 17 G3
Murray Street 18 L4
Nairn Drive 17 F4
Nairn Road 17 E5
Neil Street 21 J5
Nelson Road 17 H3
Nelson Street 19 N4
Ness Road 18 L4
Netherton Avenue 55 CC10
New Dock Lane (5) 19 Q4
Newark Avenue 18 L2
Newark House 25 X8
Newark Place 25 Z8
Newark Street (Greenock) 18 K1, L1
Newark Street (Port Glasgow) 25 Z8
Newton Gardens 19 M3
Newton Street 18 L2
Newton Street 19 N4
Newton Terrace 19 M2
Nicol Drive 18 K4
Nicol Street 18 K4, L4
Nicolson Street 19 N4, P4
Nile Street 22 P5
Nimmo Road 22 L5
Nimmo Street 22 L5
Norfolk Road 17 G5
North Road 54 AA9
North Street 18 L1
Northfield Avenue 55 BB9
Oakbank Road 55 BB9
Oakfield Terrace 23 S5
Oakleigh Drive 19 M2
Oban Terrace (1) 17 G5
Octavia Terrace 18 K1
Octavia Walk 24 W7
Old Greenock Road 55 DD9
Old Inverkip Road 21 K5
Old Largs Road 22 M6
Old Waterhouse, The 22 N6
Open Shore 19 Q4
Orangefield 19 N4
Orangefield Lane 19 N4
Orchard Crescent 24 W7
Orchard Street 23 R6
Oronsay Avenue 55 CC10
Osprey Road 21 J5
Overton Crescent 22 M6
Overton Filters 22 N7
Overton Road 22 M7
Oxford Avenue 18 J3
Oxford Road 17 F5
Papermill Road 22 M7
Park Avenue 18 J2
Park Terrace 17 G2
Parkhill Avenue 55 BB9
Parklea Road 55 DD9
Partridge Road 18 J3
Paton Street 18 L4
Patrick Street 19 N3, P3
Peat Road 22 M6
Peebles Court (8) 23 R6
Peile Lane 19 M3
Peile Street 18 L3
Pembroke Road 17 F5
Pennyfern Drive 21 K6
Pennyfern Road 21 K6
Pentland Avenue 55 BB11
Pine Street 22 N5
Pladda Avenue 55 DD10
Pleasantside Avenue 55 CC9
Plover Lane 18 K4
Plymouth Avenue 17 G4
Poplar Place 17 E3
Poplar Street 24 V7
Port Glasgow Road 24 U6, V7
Portree Terrace (3) 17 G5
Portsmouth Drive 17 G4
Pottery Street 24 U6
Preston Place 17 F2
Princes Street (Lilybank) 25 Y7
Princes Street (Greenock) 19 N4
Prospecthill Court 22 N5
Prospecthill Place 22 N5
Prospecthill Street 22 N5
Prospecthill View 22 N5
Quarrier Street 23 T6
Quarry Road 55 BB10
Queen Street 25 Y7
Queensway 17 E3
Rankin Court 21 L5
Rankin Street 21 K5, L5
Rannoch Gardens 55 CC9
Ratho Street 23 S5
Raven Road 18 J4
Ravenscraig Court 21 J5
Redpoll Place 21 K5
Redwood Court 19 N2
Regent Court 22 P5
Regent Street 22 P5
Reid Grove 24 W7
Renton Road 23 S8
Reservoir Road 17 H3
Riverside Gardens (1) 17 H2
Riverside Road 23 Q6
Roberston Street 19 M4, N3
Robert Street 25 Z8
Robin Road 18 K4
Rodney Road 17 H3
Rona Avenue 55 DD10
Rook Road 18 J4
Rose Crescent 17 F3
Rose Street 21 K5
Rosemount Place 16 C3
Roseneath Street 18 L1
Roseyard Place 25 Y8
Roslin Street 19 P3
Rosneath Road 54 Z9
Rossbank Road 24 W7
Rothesay Road 21 H6
Rowan Court 25 Y8
Rowan Gardens 23 T6
Rowan Street 18 L4
Roxburgh Avenue 22 N5
Roxburgh Street 19 N4
Roxburgh Street 22 P5
Roxburgh Way 22 N5
Royal Court 19 N4
Royal Street 17 G1
Rue End Street 23 Q5
Russell Street 24 W7
St Andrew Square (1) 23 R5
St Andrew Street (2) 23 R5
St Andrews Court 19 M2
St Andrews Drive 16 C3
St Andrews Lane 16 C3
St John's Manor 17 G1
St John's Road 17 G1
St Lawrence Street 23 R6
St Margarets Court 18 K4
Salmon Street 19 N4
Sandpiper Lane 18 K4
Sandray Avenue 55 DD11
Sandringham Terrace 19 N2
Scarlow Street 25 Y7
School Court 25 X7
School House 55 CC10
School House, The 17 G1
School Road 55 CC9
Scott House 23 R5
Scott Street 23 Q5
Scott Way 24 V6, W6
Seafield Cottage Lane 19 M1
Seafield House 19 N2
Selkirk Court (9) 23 R5
Selkirk Road 54 Z9
Serpentine Walk 23 R6, S6
Shandon Place 23 S7
Shankland Grove (1) 24 V7
Shankland Road 24 V7
Sharp Street 17 H2
Shaw Place 19 P4
Shore Street (Gourock) 17 G1
Shore Street (Lilybank) 25 X7
Sidlaw Avenue 55 BB11
Silver Birch Wynd 55 DD9
Sinclair Street 23 T6, T7
Sir Gabriel Wood Court
Sir Michael Court
Sir Michael Place (8)
Sir Michael Street
Siskin Close
Skye Crescent
Skye Road 55
Skye Street
Slaemuir Avenue 55
Smillie Street
Smith Street
Smithston Cottages
South Road 5
South Street 18 L
Southfield Avenue 5
Springhill Road
Springkell Street
Staffa Avenue 55
Staffa Street
Stafford Crescent
Stafford Road
Staffordway South
Stane Road 54
Stanners Lane (6)
Station Avenue
Station Road (Gourock)
Station Road (Lilybank)
Steel Street
Stevens Place
Stirling Drive
Stonehaven Road 2
Stoneleigh Place
Stoneleigh Road
Stroma Avenue 55 [illegible]
Stromness Place 2
Strone Crescent 2
Suffolk Road 1
Sunnyside Avenue 55
Sutherland Road
Sycamore Place 1
Tamar Court 1
Tantallon Avenue
Taransay Way 55 C
Tarbet Street 1
Tasker Street 1
Tay Street 1
Taymouth Drive 1
Terrace Road 2
Teviot Road 55 E
Thistle Court (5) 2
Thom Street 2
Thomas Muir Lane (2) 2
Thomas Muir Street 2
Tiree Avenue 55 C
Tobago Street 1
Togo Place 2
Torrance Road 2
Tower Drive 1
Tower Gardens 1
Trafalgar Street 1
Trafalgar Street 2
Tummel Gardens 55
Turnberry Avenue 16
Tweed Street 18
Uist Avenue 55 C
Union Street 19 M2
Upper Cartsburn Street 23
Urquhart Drive 16
Victoria Road 17
Virginia Street 23
Walker Street 18
Wallace Place 19
Wallace Street (Cowdenknowes) 22

ce Street 25 AA8
: Glasgow)
ck Road 17 G5
Street (1) 25 Y7
Place 19 Q4
Street 19 N3
ley Street 21 L6
Place 24 T6
Street 23 T6
eck Street 18 L1
gton Street 22 N5
gton Way 22 N5
ark Buildings 23 Q5
ark Court 22 P5
ard Lane 20 E6
ard Way 20 E7
ard Wynd 20 E7
yss Bay Street 22 N5
Barmoss 55 BB10
nue
Blackhall 19 P3, P4
et (1)
Quay 25 Y7
Road 54 AA9
Shaw Street 19 N4
Stewart Street 19 P3
Woodside 55 BB11
nue
ourn Street 19 P4
field Drive 18 L1
field Road 55 BB9
morland Road 17 G5
ray Avenue 55 DD11
mouth Crescent 17 G4
atear Close 21 J5
hill Court 22 P5
hill Crescent 23 Q7
hill Road 23 Q6
elees Road 24 V7
am Street 19 Q4
eenock)
m Street (Lilybank) 25 X7
sons Lane 25 Y8
on Street 25 Z8
d Street 18 K1
dhall Terrace 55 CC8
dlea Lane 18 J2
dstock Road 21 L6
Road 18 J4
n Road 21 J5
Road 17 G4

**x to Johnstone, Linwood, archan & Brookfield**

ey Road 33 J6
otsford Crescent 33 L9
rnethy Drive 30 H3
cia Place 32 H8
rt Road 30 E3
r Place 32 H7
rd Place 30 F2
atrick Gardens 31 J5
Street 30 H5
an Place 34 D8
our Drive 30 H3
amont Square 31 K3
our Place 30 H5
hnstone)
our Place 31 K3
nwood)
our Square 30 H5
our Street 30 H5
n Drive 32 E7
n Place 30 H2
ury Court 31 K3
Ash Place 32 H7
Ashton Way 33 M8
Aspen Place 32 H7
Atholl Place 30 H2
Auchengreoch Avenue 32 E8
Auchengreoch Road 32 E8
Auchenlodment Road 33 J6
Avon Drive 31 J2
Balmoral Road 33 J8
Bankside Avenue 30 G5
Banktop Place 30 G5
Barclay Avenue 33 J6
Barclay Drive 33 J6
Bardrain Avenue 33 K6
Barn Green 35 B5
Barnscroft 35 C4
Barochan Road 30 F2
Barrhill Crescent 34 C6
Beauly Drive 33 M7
Beech Avenue 33 K6
Beech Road 32 E7
Beeches, The 35 D2
Beith Road 32 E8, H6
Beith Road 34 B10, D9
Belmar Court 31 K3
Bemersyde Road 33 M8
Benston Road 32 F7
Berwick Crescent 30 G1
Bevan Grove 30 F5
Birch Crescent 32 H7
Blackstoun Avenue 31 J2
Blackwood Avenue 30 H2
Blackwood Terrace 32 E8
Bothwell Place 33 M8
Bothwick Way 33 M8
Braemar Drive 33 J7
Braidwood Place 30 G2
Breck Avenue 33 L9
Brediland Road (Linwood) 30 H2
Brediland Road (Paisley) 33 M9
Brewery Street 30 G5
Bridge of Weir Road 35 B3
Bridge of Weir Road 31 J2
Bridge Street 31 K2
Broom Terrace 32 H6
Broomward Drive 31 J5
Bruce Avenue 32 F8
Brydson Place 31 J2
Buchanan Grove 32 F6
Buchanan Street 32 F6
Buchanan Way 32 F6
Burnbrae Avenue 31 K3
Burnbrae Drive 31 L4
Burnbrae Road 31 J4
Burns Drive 32 F8
Burnside Avenue 35 D3
Burnside Gardens 34 C6
Burnside Grove 32 F6
Burnside Road 33 K7
Burnside Terrace 34 C6
Burntshields Road 35 A5
Bute Drive 32 E7
Byres Road 33 L6
Cairn Drive 31 J2
Caldwell Avenue 30 H3
Campbell Street 32 G6
Canal Avenue 32 G6
Canal Gardens 31 L5
Canal Road 32 G6
Canal Street (Elderslie) 31 L5
Canal Street (Johnstone) 30 H5
Candren Road 31 L2
Carradale Place 30 H2
Cartside Avenue 32 E7
Cartside Terrace 34 D6
Castle Avenue 33 J7
Castle Road 31 K5
Cedar Avenue 32 G8
Cedar Court 35 B5
Charnwood Avenue 32 E8
Cherry Place 32 H7
Cherrywood Road 33 K6
Chestnut Place 32 H8
Chiron House (3) 31 M3
Chuckie Lane 35 D2
Church Close (1) 30 G5
Church Street (Johnstone) 30 G5
Church Street (Kilbarchan) 35 B5
Churchill Avenue 34 D9
Churchill Place 35 B5
Clark Street 30 G5
Clifton Terrace 32 H6
Clippens House 30 H2
Clippens Road 30 G1
Clippens Road 31 J3
Clochoderick Avenue 34 C6
Clyde Place 34 D8
Cochrane Square 31 J2
Cochranemill Road 34 D7
Collier Street 30 G5
Co-operative Terrace 30 H5
Corseford Avenue 34 D8
Coruisk Way 33 M8
Cotton Avenue 31 J3
Cowal Drive 30 H3
Craig Road 30 G1
Craigbog Avenue 32 E7
Craigburn Avenue 30 E1
Craigburn Crescent 30 E1
Craigburn Place (1) 30 E1
Craigdonald Place 32 G6
Craigends Drive 35 C5
Craigends Road 30 E1
Craigenfeoch Avenue 32 E7
Craigston Place 32 G6
Craigston Road 32 F6
Craigview Avenue 32 E8
Craigview Terrace (1) 32 E7
Crosbie Drive 33 M9
Cross, The 35 B5
Crosslee Road 35 B1
Cuninghame Road 35 C5
Curlew Place 34 D9
Currie Court 32 F7
Cyprus Avenue 33 J6
Dalhousie Road 34 C6
Darluith Park 35 D2
Darluith Road 30 F2
Dee Place 34 D8
Dimity Street 32 G6
Don Place 34 D8
Douglas Avenue 33 J6, J7
Drygait 34 B10
Duart Drive 33 J7
Dunbar Avenue 32 F8
Duncraig Crescent 32 E8
Dundonald Avenue 32 E7
Dunlop Street 31 K2
Dunrobin Avenue 33 K7
Dunvegan Avenue 33 J7
East Road 35 B4
Easwald Bank 34 C6
Edmiston Drive 30 G2
Edzell Drive 33 L6
Eldin Place 33 J6
Ellerslie Street 30 H5
Elliot Avenue 33 M9
Ellon Drive (4) 30 G3
Elm Drive 32 G8
Elmlea 33 J6
Erskinefauld Road 30 H2
Esk Drive 33 M7
Esk Way 33 M7
Ettrick Oval 33 M8
Ettrick Terrace 34 D8
Ewing Street 35 B5
Fairways, The 32 E9
Falcon Road 32 E9
Farrier Court 30 G5
Ferguson Street 30 F5
Finch Place 32 E9
Finlay Drive (3) 30 G3
Fir Place 32 H7
Floors Street 32 F6
Floorsburn Crescent 32 F6
Forehouse Road 35 A4
Forth Avenue 33 M7
Forth Place 34 D8
Foxbar Crescent 33 M9
Foxbar Drive 33 M9
Foxbar Road 33 L9
Fraser Avenue 32 H6
Fulmar Place 32 E10
Fulton Crescent 35 C5
Fulton Drive 30 F1
Fulwood Avenue 31 J2
Fyffe Place 30 H5
Gas Street 30 H5
Gateside Place 35 B5
George Street 30 G5
Gibson Crescent 32 F6
Gilfillan Way 33 M8
Gilmartin Road 30 G2
Gladstone Avenue 32 E8
Glamis Avenue 33 K7
Glen Gardens 31 K5
Glenallan Way 33 L9
Glencart Grove 34 D7
Glendower Way 33 M8
Gleniffer Crescent 33 K7
Glenmalloch Place 31 K5
Glenpatrick Buildings 33 K7
Glenpatrick Road 31 L5
Glenpatrick Road 33 K7
Glentyan Avenue 35 B4
Gordon McMaster Gardens 30 H5
Gordon Square 32 G6
Gowanbank Gardens 32 F6
Graham Street 32 F6
Green Farm Road 31 J2
Greenend Avenue 32 E7
Greenfield Avenue 32 F7
Greenhill Crescent (Elderslie) 33 L6
Greenhill Crescent (Linwood) 31 K2
Greenhill Drive 31 K3
Greenwood Drive 32 F8
Griffen Avenue 31 M3
Grove, The 35 B4
Hagg Crescent 30 F5
Hagg Place 30 F5
Hagg Road 32 F6
Hallhill Road 34 D9
Hanover Court 30 G5
Hart Street 31 J3
Hawthorn Avenue 32 H7
Hazel Avenue 32 H7
Hazelwood Avenue 33 M9
Heather Place 32 H6
Helmsdale Drive 33 M6

Heriot Avenue 33 M8
Heron Place 32 E9
High Barholm 35 B5
High Kirk View 32 G6
High Street 30 G5
Highcraig Avenue 32 E7
Hillman Crescent 31 M4
Hillman Road 31 M4
Hillview Road 33 J6
Hogg Avenue 32 F7
Holly Place 32 H8
Holm Place 31 J1
Holms 34 D9
Houston Place 33 K6
Houstoun Court 30 G5
Houstoun Square 30 G5
Howden Drive (5) 30 G3
Hunter Place 34 B6
Huntersfield Road 34 D7
Inglewood Crescent 33 M6
Irvine Drive 30 G1
Janefield Avenue 32 F6
Jarvie Way 33 M8
John Lang Street 30 H5
Jubilee Terrace 32 E6
Juniper Place 32 H8
Kestrel Place 32 E9
Kibbleston Road 34 A8
Kibbleston Road 35 A5
Kilbarchan Road (2) 34 D6
Kilbarchan Road 32 E6
Kilbarchan Road 35 A3
Kilbrennan Road 31 J2
Killin Drive 30 G3
Kilnknowe Cottages 34 B10
Kings Crescent 31 L5
King's Road 33 J6
Kinloch Avenue 30 H3
Kinnaird Drive 31 J2
Kintyre Avenue 30 H3
Kirkland Grove 30 G5
Kirkshaw Court 30 G5
Laburnum Place 32 H8
Ladeside Drive 32 E6
Ladysmith Avenue 34 D6
Laighcartside Street 30 H5
Lang Place 30 G5
Langholm Drive 31 K3
Langside Drive 34 B6
Langside Park 34 B6
Larch Place 32 G8
Lauder Drive 31 J3
Leitchland Road 33 L8
Leven Way 33 M7
Lewis Crescent 34 D6
Lexwell Avenue 31 L5
Liddlesdale Avenue 33 L9
Lilac Place 33 J7
Lilybank Wynd 30 G5
Linclive Terrace 31 L3
Lindsay Place 30 H5
Linn Brae 32 G6
Linn Park Gardens 32 H6
Linn-Clive Spur 31 M2
Linnet Avenue 34 D9
Linwood Road 31 L3
Lismore Drive (1) 30 G3
Lismore Gardens 34 D6
Loanhead Avenue 30 H2
Loanhead Lane (1) 30 H2
Loanhead Road 30 H2
Locher Road 35 A3
Lochhead Avenue 31 J3
Locksley Road 33 M7
Lomond Gardens 33 K6
Longmeadow 32 E7

Loom Walk 35 B5
Lorne Drive 30 H3
Loudon Gardens 30 H5
Low Barholm 34 C6
Ludovic Square 30 G5
Lyon Road 31 J4
McCrorie Place 35 B5
McDonald Avenue 32 F7
MacDowall Street 30 G5
McKay Crescent 32 H6
MacKenzie Drive 34 C7
McLaurin Crescent 32 E7
Mackie's Mill Road 33 L8
MacLay Avenue 34 B6
Magdalen Way 33 L9
Main Road 31 J5
Malloch Crescent 33 J6
Mannering Road 33 M8
Mannering Way 33 M8
Maple Drive 32 G8
Maple Place 32 H8
Marmion Road 33 M8
Martlet Drive 34 D9
Mary Street 30 H5
Mavisbank Terrace 32 G6
Mayfield Court 34 A10
Mayfield Crescent 34 A10
Mayfield Drive 34 A10
Meadowside Avenue 33 L6
Meadside Avenue 35 B4
Meadside Road 35 B4
Melfort Gardens 34 D7
Melfort Mews 34 D7
Melrose Avenue 31 J3
Menzies Lane 34 D6
Merchants Close 35 B5
Merchiston Avenue 30 G3
Merchiston Drive 30 E3
Middleton Road 31 L1
Midton Cottages 34 C10
Midton Road 34 D9
Mill Place 30 H2
Miller Street 31 J5
Millford Drive 31 J3
Milliken Drive 34 D6
Milliken Park Road 34 D7
Milliken Place 34 D6
Milliken Road 34 D6
Millview Crescent 30 G5
Montclair Place 31 J2
Montgomery Drive 35 B4
Montrose Place 30 H2
Moorburn Place 30 G2
Morar Drive 30 H3
Moray Place 30 H2
Morven Drive 30 H3
Moss Avenue 31 J2
Moss Road 31 K2
Muirhead Drive 30 H3
Napier Gardens 31 K2
Napier Street (Johnstone) 30 F5
Napier Street (Linwood) 31 K2
Ness Avenue 34 D8
New Street 35 B5
Newlandcraigs Avenue 33 L7
Newlandcraigs Drive 33 L7
Newlands Gardens 33 K7
Newton Avenue 31 M5
Newton Drive 31 M5
Nightingale Place 32 E10
Nith Place 34 D8
North Drive 31 J2
North Iverton Park Road 31 J5

North Lane 31 K2
North Road 32 F6
Oaks, The 32 F6
Old Road 31 K5
Old School Square 35 B5
Oliphant Crescent 33 M8
Oliphant Oval 33 M8
Overton Crescent 31 J5
Overton Road 32 H6
Oxford Drive 31 J2
Palmerston Place 34 D9
Park Avenue 33 K6
Park Gardens 35 B4
Park Place 32 G6
Park Road 32 G6
Park View 35 B4
Patrickbank Crescent 33 K7
Patrickbank Gardens 33 K7
Patrickbank Wynd 33 L7
Pearson Place 31 J3
Pegasus Avenue 31 L3
Pend Close 32 G7
Pentland Avenue 30 H3
Peockland Gardens 30 H5
Peockland Place 30 H5
Perimeter Road 31 J3
Phoenix House (1) 31 M3
Phoenix Place 31 L5
Pine Crescent 32 H7
Planetree Place 32 H7
Plover Place 34 D9
Polson Drive 32 F6
Poplar Avenue 32 H7
Provost Close 30 G5
Quarrelton Grove 32 G7
Quarrelton Road 32 F6
Quarry Street 30 G5
Quarrybank 34 D6
Queen's Road 33 K6
Ramsay Avenue 32 F7
Ramsay Crescent 34 C6
Ramsay Place 32 F7
Rankine Place 30 G5
Rankine Street 30 G5
Rannoch Road 32 F7
Ravenswood Avenue 33 M9
Reid Avenue 31 J3
Renshaw Road 33 K7
Rhumhor Gardens 34 D6
Richmond Drive 30 H1
Ritchie Crescent 31 K5
Ritchie Park 31 J5
Robertson Place 34 D6
Rock Drive 34 C6
Rosebank Gardens 32 H6
Rosedale Avenue 33 L9
Roundhill Drive 31 M5
Rowan Road 30 G1
Rowanlea 32 F6
Rowanlea Avenue 33 L9
Rowantree Place 32 G7
Rowantree Road 32 G7
Roxburgh Road 33 L9
Russell Place 30 G2
Russell Street 30 H5
Rye Way 33 M7
Ryefield Avenue 32 E7
Ryefield Place 32 E7
Ryewraes Road 31 J3
St Barchan's Road 34 C6
Sanderling Place 32 E10
Sandholes Road 35 D2, D3
Sandringham Drive 33 J7
Saturn Avenue 31 M4
Scarffe Avenue (2) 30 G3
Scott Avenue 32 F8

Scott Place
Semple Place
Shanks Crescent
Shaw Place
Sheldrake Place
Shuttle Street
South Drive
South William Street
Spateston Road
Speirs Place
Spencer Drive
Spey Avenue
Spey Place
Spiers Road
Springfield Park
Springfield Woods
Spruce Avenue
Stanley Drive
Stanley Lane
Station Road
Station Wynd
Steeple Square
Steeple Street
Stirling Drive (Johnstone)
Stirling Drive (Linwood)
Stirling Gate
Stoddard Square
Swallow Drive
Swan Place
Swift Place
Sycamore Avenue
Talisman Road
Tandlehill Road
Tannahill Crescent
Tay Place
Taylor Avenue
Tern Place
Teviot Avenue
Teviot Terrace
Thomson Avenue
Thomson Street
Thorn Brae
Thorn Court
Thorndene
Thornhill Avenue
Thornhill Drive
Thornhill
Thornside Road
Thrush Place
Toppersfield
Torbracken
Tower Place
Tower Road
Traquair Avenue
Trojan House (2)
Troubridge Avenue
Troubridge Crescent
Tweed Place
Ulundi Road
Vernon Drive
Victoria Road
Victory Drive
Walker Drive
Walkinshaw Court
Walkinshaw Street
Wallace Avenue
Wallace Gait
Walnut Crescent
Walpole Place
Waterside Lane (4)
Waterside Terrace (1)
Waterside Way (3)
Waterside Yard
Watson Avenue

ley Gardens 33 L6
er Lane 35 B4
ers Court 35 B5
e Drive 30 H2
Road 35 B5
Avenue 31 L4
Road 35 B4
tlands Drive 35 B4
tlands Farm Road 35 B4
n Street 30 G5
nson Place 33 J6
v Avenue 33 K6
v Drive 32 H7
v Place 32 H6
n Avenue 30 H3
sor Crescent 33 J7
bank Crescent 32 G6
burn Place 30 F1
lend Place 33 J6
ford Place 30 H2
lands Crescent 32 F8
side Lane 30 E2
side Road 30 E2
stock Way 33 M8
Place 32 E9
Place 32 G7

**k to Paisley**

y Close 49 J6
y Place 49 J6
t Street 45 J4
tsburn Way 45 G2
tsford Crescent 50 B11
tsinch Road 45 H1
corn Street 45 J3
ne Drive 51 J9
ia Drive 50 E9
rd Place 49 M8
Crescent 50 E9
ay Drive 50 D9
Drive 52 L9
Way 50 C9
Court 51 G11
Drive 51 G11
ny Way 45 H2
n Gate 45 G4
n Street 45 H4
andra Drive 47 E7
andra Gate 47 H7
Street 47 H8
Way 48 N1
way Avenue 52 L10
vay Crescent 52 L10
vay Drive 52 L10
vay Grove 52 M10
ond Crescent 46 C8
Road 49 M6
assador Way 48 N1
chrie Drive 50 D10
chrie Glen 50 D10
chrie Road 50 D10
chrie Way 50 C9
hor Avenue 49 K6
hor Crescent 49 K7
hor Drive 49 K6
hor Mills 49 J6
hor Wynd 49 K6
rew Street 45 H4
on Way (5) 48 M1
gowan Avenue 49 J7
gowan Street 49 J7
osy Way 48 M1
yle Street 47 G6
yll Avenue 45 H1
eston Court 48 L2

Arkleston Crescent 48 L3
Arkleston Drive 48 L4
Arkleston Road 48 L2
Arkleston Road 48 L5
Arkwrights Way 47 E7
Arniston Way 45 K3
Arran Avenue 45 H1
Arran Drive 51 H11
Arthur Road 51 H10
Arthur Street 44 F5
Ashton Way 50 B10
Auchentorlie Quadrant 49 L6
Auldbar Terrace 49 K8
Avenue 3 49 M8
Avondale Drive 48 L4
Back Sneddon Street (1) 45 H5
Balfron Road 48 N5
Balgair Drive 48 L5
Balgonie Avenue 50 D9
Balgonie Drive 51 F9
Balgonie Woods 51 F9
Ballater Drive 51 J9
Bank Street 45 J5
Bank Street 49 J6
Bankfoot Road 44 E4
Barclay Square 48 L1
Barcraigs Drive 51 J10
Bardrain Road 51 F11
Bargarron Drive 45 K3
Barnsford Road 44 D1
Barochan Crescent 46 D6
Barochan Way 46 D6
Baron Road 45 K4
Baronscourt Drive 46 C6
Baronscourt Gardens 46 C6
Baronscourt Road 46 C6
Barr Place 47 G6
Barra Avenue 48 M1
Barrhead Road 49 K8
Barscube Terrace 49 K8
Barshaw Drive 45 K4
Barshaw House 48 M5
Barshaw Place 48 N5
Barskiven Road 46 C6
Barterholm Road 49 J8
Beauly Drive 50 B9
Beech Avenue 52 K9
Beechwood Drive 48 M1
Belltrees Crescent 46 D6
Belmont Road 45 K4
Ben Alder Drive 52 N9
Ben Buie Way 52 N9
Ben Hope Avenue 52 N8
Ben Lawers Drive 52 N8
Ben Ledi Avenue 52 N8
Ben Loyal Avenue 52 N8
Ben Lui Drive 52 M9
Ben More Drive 52 N8
Ben Nevis Road 52 M9
Ben Vane Avenue 52 M9
Ben Venue Way 52 N9
Ben Wyvis Drive 52 M9
Benn Avenue 49 J7
Benview Terrace 49 L8
Beresford House 49 M8
Birchwood Drive 50 E9
Birkenshaw Way 45 H2
Birmingham Road 48 L1
Blackford Road 49 K7
Blackhall Lane 49 J7
Blackhall Street 49 J7
Blackland Grove 51 F10
Blacklaw Lane 45 H5
Blackstoun Oval 44 E5
Blackstoun Road 44 D2, E5

Bladda Lane 49 J6
Blairmore Avenue 48 M5
Blythswood Drive 45 H4
Bobbins Gate 47 E7
Bothwell Place 50 B10
Bothwick Way 50 B10
Brabloch Crescent 45 J4
Brabloch Park 45 J4
Braefoot Crescent 51 J11
Braehead Road 51 F12
Braemar Crescent 51 J9
Braemount Avenue 51 F12
Braeview Avenue 50 E11
Braeview Drive 50 E11
Braeview Gardens 50 E11
Braeview Road 50 E11
Braids Circle 51 H9
Braids Court 51 G9
Braids Gait 51 G9
Braids Road 51 H9
Brediland Road 50 C9
Brewster Avenue 45 K3
Brick Lane (6) 45 J5
Bridge Lane 47 E7
Bridge Street 49 J6
Britannia Way 48 M1
Broadloan 48 N1
Brodie Park Avenue 47 H8
Brodie Park Crescent 47 G8
Brodie Park Gardens 47 H8
Broomdyke Way 45 G2
Broomlands Court 47 F6
Broomlands Lane 47 E6
Broomlands Street 47 F6
Brown Street 45 G5
Browns Lane 47 H6
Brownside Avenue 51 F11
Bruce Avenue 45 K4
Bruce Road 45 K1
Bruce Road 45 K4
Burnbrae Drive 46 A6
Burnbrae Road 46 A5
Burnfoot Crescent 51 F10
Burnside Place 44 D3
Burnside Road 46 A8
Bushes Avenue 51 G9
Bute Avenue 48 N1
Bute Crescent 51 G11
Bute Road 45 G1
Byres Avenue 45 K4
Byres Crescent 45 K4
Byres Road 46 A8
Cairngorm Crescent 51 H9
Calder Road 44 D5
Caledonia Court 45 G4
Caledonia House 45 G4
Caledonia Street 45 G4
Caledonia Way 45 G1
Caledonia Way East 45 H1
Caledonia Way West 45 G1
Calside 47 H7
Calside Avenue 47 G7
Calside Court 47 H8
Camphill 47 G7
Camphill Court 47 G7
Campsie Drive (Glenburn) 51 G10
Campsie Drive (Glasgow Airport) 45 H1
Campsie Drive (Moorpark) 48 L2
Canal Gardens 46 A7
Canal Street 46 A7
Canal Terrace 47 H6
Candren Road (Linclive) 46 A5

Candren Road (Ferguslie Park) 44 D5
Candren Way 44 D5
Cannich Drive 52 L9
Caplaw Road 51 F12
Caplethill Road 51 H11, J11
Caravelle Way 48 N1
Carbrook Street 47 F6
Cardell Avenue 46 D7
Cardell Drive 46 D7
Cardell Road 46 D7
Carlile Place 45 H4
Carriagehill Avenue 47 H8
Carriagehill Court 47 H7
Carriagehill Drive 47 H8
Carron Way 45 K3
Carsegreen Avenue 50 E11
Cart Lane 45 H4
Cart Walk 49 J6
Cartha Crescent 49 L7
Cartvale Lane 45 H4
Castle Gait 47 H7
Castle Gardens (Millarston) 46 D7
Castle Gardens (Castlehead) 47 G7
Castle Street 47 F6
Castleview Avenue 50 D11
Castleview Drive 50 D11
Castleview Place 50 D11
Cathcart Crescent 49 K7
Causeyside Street (5) 47 H6
Central Road 45 H5
Central Way 45 H5
Chapelhill Road 52 L9
Charleston Gate 47 H7
Charlotte Place (3) 47 H8
Cheviot Road 51 H9
Chiron House (3) 46 B5
Christie Lane 45 H5
Christie Street 45 J5
Church Hill 45 H5
Clairinsh Gardens (2) 48 M1
Clarence Drive 49 K6
Clarence Street 45 K5
Clark Street 44 F4
Claud Road 45 K4
Claverhouse Place 49 K7
Clavering Street East 44 F5
Clavering Street West 47 F6
Cluny Drive 45 K4
Clyde Road 48 L3
Clyde View 49 L8
Clyde Way 48 L3
Clydesdale Avenue 45 K1
Coats Drive 47 E7
Cochran Street 49 J6
Cockles Loan 48 L1
Coldstream Drive 50 D9
Colinslee Avenue 51 J9
Colinslee Crescent 51 J9
Colinslee Drive 51 J9
Coll Avenue 48 N1
Colonsay Avenue 48 M1
Colonsay Road 51 G11
Convair Way 48 N1
Conval Way 45 G2
Corsebar Avenue 47 F8
Corsebar Crescent 51 F9
Corsebar Drive 47 F8
Corsebar Lane 50 E9
Corsebar Road 47 F8
Corsebar Way 47 F8
Coruisk Way 50 B10
Cottages, The 49 M8
Cotton Street 49 J6

Counting House, The 47 E7
County Place (4) 45 H5
County Square (3) 45 H5
Crags Avenue 51 J9
Crags Crescent 49 J8
Crags Road 51 J9
Craigendon Oval 51 F12
Craigendon Road 51 F12
Craigfaulds Avenue 47 E8
Craigiebar Drive 51 F10
Craigielea Drive 44 F5
Craigielinn Avenue 50 E12
Craigmount Avenue 51 F12
Craw Road 47 F7
Crawfurd Drive 44 E4
Crestlea Avenue 51 H10
Cromer Way 45 G3
Cromptons Grove 47 E7
Crosbie Drive 50 B11
Crosbie Wood 50 E9
Cross Road 47 E8
Cross Street 47 F6
Cross, The 45 H5
Crossflat Crescent 45 K5
Cruachan Avenue 51 H10
Cruachan Avenue 48 M1
Cumbrae Road 51 H11
Cumbrae Road 48 N1
Cyril Crescent 49 K6
Cyril Place 49 K6
Cyril Street 49 K6
Dakota Way (8) 48 N1
Dalmary Drive 48 L5
Dalskeith Avenue 44 D5
Dalskeith Crescent (3) 44 D5
Dalskeith Road 46 D6
Darkwood Court 44 E4
Darkwood Crescent 44 E4
Darkwood Drive 44 E4
Davaar Drive 51 H11
Davaar Road 48 N1
David Place 48 L3
David Way 48 L3
Dee Avenue 46 C8
Dee Drive 50 C9
Denewood Avenue 51 G10
Deveron Way 50 C9
Dinmont Avenue 50 C9
Dinmont Way 50 C9
Direlton Drive 50 D9
Dixon Street 49 J6
Don Drive 50 C9
Donaldswood Park 51 F10
Donaldswood Road 51 F10
Douglas Road 45 K2
Douglas Street 44 F5
Drums Avenue 44 F4
Drums Crescent 44 F4
Dryburgh Avenue 50 D9
Duke Street 47 H8
Dunard Way 45 G3
Dunbar Road 50 D9
Dunchurch Road 48 N5
Dundonald Road 45 K3
Dunearn Place 49 K7
Dunn Square 47 H6
Dunn Street 49 K6
Durrockstock Crescent 50 C11
Durrockstock Road 50 C11
Durrockstock Way 50 C11
Durward Crescent 50 C9
Durward Way 50 C9
Dyers Wynd 45 H5

Dykebar Cottages (1) 52 M10
Dykebar Crescent 49 L8
East Buchanan Mews (7) 45 J5
East Buchanan Street 45 J5
East Candren 44 D3
East Lane 49 K6
Edzell Drive 46 A8
Elizabeth Way 48 M1
Elliot Avenue 50 B11
Ellon Grove 45 J3
Ellon Way 45 K3
Elm Road 52 K9
Endrick Drive 48 L4
Esk Drive 50 B9
Esk Way 50 B9
Espedair Street 47 H7
Ettrick Oval 50 B10
Fairfield Drive 48 N1
Fairway Avenue 51 G10
Falcon Crescent 44 E4
Falcon House 45 H3
Falside Avenue 51 H9
Falside Road 51 G9
Fauldswood Crescent 47 E8
Fauldswood Drive 47 E8
Fereneze Avenue 48 L2
Fereneze Drive 51 F10
Fergus Avenue 44 D5
Fergus Drive (4) 44 D5
Ferguslie 47 E6
Ferguslie Park Avenue 44 D5
Ferguslie Park Avenue 46 D6
Ferguslie Park Crescent 46 D6
Ferguslie Walk 47 E6
Fifth Avenue 48 M1
Finart Drive 52 L9
Findhorn Avenue 50 C9
Finglas Avenue 52 L9
Fintry Avenue 51 H11
Fischer Gardens 44 C5
Fisher Avenue 46 C6
Fisher Drive 46 C6
Fisher Way 46 C6
Fitzalan Drive 45 K4
Fitzalan Road 45 K1
Fleming Street 45 H3
Forbes Place 47 H6
Forest Place (4) 47 H8
Forth Avenue 50 B9
Fountain Court 45 H4
Foxbar Crescent 50 B11
Foxbar Drive 50 B11
Foxbar Road 50 B11, D11
Friarshall Gate 47 G8
Friendship Way 48 N1
Fulbar Crescent 46 C8
Fulbar Gardens 46 C8
Fulbar Road 46 C7
Fullerton Street 45 G3
Gallacher Avenue 50 D9
Gallacher Court 44 F5
Gallow Green (1) 47 F6
Galloway Avenue 45 G3
Galloway Terrace 45 G3
Gallowhill Court 45 K2
Gallowhill Road 45 K4
Gareloch Avenue 46 D8
Garry Drive 46 D8
Garthland Cottages 45 J5
Garthland Lane 45 J5
Gartmore Road 49 M6
Gauze Street 45 H5

George Court 47 G6
George Lane 49 M6
George Place 47 H6
George Street 47 G6
Gibson Road 48 L1
Gifford Wynd 46 C8
Gilfillan Way 50 B10
Gilmour Street 45 H5
Glasgow Road 45 K5
Glen Lane 45 H5
Glen Street 45 H5
Glenapp Avenue 52 L9
Glenapp Road 52 L9
Glenarklet Crescent 52 K10
Glenarklet Drive 52 K9
Glenashdale Way 52 K9
Glenbrittle Drive 52 K9
Glenbrittle Way 52 K9
Glenburn Crescent 51 G10
Glenburn Road 51 G11
Glencairn Court 45 K2
Glencairn Road 45 K3
Glencally Avenue 52 L9
Glenclora Drive 52 K9
Glencoats Crescent 44 E5
Glencoats Drive 44 D5
Glencorse Road 47 F8
Glendower Way 50 B10
Glenfield Avenue 51 G11
Glenfield Crescent 51 H12
Glenfield Gardens 51 G12
Glenfield Grange 51 H12
Glenfield Grove 51 G12
Glenfield Road 51 G12
Glenfruin Crescent 52 L9
Glengavin Way 52 L9
Glenholme Avenue 50 E9
Gleniffer Court 50 E11
Gleniffer Road (Glenburn) 50 E11, C12
Gleniffer Road (Moorpark) 48 L2
Glenpatrick Road 46 A8
Glenshiel Avenue 52 K9
Glenshira Avenue 52 K9
Glentaner Court 49 K6
Glenvilla Circle 51 G12
Glenvilla Crescent 51 G12
Glenvilla Place 51 G12
Glenvilla Road 51 G12
Glenvilla Wynd 51 G12
Gockston Road 45 G3
Golf Drive 49 M6
Gordon Street 47 H6
Goudie Street 45 G3
Grahamston Court 52 M10
Grahamston Crescent 52 M10
Grahamston Place 52 M10
Grahamston Road 52 M12
Grampian Avenue 51 G10
Grants Avenue 51 G9
Grants Crescent 51 G9
Grants Place 51 G9
Grants Way 51 G9
Great Hamilton Street 47 H8
Green Road 46 D7, E7
Greenbank Drive 51 G11
Greenhill Crescent 46 A8
Greenhill Road 44 F4
Greenlaw Avenue 45 K5
Greenlaw Crescent 45 K4
Greenlaw Drive 45 K5
Greenlaw Gardens 45 K4

Greenock Road
Greenways Avenue
Greenways Court
Griffen Avenue
Gryffe Crescent
Halifax Way (7)
Hamilton Court
Hamilton Street
Hampden Way (10)
Hannay Street
Hannover Court
Hanover Gardens
Harbour Lane
Harbour Road
Harelaw Crescent 5
Hartfield Terrace
Hawick Avenue
Hawkhead Avenue
Hawkhead Road 49 L
Hazelwood Avenue 5
Helemsdale Drive 4
Henderson Street 4
Herald Way 4
Hercules Way 4
Heriot Avenue 50
Heriot Way 50
Heron Way 4
High Calside 4
High Road
High Street 4
Highfield Avenue 51
Highfield Crescent 51
Hillcrest Avenue 51
Hillman Crescent 4
Hillman Road 4
Hillpark Avenue 5
Hillside Road 4
Hollows Avenue 50
Hollows Crescent 50
Hollybush Avenue 50
Holm Avenue 4
Holmes Avenue 4
Howard Street 4
Hunter Street 4
Hunterhill Avenue 4
Hunterhill Road 4
Huntly Terrace 5
Hurlet Road 52
Inchinnan Road 4
Incle Street 4
Inglewood Crescent 4
Inverkar Drive 4
Iona Drive 51
Iona Road 48
Islay Crescent 51
Ivy Gardens 4
Ivanhoe Road 5
Ivanhoe Way 5
Jarvie Way 50
Jedburgh Drive 5
Jenny's Well Court 4
Jenny's Well Road 4
Jessiman Square 4
Johnston Street 47
Jura Avenue 48
Jura Road 51
Katrine Drive 46
Kelburne Court 45
Kelburne Drive 4
Kelburne Gardens 45
Kelburne Oval 45
Kelso Avenue 50
Kemp Avenue 45
Kenilworth Avenue 50

worth Way 50 C9
Street 45 G5
rn Road 48 L3
rn Square 48 L3
rn Way 48 L3
h Avenue 44 D5
h Lane (1) 44 D5
h Road 44 D5
h Way (2) 44 D5
roft Lane 51 H9
ide Lane 45 J5
ide Road 45 J5
trick Avenue 47 E8
trick Crescent 51 G10
net Way 45 K3
Street 44 F5
s Court 44 F4
s Crescent 46 A7
sburgh Drive 48 L5
ch Road 48 L1
urnie Road 48 N5
ea Gardens 44 D5
k Way 45 K3
khill Road 48 L1
ckside Avenue 51 G11
we Road 48 L3
x Street 47 F6
Street 45 K5
Lane 47 G6
yburn Street 49 K6
ykirk Crescent 49 J7
h Kirk Lane 47 H6
hpark View 45 H3
mermuir Court 51 H9
mermuir Drive 51 H10
caster Way (3) 48 M1
fine Road 49 L6
g Avenue 48 N1
g Street 49 K6
gcraigs Court 51 F10
gcraigs Drive 51 G12
gcraigs Terrace 51 F12
sbury Gardens 45 G3
sley Avenue 51 H9
kin Gardens 45 G3
ren Way 50 C9
vers Road 48 M1
wn Street 45 J5
abank Avenue 51 H10
tchland Road 50 B10
nnox Terrace 45 K2
ven Way 50 B9
wis Avenue 48 N1
xwell Avenue 46 A7
necraigs Avenue 51 F11
necraigs Crescent 51 F11
necraigs Road 51 F11
neview Avenue 50 E11
neview Crescent 50 E11
neview Road 50 E11
neview Way 50 E11
nclive Terrace 46 A5
n Crescent 51 F11
n-Clive Spur 46 B4
nside Avenue 49 L6
nwell Crescent 51 G11
nwood Road 46 A5
smore Avenue 48 N1
smore Drive 51 G11
thgow Crescent 49 K8
chaline Avenue 46 D8
chalsh Drive 46 D8
chard Drive 50 D9
chbroom Drive 46 D8
Lochearn Crescent 46 D8
Lochfield Crescent 51 J9
Lochfield Drive 52 K9
Lochfield Road 51 J9
Lochfield Road 52 L9
Lochinver Crescent 46 D8
Lochore Avenue 45 K3
Locksley Road 50 C9
Locksley Way 50 C9
Lomond Avenue 48 L1
Lomond Crescent 51 G10
Lonend 49 J7
Lothian Crescent 51 G9
Lounsdale Avenue 47 E7
Lounsdale Crescent 47 E8
Lounsdale Drive 47 E8
Lounsdale Grove 47 E8
Lounsdale House 50 D9
Lounsdale Road 47 E8
Lounsdale Way 47 E7
Love Street 45 H4
Low Road 47 F7
Lyle Place 49 J8
Lylesland Court 47 H8
Lyon Road 50 C9
Lysander Way (9) 48 M1
MacDowall Street 45 G4
MacKean Street 44 F4
McFarlane Lane (6) 45 J5
McFarlane Street 44 F3
McGown Street 45 G4
McIntyre Place 47 H8
McKenzie Street 44 F5
McKerrell Street 45 K5
McLaren Avenue (1) 48 M1
McLean Place 45 G3
Magdalen Way 50 B11
Main Road 46 A7
Malvern Way 45 G2
Mannering Road 50 B10
Mannering Way 50 B10
Manor Park Avenue 50 E9
Manor Road 50 C9
Mansionhouse Road 45 K5
Marchburn Drive 45 H2
Marchfield Avenue 45 G2
Marchfield Drive 45 H2
Marchmont Gardens 47 G8
Maree Road 46 D8
Marjory Drive 48 L3
Marjory Road 45 K1
Marmion Road 50 B10
Marnock Terrace 49 K8
Marshalls Lane 47 H6
Mary Street 47 H8
Mathieson Street 48 L5
Mavisbank Terrace 49 J7
Maxwell Street 45 H5
Maxwellton Court 47 F6
Maxwellton Road 47 E6
Maxwellton Street 47 F7
May Road 51 H11
Meadowside Avenue 46 A8
Meetinghouse Lane 45 H5
Meikleriggs Court 47 E8
Meikleriggs Drive 50 D9
Melford Way 45 K3
Melrose Avenue 50 D9
Merksworth Way 45 H3
Merlin Way 48 L3
Methven Road 45 J1
Mews Lane 45 J3
Middleton Road 44 E4
Mill Street 49 J6
Millar Street 45 J5
Millarston Avenue 46 D6
Millarston Drive 46 D6
Millstream Court 49 K6
Mirrin Drive 45 G3
Mirrin Wynd 45 G3
Mirren Court 45 J3
Mogarth Avenue 50 C10
Montcrieff Street 45 H5
Montgomery Avenue 48 L3
Montgomery Court 48 L3
Montgomery Road 45 K2
Montrose Road 50 C10
Montrose Way 50 C10
Moorfoot Avenue 51 G9
Moorfoot Path 51 G10
Moorhouse Avenue 47 E8
Moorings, The 47 F7
Morar Drive 46 C8
Moredun Drive 50 E9
Moredun House 51 F9
Moredun Road 50 E9
Morton Avenue 52 M9
Morton Drive 49 M8
Morven Avenue 51 G10
Moss Street 45 H5
Mossland Road 48 N2
Mosslands Road 45 G2
Mossneuk Drive 51 F10
Mossvale Lane 45 G4
Mossvale Square 45 G4
Mossvale Street 45 G4
Motehill Road 45 K4
Muir Terrace 45 K3
Muirdykes Road 44 E3
Mull Avenue 51 H11
Mull Avenue 48 M1
Murray Street 45 G4
Navar Place 49 K8
Neilston Road 47 H7
Nethercraigs Court 50 E11
Nethercraigs Drive 51 F10
Nethercraigs Road 50 E11
Netherhill Cottages 48 L2
Netherhill Crescent 45 K4
Netherhill Road 45 J4
Netherhill Way 48 L3
Nevis Road 48 L1
Nevis Way 45 H1
New Cottages (2) 52 M10
New Inchinnan Road 45 H3
New Sneddon Street (2) 45 H5
New Street 47 H6
Newark Drive 51 F10
Newlandcraigs Avenue 46 A8
Newlandcraigs Drive 46 A8
Newmains Road 48 M1
Newton Avenue 46 B7
Newton Drive 46 B7
Newton Street 47 F6
Newton Terrace 46 C7
Newton Way 48 L3
Newtyle Road 49 M6
Niddry Street 45 J5
North Boulevard 49 M8
North Corsebar Road 47 F8
North Croft Street 45 J5
North Street 45 H4
Oak Road 52 K9
Oakshaw Brae 45 G5
Oakshawhead 45 G5
Oakshaw Street East 45 H5
Oakshaw Street West 45 G5
Oakwood Avenue 50 E9
Ochil Drive 51 G10
Ochil Road 48 L1
Ogilvie House 44 E5
Oldhall Road 48 N5
Old Mill Road 47 E7
Old Sneddon Street 45 H5
Oliphant Court 50 C10
Oliphant Crescent 50 B10
Oliphant Oval 50 B10
Orchard Street 47 H6
Orchy Crescent 50 C9
Orr Square 45 H5
Orr Street 45 H5
Orr Street 47 H7
Osprey Crescent 45 G2
Osprey House 45 H2
Osprey Road 45 G2
Osprey View 45 G2
Paisley Road 48 L1
Park Avenue 51 F9
Park Grove 51 F9
Park Lane (Gallowhill) 48 L3
Park Lane (Millarston) 46 D6
Park Road 47 G8
Park View 47 G8
Patrick Street 49 J7
Peacock Avenue 46 C8
Peacock Drive 46 C8
Pegasus Avenue 46 A5
Penilee Road 48 N2
Pentland Crescent 51 G10
Pentland Drive 48 L2
Percy Road 45 K2
Peter Coats Building 47 H7
Phoenix House (1) 46 A5
Phoenix Place 46 A7
Pine Street 49 K8
Pinkerton Lane 48 N1
Pladda Road 48 N1
Plaintrees Court 47 H8
Polsons Crescent 47 G8
Portland Street 49 L7
Potterhill Avenue 51 H10
Princess Crescent 48 L4
Priory Avenue 45 K3
Quarry Road 51 J9
Queen Street 47 F6
Raasay Drive 51 G11
Raeburn Avenue 49 K6
Ralston Street 49 K6
Rannoch Place 49 K7
Ravenscraig Avenue 47 F8
Ravenswood Avenue 50 B11
Redhurst Crescent 51 F11
Redhurst Lane 51 F11
Redhurst Way 51 F11
Regent Street 48 L5
Renfrew Road 45 J4
Renshaw Road 46 A8
Riccartsbar Avenue 47 F7
Roaden Avenue 50 C11
Roaden Road 50 C11
Robertson Gait 47 H7
Rockwell Avenue 51 F10
Roffey Park Road 48 N5
Rooksdell Avenue 51 F9
Rosewood Avenue 50 E9
Ross Avenue 45 K1
Ross House 49 M8
Ross Street 49 K7
Rosshall Avenue 49 M6
Rotherwood Avenue 50 C10
Rotherwood Way 50 C10

Roundhill Drive 46 B7
Rowan Court 47 H8
Rowan Gardens 49 J8
Rowan Street 47 H8
Rowan Wynd 49 J8
Rowans Gate 49 J8
Rowanlea Avenue 50 B11
Russell Street 45 G3
Rye Way 50 B9
St Abbs Drive 50 D9
St Andrew's Avenue 44 F1
St Andrew's Crescent 44 F2
St Andrew's Drive 45 G2
St Andrew's Drive West 44 F1
St Andrew's Oval 44 F2
St Andrew's Way 45 G2
St Boswells Crescent 50 D9
St Georges Gate 47 H6
St James Avenue 44 E3
St James Street 45 H5
St Margarets Avenue 45 J3
St Margaret's Court 45 J3
St Mirren Street 47 H6
St Ninians Crescent 49 J8
St Ninians Road 49 J8
St Peters Close 51 F11
Sanda Way 51 G11
Sanderling Road 45 H2
Sandholes Street 47 F6
Sandy Road 48 M1
Sandyford Road 45 K2
Saturn Avenue 46 B6
Saucel Street 49 J6
Saucel Crescent 47 H6
Saucel Place 47 H6
Saucel Hill Terrace 49 J7
Scadlock Road 44 E5
Schaw Road 45 K4
School Houses 50 D10
School Wynd 45 H5
Scotscraig 51 G9
Scotts Road 49 M7
Seedhill 49 J6
Seedhill Road 49 J6
Selkirk Avenue 50 D9
Sergeant Law Road 50 D12
Sherwood Avenue 45 K4
Shortroods Avenue 45 H3
Shortroods Road 45 G3
Shuttle Street 47 H6
Silk Street 45 J5
Sir James Clark Building 49 J6
Sir Michael Place 47 G6
Sixth Avenue 48 M1
Skye Avenue 48 M1
Skye Crescent 51 G11
Smithhills Street 45 H5
Smiths Lane 45 H4
Somerled Avenue 45 J1
South Avenue 51 J10
South Boulevard 49 M8
South Campbell Street 47 H7
Southfield Avenue 51 H10
Southpark Drive 47 H8
Spey Avenue 50 B9
Spiersfield Court 47 G7
Spiersfield Gardens 47 H7
Spinners Gardens 47 E7
Spoolers Road 47 E7
Springbank Road 45 G3
Springbank Terrace 45 G3
Springfield Avenue 49 L6
Springvale Drive 46 C8
Stable Grove 47 E6
Stables, The 47 E6
Staffa Avenue 48 M1
Staffa Drive 51 H11
Stanely Avenue 50 E9
Stanely Crescent 50 E10
Stanely Drive 51 F9
Stanely Grange 50 E11
Stanely Grove 50 E10
Stanley Road 51 F9
Station House 51 H10
Station Road 46 D7
Stevenson Street 47 H7
Stewart Avenue 48 L1
Stewart Road 51 J10
Stirling Way 48 N1
Stirrat Crescent 44 F4
Stirrat Street 44 E3
Stock Avenue 47 H8
Stock Street 47 H8
Stockholm Crescent 47 H7
Stoddard Square 46 A7
Stonefield Avenue 51 J9
Stonefield Crescent 51 J9
Stonefield Drive 51 J9
Stonefield Gardens 51 J9
Stonefield Green 51 H9
Stonefield Grove 51 H9
Stonefield Park 51 H10
Stoney Brae (Glenburn) 51 H10, J11
Stoney Brae (Paisley) 45 H5
Storie Street 47 H6
Stow Brae 47 H6
Stow Street 47 H6
Stranka Avenue 47 F7
Strathcarron Crescent 52 L10
Strathcarron Drive 52 L9
Strathcarron Green 52 L9
Strathcarron Place 52 L10
Strathcarron Road 52 L10
Strathcarron Way 52 L9
Strathcarron Wynd 52 L9
Strathdon Avenue 47 F8
Stravaig Path 50 D11
Stravaig Walk 50 D11
Sunnylaw Drive 47 E8
Sunnyside Oval 51 H9
Sunnyside Road 51 G9
Sutherland Street 45 G5
Tait House 49 M8
Talisman Road 50 B11
Tannahill Road 44 E4
Tannahill Terrace 44 E4
Tannahills Cottage (2) 47 F6
Tantallon Drive 50 D9
Tenters Way 47 E7
Teviot Avenue 50 B10
Thistle Street 47 F8
Thomas Street 47 E6
Thompson Brae 47 H7
Thornly Park Avenue 51 J10
Thornly Park Court 51 H10
Thornly Park Drive 51 J10
Thornly Park Gardens 51 H9
Thornly Park House 51 H10
Thornly Park Road 51 J10
Thornwood Drive 50 E9
Thrushcraig Crescent 49 J8
Tillet Oval 45 G3
Tinto Square 48 L1
Tiree Avenue 51 G11
Tiree Avenue 48 M1
Todburn Drive 51 J10
Todholm Crescent 49 L8
Todholm Road 49 L8
Todholm Terrace 49 L8
Toward Way 51 G11
Tower Terrace (3) 47 G6
Townhead Terrace 47 G6
Traquair Avenue 50 B10
Trident Way 48 M1
Trojan House (2) 46 B5
Tummel Way 50 C9
Turner Road 45 J2
Turners Avenue 47 E7
Tweed Avenue 46 C8
Tylney Road 48 N5
Underwood Court 45 G5
Underwood Lane 45 G5
Underwood Road 45 G5
Union Court 47 H8
Union Street 47 H8
Unsted Place 49 K6
Vanguard Way 48 M1
Victoria Gardens 47 F8
Victoria Road 47 F8
Vigilant House 45 H3
Viking Way 48 M1
Violet Street 49 K6
Viscount Avenue 48 M1
Walker Street 47 G6
Walkinshaw Way 45 G3
Wallace Gait 46 A7
Wallace Road 45 K1
Wallace Street 45 H4
Wallneuk 45 J5
Wallneuk Road 45 J5
Wardhouse Road 51 F11
Wardrop Street 47 H6
Washington Road 45 J2
Waverley Gardens 46 A8
Waverley Road 50 C10
Waverley Way 50 C11
Weaver Terrace 49 K7
Weavers Avenue 47 E7
Weavers Gate 47 E7
Weavers Road 47 E7
Weighhouse Close 47 H6
Weir Street 45 J5
Well Street 44 F5
Well Street 47 G6
Wellington Street 45 G5
Wellington Way (6) 48 M1
Wellmeadow Street 47 G6
Wendour Way 45 H2
Wenlock Road 49 J8
West Avenue 46 A6
West Brae 47 G6
West Buchanan Place (4) 47 G6
West Campbell Street 47 E6
West Dykebar Farm Cottages 52 K10
West Lane 47 E6
West Street 47 F6
Westburn Avenue 44 D5
Wester Carriagehill (2) 47 H8
Westerfield 47 G7
Westlands Gardens (1) 47 G8
Westpark Drive 44 E5
Westward House 45 H5
Westwood Gardens 44 E5
Whinhill Road 49 L8
White Cart Road 45 H2
Whiteford Road 49 K8
Whitehaugh Avenue 48 L5
Whitehaugh Drive 48 L5
Whites Bridge Avenue 4
Whites Bridge Avenue 4
Whites Bridge Close 4
Wickets, The 4
William Street 4
Williamsburgh Court 4
Williamsburgh Terrace 4
Wilson Street 4
Windsor Crescent 4
Wood Street 4
Woodland Avenue 51
Woodside Crescent 4
Woodstock Avenue 50
Woodstock Way 50
Woodvale Drive 4
Wright Street 4
York Way 4

## Index to Renfrew

Abbotsinch Road 56
Abercorn Avenue 57
Accord Place 60
Afton Drive 57
Ailsa Road 56
Ainslie Avenue 57 V
Ainslie Road 59 V
Albert Road 56
Alexandra Drive 57
Allan Avenue 57 U
Allanton Avenue 60 U
Allanton Drive 59
Allen Way 57
Alloway Grove 60
Almond Avenue 57 U
Alton Road 60
Ambassador Way 57
Anderson Drive 57
Andrew Avenue 57 U
Angus Avenue 61 Y
Angus Oval 61 X
Angus Place 61 X
Anne Avenue 57
Anson Way (4) 56 S
Aranthrue Crescent 56
Aranthrue Drive 56
Arbroath Avenue 61 X
Ard Road 56
Ardsloi Lane (1) 57 V
Ardsloi Place 57 V
Argosy Way (5) 56 S
Argyll Avenue 56
Arisaig Drive 61 Z
Arkleston Court 56 R
Arkleston Road 56 S
Aros Drive 61 Z
Aros Lane 61 Z
Arran Road 57 T
Arrol Street 58 U
Athol Avenue 57 U
Athol Crescent 58 U
Auchmannoch Avenue 58 U
Avenue 3 60 S
Baird Avenue 57 U
Baldovie Road 61 Y
Balfron Road 58 T
Ballantyne Avenue 59 W
Ballochmyle Drive 61 W2
Bankfoot Drive 59 X
Bankfoot Road 61 X
Barclay Square 56 R
Bargany Court 61 W2
Bargany Place 61 W2

ny Road 61 W20
ran Road 61 X18
rron Drive 56 Q13
eth Road 61 X19
han Place 61 X18
han Road 61 X18
Street 56 S11
Avenue 56 S12
Road 59 W14
aw Close 58 U15
aw Court 58 V15
aw Drive 58 V15
aw House 58 S16
aw Place 58 T16
aw Road 58 U15
jo Avenue 60 U17
ord Drive 59 X16
hwood Drive 56 S12
Street 57 T9
ew Court 57 T9
es Drive 59 Y16
es Gardens 59 Y16
ees Avenue 61 W20
ees Crescent 61 W20
ees Road 61 W20
Alder Drive 60 T20
Buie Way 60 T20
Hope Avenue 60 T19
Lawers Drive 60 T19
Ledi Avenue 60 T19
Loyal Avenue 60 T19
Lui Drive 60 T20
More Drive 60 T19
Nevis Road 60 S20
Vane Avenue 60 S20
Venue Way 60 T20
Wyvis Drive 60 S20
esford House 60 S19
yknowes Avenue 59 Y16
yknowes Drive 59 Z16
yknowes Lane 59 Y16
yknowes Road 59 Y16
wick Drive 61 X17
h Place 56 R11
h Way 56 R11
hall Avenue 60 V17
hall Lane 61 W17
ningham Road 56 R12
nock Avenue 57 U12
cksey Burn Drive 60 V19
ckstone Crescent 61 Y20
ir Road 58 U16
irgowrie Road 61 Y17
irmore Avenue 58 S16
thswood Avenue 57 T9
gmoor Place 59 Y12
gmoor Road 59 Y13
nnyholm Avenue 61 W18
swell Square 58 V14
wden Drive 59 X15
wfield Avenue 58 V15
wfield Crescent 58 V15
wfield Drive 58 V15
wfield Path 58 V15
wfield Place 58 V15
aidcraft Road 61 Y20
aidcraft Terrace 61 Z20
aids Drive 60 V20
aille Crescent 57 V12
ewster Avenue 56 Q13
itannia Way 56 S12
oadloan 56 S11
ockburn Road 61 W19
ook Place 61 W20

Brora Drive 57 U10
Brown Street 56 R11
Brown Street North 56 S10
Bruce Road 56 Q12
Buccleuch Avenue 57 U13
Buchlyvie Road 58 U16
Bucklaw Gardens 61 Y17
Bucklaw Place 61 Y17
Bucklaw Terrace 61 Y17
Bullwood Court 60 V20
Bullwood Drive 60 V20
Bullwood Gardens 60 V20
Bullwood Place 60 V20
Burnfoot Drive 59 X16
Burnham Road 57 W9
Bute Avenue 57 T12
Byrebush Road 61 Y20
Cairn Avenue 57 U12
Cairnban Street 59 Z15
Cairnhill Circus 60 V18
Cairnhill Drive 60 V18
Cairnhill Place 60 V18
Calfhill Road 61 X18
Cambridge Road 56 S11
Cameron Court 58 V14
Cameron Street 58 V14
Camps Crescent 57 U11
Campsie Drive 56 Q13
Canal Street 57 T9
Caravelle Way 57 T12
Cardonald Court 59 W16
Cardonald Drive 61 W17
Cardonald Gardens 61 X17
Cardonald Place Road 61 X17
Carham Crescent 59 Y16
Carham Drive 59 Y16
Carleith Quadrant 59 Z14
Carlyle Avenue 57 V13
Carnegie Road 59 W15
Cassley Avenue 57 V11
Castlehill Crescent 57 T9
Cayzar Court 58 U16
Charles Avenue 57 T9
Chirmorie Crescent 61 W20
Chirmorie Place 61 W20
Chirnside Place 59 W15
Chirnside Road 59 W15
Clairinsh Gardens 56 S12
Clark Street 56 R10
Clavens Road 58 U15
Claverhouse Road 58 V14
Clydesdale Avenue 56 Q12
Cockles Loan 56 R12
Cockles Loan 57 U12
Coll Avenue 57 T12
Colonsay Avenue 56 S12
Colquhoun Avenue 59 W14
Colquhoun Park 59 W14
Convair Way (9) 57 T12
Corkerhill Place 61 Z19
Corkerhill Road 61 Z19
Corrie Drive 60 U17
Corse Road 58 U15
Cowden Street 59 Z14
Cowdray Crescent 57 T10
Craigielea Court 56 S9
Craigielea Park 56 S10
Craigielea Road 56 S10
Craigmuir Crescent 58 V15
Craigmuir Place 58 U15
Craigmuir Road 58 U15
Cramond Avenue 57 U11
Creran Drive 56 R9
Croft Way 57 T12

Crofton Avenue 57 U9
Cronberry Quadrant 60 V18
Cronberry Terrace 60 V18
Crookston Avenue 61 W17
Crookston Court 61 W17
Crookston Drive 60 V17
Crookston Gardens 60 V17
Crookston Grove 61 W17
Crookston Path (1) 60 V18
Crookston Place (3) 60 V17
Crookston Quadrant 60 V17
Crookston Road 61 W19
Crookston Terrace (4) 61 W17
Crookstonhill Path (2) 60 V17
Crosstobs Road 61 W20
Cruachan Avenue 56 S12
Cumbrae Road 57 T12
Cunningham Road 57 V13
Daer Avenue 57 U12
Dakota Way (8) 57 T12
Dalfoil Court 60 V17
Dalmellington Road 61 W20
Dalziel Road 57 V13
Damshot Crescent 61 Z20
Darvel Crescent 60 T17
Davaar Road 57 T12
Daviot Street 59 Z15
Dean Park Road 57 U11
Deanfield Quadrant 58 V15
Deanside Road 57 W13
Dee Avenue 57 U10
Dermontside Close 60 V19
Dochart Avenue 57 U12
Don Avenue 57 U11
Donaldson Drive 57 T10
Dormanside Court 61 X18
Dormanside Gate 61 X18
Dormanside Grove 61 X18
Dormanside Place 61 Y19
Dormanside Road 61 X18
Douglas Road 56 Q13
Dowrie Crescent 61 X20
Drumcross Road 61 Y20
Drummond Drive 60 T17
Drums Road 61 W18
Dryburn Avenue 59 W16
Duchray Drive 60 V17
Dunchurch Road 58 T16
Dundee Drive 61 X18
Dunlop Crescent 57 T9
Dunlop Street 57 T9
Dunvegan Quadrant 56 R9
Earl Haig Road 58 V14
Earn Avenue 57 U11
East Avenue 57 T10
Eden Place 57 U11
Edgam Drive 59 Y16
Edison Street 57 U13
Edward Avenue 57 U9
Elder Grove Avenue 59 Z14
Elder Grove Court 59 Z14
Elder Grove Place 59 Z14
Elizabeth Way 56 S12
Elm Avenue 56 S9
Erskine Square 58 V14
Esk Avenue 57 U11
Ettrick Avenue 57 V11
Ettrick Way 57 V11
Everton Road 61 Y18
Fairfield Drive 57 T12
Faulds Head Road 57 T10
Fereneze Avenue 56 R13
Ferguson Avenue 57 T10
Ferguson Street 56 S10

Ferry Road 57 T9
Fife Avenue 61 X17
Fifth Avenue 56 S11
Fifty Pitches Place 59 X14
Fifty Pitches Road 59 X14
Fifty Pitches Way 59 X14
Findhorn Avenue 57 U10
First Avenue 56 S11
Fitzalan Road 56 Q12
Fleet Avenue 57 U12
Fochabers Drive 59 Y15
Forfar Avenue 61 X17
Fourth Avenue 56 S11
French Street 56 R11
Friendship Way 57 T12
Fulbar Avenue 56 S9
Fulbar Court 57 T9
Fulbar Lane 57 T9
Fulbar Road 59 Y14
Fulbar Street 57 T9
Gadie Avenue 57 U11
Gala Avenue 57 U11
Gallowhill Court 56 Q13
Gartartan Road 58 V16
Gartmore Road 60 S17
Gauldry Avenue 61 Y18
Gibson Road 56 R12
Gifford Drive 59 W16
Gladsmuir Road 59 W15
Glasgow Road (Oldhall) 58 S16, U16
Glasgow Road (Renfrew) 57 U10
Globe Street 57 T10
Glencairn Court 56 Q13
Glencairn Road 56 Q13
Gleddoch Close 58 U15
Glenddoch Court 58 U15
Glenddoch Gate 58 V15
Glenddoch Road 58 U15
Glendee Gardens 57 T11
Glendee Road 57 T11
Glengarry Drive 59 Y16
Gleniffer Road 56 R13
Glensax Drive 57 U12
Glenside Avenue 61 X19
Golf Drive 60 S17
Gordon Avenue 57 U13
Gosford Lane 57 W9
Govan Road 59 Z12
Greengairs Avenue (1) 59 Z13
Greenloan Avenue 59 Z13
Haining Road 57 T10
Haining, The 57 T11
Hairst Street 57 T9
Halifax Way (3) 56 S12
Hallidale Crescent 57 V11
Hallrule Drive 59 Y16
Hampden Way (7) 57 T12
Hapland Avenue 61 Y19
Hapland Road 61 Y19
Hardgate Drive 59 Y13
Hardgate Gardens 59 Y13
Hardgate Place 59 Y13
Hardgate Road 59 Y13
Hardridge Road 61 Z19
Hartlaw Crescent 59 W15
Hatton Gardens 61 W17
Hatton Path 61 W17
Hawkhead Road 60 S18
Hepburn Road 59 X14
Herald Way 56 S12
Hercules Way (10) 57 T12
Heron Way 56 S12

High Mair 56 S11
High Street 57 T10
Highgrove Court 57 U10
Highgrove Road 57 U10
Hillbrae Street 59 Z15
Hillington Gardens 61 Y17
Hillington Park Circus 59 Y16
Hillington Quadrant 59 W16
Hillington Road 59 W14
Hillington Road South 59 W16
Hillington Terrace 59 W16
Hollybush Road 58 V16
Holmes Avenue 56 S12
Honeybog Road 58 U15
Houston Court 57 T9
Houston Street 57 T9
Howford Road 61 X17
Huntly Road 57 V13
Hurlet Road 60 S20
Hyndal Avenue 61 Y20
Hyndlee Drive 59 Y16
Inchbrae Road 61 Y17
Inchinnan Road 56 Q9
Inkerman Road 58 V16
Innerwick Drive 59 X16
Inverglas Avenue 57 V12
Invergyle Drive 59 X16
Invergyle Lane 59 X16
Inverness Street 59 Z15
Iona Road 56 S12
Jennys Well Road 60 S19
Jessiman Square 56 R12
Johnstone Avenue 59 X14
Jubilee Court 58 V14
Jura Avenue 57 T12
Kelhead Avenue 58 V16
Kelhead Drive 58 V16
Kelhead Path 58 V16
Kelhead Place 58 V16
Kelvin Avenue 57 V13
Kemp Avenue 56 Q12
Kempsthorn Crescent 61 X20
Kempsthorn Path 61 X20
Kempsthorn Place 61 X20
Kempsthorn Road 61 W20
Kenley Road 57 U9, V10
Killearn Drive 60 V17
Kilpatrick Drive 56 R13
Kincraig Street 59 Z15
King George Court 57 U12
King George Gardens 57 U11
King George Park Avenue 57 U12
King George Place 57 U12
King George Way 57 U12
Kings Inch Drive 57 W11
Kings Inch Drive 59 X12
Kings Inch Place 57 V11
Kings Inch Road 57 V10
Kiingsberry Court 57 U9
Kingsland Crescent 59 X15
Kingsland Drive 59 Y15
Kingsland Lane 59 Y15
Kinloch Road 56 R12
Kinnell Avenue 61 Y18
Kinnell Crescent 61 Y18
Kinnell Path 61 Y18
Kinnell Place 61 Z18
Kinnell Square 61 Y18
Kinpurnie Road 58 T16
Kinross Avenue 61 X17
Kinsail Drive 58 V15
Kirkaig Avenue 57 V11
Kirkfield Gardens 56 R10
Kirklandneuk Crescent 56 Q9
Kirklandneuk Road 56 Q9
Kirklands 56 R10
Kirriemuir Avenue 61 Y17
Kirriemuir Place 61 Y17
Knockhill Road 56 R12
Lade Terrace 61 W17
Ladykirk Crescent 59 X15
Ladykirk Drive 59 X15
Ladymuir Crescent 61 Y18
Laggan Terrace 56 R9
Lamberton Drive 59 X15
Lamington Road 59 X16
Lammermoor Avenue 61 Y17
Lancaster Way (1) 56 S12
Lanfine Road 60 S17
Lang Avenue 56 S11
Langcroft Place 59 Y14
Langcroft Road 59 Z14
Langcroft Terrace (1) 59 Z14
Langhaul Avenue 60 V20
Langhaul Court 60 V20
Langhaul Place 60 V20
Langhaul Road 60 V20
Langlands Avenue 59 Z14
Langlands Drive 59 Y13
Langlands Road 59 Z14
Langlook Road 60 V20
Langstile Place 58 V16
Langstile Road 58 V16
Langton Crescent 61 Y20
Langton Road 61 Y20
Lanton Drive 59 X16
Lapwing Road 57 U9
Latimer Gardens 61 W17
Latimer Path 61 W17
Lawers Road 56 S12
Laymoor Avenue 57 V10
Leander Crescent 57 U11
Lednock Road 59 W16
Leithland Avenue 61 X20
Leithland Road 61 X20
Lennox Terrace 56 Q13
Leven Square 56 R9
Leverndale Court 60 V20
Leverndale Road 60 V20
Levernside Crescent 61 X20
Levernside Road 61 X20
Lewis Avenue 57 T12
Libo Avenue 61 Z20
Linburn Place 59 W15
Linburn Road 58 V14
Linthaugh Road 61 W18, Z18
Linthaugh Terrace 61 Z20
Lintlaw Drive 59 X15
Lismore Avenue 57 T12
Lister Place 59 W14
Lister Road 59 W14
Livingstone Avenue 57 W13
Loanhead Avenue 57 T10
Lobnitz Avenue 57 T10
Lochar Crescent 61 Z18
Lochmaben Road 60 V17
Lochy Avenue 57 V12
Lomond Avenue 56 R12
Longcroft Drive 56 S9
Lorne Road 57 V13
Lossie Crescent 57 V11
Lothian Street 57 U13
Lourdes Avenue 61 Z17
Lourdes Court 61 Z17
Lovat Place 58 U14
Loyne Drive 57 V11
Luma Gardens 59 Y14
Lyoncross Road 61 X18
Lysander Way (6) 57 T12
McClue Avenue 56 R10
McClue Road 56 S9
McCracken Avenue 56 R11
McGregor Avenue 56 R11
McLaren Avenue (1) 56 S12
Maitland Place 56 R11
Mallaig Road 59 Z14
Manse Street 57 T9
Mansfield Road 58 V14
Marchbank Gardens 60 T17
Marchglen Place (1) 59 Z14
Marjory Road 56 Q12
Markdow Avenue 60 T17
Markdow Avenue 61 W20
Meikle Avenue 56 S11
Meiklerig Crescent 61 Y19
Meiklewood Road 59 Z15
Meldon Place (4) 59 Z14
Melness Place (2) 59 Z14
Melvick Place (3) 59 Z14
Memus Avenue 61 Y17
Merlinford Avenue 57 U10
Merlinford Crescent 57 U10
Merlinford Drive 57 U10
Merlinford Way 57 U10
Merton Drive 59 W16
Methuen Road 56 P12
Midfaulds Avenue 57 U11
Midlem Drive 59 Y16
Midlem Oval 59 Y16
Mill Vennel 57 T10
Millburn Avenue 57 T10
Millburn Drive 57 U10
Millburn Road 57 T10
Millburn Way 57 U10
Mitchell Avenue 56 R11
Moidart Avenue 56 R9
Mondyke House 57 T10
Monifieth Avenue 61 Z17
Montgarrie Street 59 Z15
Montgomery Avenue 56 R13
Montgomery Road 56 Q13
Montrave Path 61 Z17
Montrave Street 61 Z17
Moorpark Avenue 58 V15
Moorpark Court 56 R11
Moorpark Drive 59 W15
Moorpark Place 58 V15
Moorpark Square 56 R11
Morar Place 56 R9
Morefield Road 59 Z14
Morriston Crescent 57 V12
Morton Avenue 60 S20
Morton Drive 60 S19
Moss Heights Avenue 59 Z16
Mossland Road 57 V12, U13
Mosspark Boulivard 61 Z17
Mosspark Drive 61 Y17
Mossview Lane 59 Y16
Mossview Quadrant 59 Y16
Moulin Circus 61 W17
Moulin Place 61 W17
Moulin Road 61 W17
Moulin Terrace 61
Mountgarrie Road 5
Moyne Road 61
Muir Street
Muirdrum Avenue 6
Muirdykes Avenue 59
Muirdykes Road 59
Muirpark Avenue 5
Mull Avenue 56
Munlochy Road (5) 5
Murray Street 56
Murroes Road 5
Mybster Place 59
Napier Road 57
Nasmyth Road 59
Nasmyth Road North 59
Nasmyth Road South 59
Neilsland Oval 61
Neilsland Square 61
Ness Road 5
Netherdale Drive 60
Nethergreen Crescent 56
Nethergreen Road 56
Nethergreen Wynd 56
Nethy Way 57
Nevis Road 56
Newham Road 60
Newmains Road 56
Newtyle Drive 60
Newtyle Place 60
Newtyle Road 60
Nissen Place 60
Nith Drive 57
Nith Way 57
North Lodge Road 56
Ochil Road 56
Old Govan Road 57
Oldhall Road 58
Orchard Street 57
Ossian Avenue 58
Oxford Lane 56
Oxford Road 56
Oxton Drive 59
Paisley Road 56
Paisley Road West 61 W17,
Parklands Oval 60
Parklands View 60
Pearson Drive 57
Penilee Road 58
Penilee Terrace 58
Penneld Road 58
Pentland Drive 56
Percy Road 56
Pinkerton Lane 57
Pioneer Place 57
Pitlochry Drive 61
Pladda Road 57
Porterfield Road 56
Potterhill Road 61
Provost Driver Court 57
Queen Elizabeth Avenue 58
Queen Street 57
Queensberry Avenue 58
Queensland Court 59
Queensland Drive 59
Queensland Gardens 59
Queensland Lane East 59
Queensland Lane West 59

n Avenue 60 V17
n Court 60 V17
n Drive 60 V17
n Path 60 V17
n Place 60 V17
rley Road 58 V16
och Drive 56 S9
ath Drive 59 X16
nank Avenue 57 U9
eld Street 57 T9
ew Road 56 Q13
sley)
ew Road 57 W12
nfrew)
haw Drive 59 X15
on Drive 59 X15
nds Gate 56 S9
nds Way 56 S10
uir Road 59 Y15
sdale Lane 57 W9
rtson Avenue 56 R10
rtson Drive 56 R10
y Park Road 58 T16
Avenue 56 Q12
Hall Place 57 T10
House 60 S19
hall Avenue 60 S17
hill Avenue 58 V16
hill Road 58 V16
erwick Drive 60 U17
Avenue 59 X12
an Avenue 56 S9
es Crescent 58 U15
es Place 58 U15
es Road 58 U15
St Andrews Road 56 S11
St Kenneth Drive (1) 59 Z13
Sandwood Crescent 59 W16
Sandwood Path 59 W15
Sandwood Road 59 W16
Sandy Road 56 S12
Sandyford Road 56 Q13
School Road 58 U16
Scott Road 57 V13
Scotts Road 60 U18
Seaforth Road 59 W14
Seaforth Road North 59 W14
Seaforth Road South 59 W14
Second Avenue 56 S11
Selkirk Avenue 61 Y17
Selvieland Road 58 V16
Shearers Lane 56 S10
Shieldburn Road 59 Z14
Shieldhall Gardens 59 Y14
Shieldhall Road 59 Y14
Silver Glade 61 X17
Sixth Avenue 56 S12
Skipness Drive 59 Z13
Skye Avenue 56 S12
Somerled Avenue 56 P12
South Avenue 57 T10
South Street 57 W9
Southwold Road 58 U16
Spey Drive 57 U11
Stables, The 61 W18
Staffa Avenue 56 S12
Station Crescent 57 T9
Station Road 57 T9
Staybrae Drive 60 V20
Staybrae Grove 60 V20
Stephenson Street 57 U13
Stewart Avenue 56 R12
Stirling Way 57 T12
Strathcarron Drive 60 S20
Strathmore Avenue 60 T17
Sunart Avenue 56 R9
Swinton Drive 59 X16
Swinton Place 59 X16
Tait House 60 S19
Talla Road 59 W16
Tanar Avenue 57 V12
Tanar Way 57 U12
Tannadice Avenue 61 Y17
Tannadice Path 61 Y17
Tarfside Avenue 61 Y17
Tarfside Gardens 61 Z17
Tarfside Oval 61 Z18
Tarras Drive 57 U12
Tay Avenue 57 U10
Tealing Avenue 61 Y17
Tealing Crescent 61 Y17
Teith Avenue 57 V11
Templeland Road 61 Y19
Tennant Street 57 T9
Third Avenue 56 S11
Thompson Street 56 S11
Thorndon Lane 57 W9
Thurston Road 59 W16
Tinto Square 56 R12
Tinwald Path 59 W16
Tiree Avenue 56 S12
Tirry Avenue 57 V11
Tirry Way 57 V11
Tormore Street 59 Z15
Torridon Drive 57 U11
Towerside Crescent 61 W19
Towerside Road 61 W19
Traquair Drive 61 X17
Trident Way 56 S12
Trinity Avenue 61 Y17
Tweed Crescent 57 U10
Tweedsmuir Road 59 X16
Tylney Road 58 T16
Urquhart Crescent 56 S11
Vanguard Way 56 S12
Vennacher Road 56 R9
Victoria Drive East 56 S11
Victoria Drive West 56 R10
Viewpark Gardens 56 R11
Viking Way 56 S12
Viscount Avenue 56 S12
Walkerburn Road 61 X17
Wallace Road 56 Q12
Watt Road 58 V14
Wedderlea Drive 59 W16
Wellington Way (2) 56 S12
West Avenue 57 T10
West Lodge Road 56 R9
Westfield Drive 59 W16
Whinhill Gardens 61 W18
Whinhill Place 61 W18
Whinhill Road 61 W18
Wilson Street 57 T9
Windsor Road 56 S11
Woodend Drive 60 T17
Wright Street 56 Q12
Yair Drive 59 W15
York Way 56 S12
Zetland Road 57 V13

# NOTES

# NOTES